# THE FUTURE OF WETLANDS

# THE FUTURE
# OF WETLANDS

## Assessing Visual-Cultural Values

*Edited by*
*RICHARD C. SMARDON*

ALLANHELD, OSMUN   Publishers

ALLANHELD, OSMUN & CO. PUBLISHERS, INC.

Published in the United States of America in 1983
by Allanheld, Osmun & Co. Publishers, Inc.
(A Division of Littlefield, Adams & Company)
81 Adams Drive, Totowa, New Jersey 07512

**Library of Congress Cataloging in Publication Data**
Main entry under title:

The Future of wetlands.

   Includes bibliographical references and index.
   Contents: Introduction and overview – State of the
art in assessing wetland visual-cultural values /
by Richard C. Smardon – Wetland policy and visual-
cultural values in the United States / by Richard C.
Smardon – [etc.]
   1. Wetland conservation. 2. Environmental impact
analysis. 3. Landscape assessment. I. Smardon,
Richard C.
QH75.F87            333.91'816            78-72316
ISBN 0-86598-020-9                       AACR2
83  84  85  /  10  9  8  7  6  5  4  3  2  1

Printed in the United States of America

This book is dedicated to my mother, whose spirit lives on.

# Contents

# Foreword

While touring the Georgia lowlands recently, I was stunned to see large advertisements posted by local real estate offices extolling the values and virtues of Marshfront Properties. Nothing is more honest than the marketplace, and here it was announcing that twenty years of frustrating effort had paid off. We had convinced people that wetlands were beautiful as well as biologically productive, at least here in the coastal plain. We had convinced them so well that they were willing to pay premium prices for land that bordered the salt marsh. Our "ugly duckling" had grown up to be a beautiful goose that was laying golden eggs.

My signal that the turning point had come came from the U.S. Army Corps of Engineers, who had inherited the nation's wetland protection program in 1972 by a strange bit of political maneuvering. The Washington brass, having made a behind-the-scenes decision about wetlands that would send a shock wave across the country, invited me to come and lecture the generals and high civilian staff on the values of wetlands, specifically including any "resources of the mind" that the strange landscape might harbor. By "resources of the mind" the Corps meant aesthetic, heritage, cultural, spiritual, and psychological values. I accepted this intriguing assignment knowing that something quite unusual was about to happen. It did. Less than a week after my lecture in April 1976, the Chief of Civil Engineers announced that the Corps was denying permits for units of a mammoth Deltona Project in Florida, which would have eventually converted 20,000 acres of mangrove wetlands into lots and canals. The Corps had spent eight months searching its institutional soul, had rejected the testimony of the greatest collection of high-powered experts ever brought into a wetlands case, had overridden the governor of Florida, and declared itself ready to provide a reasonable measure of protection for all wetlands within its authority. As brought out in the pages that follow, the Corps subsequently included aesthetic and amenity values as properties of wetlands that it could legitimately protect.

Surveys of public opinion show that wetland appreciation is high among the public. For example, a statewide survey of Floridians, taken in the fall of 1981, showed that 60 percent of the populace knew that wetlands purified the water that flows through them. In another example, a survey by the Philadelphia District of the

Corps found that 90 percent of the inhabitants of the Atlantic City, N.J., area believed that wetlands should be protected, even if economic growth is adversely affected. This is a much higher percentage than I would expect to find across the country. I believe that nationally one would find about two out of three people supporting protection for the 3 percent of our national landscape that is wetland. Twenty years ago I would have hazarded a guess that less than one out of ten would be supportive.

I am firmly convinced that public support for wetlands conservation will remain high permanently. Only the truly mean-spirited now talk about wetlands being wastelands. This attitude is a holdover from olden times when people needed to believe there were special places on earth where evil was bred. If you needed to believe this, what better candidate than an impenetrable and mysterious swamp. In this century wetlands have been more the victims of technological bravado than superstitious belief. Places that were neither land nor water challenged our inventiveness. We couldn't drive across them nor boat through them with any ease. We couldn't easily farm them nor build upon them. The solution was to convert them to either land or water or both by draining, diking, or filling. But now the mood has changed. Wetlands are recognized as among the most important resources we have.

Also contributing to the future security of wetlands is a mellowing of the technological imperative. Events of the last ten years have shown us that there are, and should be, limits on technology. As a nation we are just beginning to practice restraint, to not do some things we are technologically capable of doing. Rejecting massive wetland conversion projects as a restraint on technology is becoming a reality.

Many of the authors of this volume were already deeply into analysis of wetlands-connected "resources of the mind" and, in fact, had contributed strongly to the foundation of legitimacy by which wetlands are now being protected. It is heartening to see that the research is being continued in academies and agencies around the globe and that some of the best is reported here. Although 40 percent of the nation's original inventory of wetlands has been obliterated, we are having good success in conserving the remaining 60 percent (about 70 to 75 million acres). While this volume of papers shows excellent progress, much important work remains to be done in the analysis of visual-cultural values in support of the conservation and land use actions of the future.

JOHN R. CLARK
*The Conservation Foundation*
*Washington, D.C.*

# Acknowledgments

Many acknowledgments need to be made when one edits a book with contributed chapters. I would first like to thank all the contributing authors, Edmund Penning-Rowsell, Michael Lee, Jim Palmer, Bill Hammitt, Molly Mooney, Rowan Rowntree, and Julius Fabos, whose efforts are critical to the work's integrity. Special thanks go to Mike Hunter and Brian Dick for their obvious efforts; to Susan Fichter, Anne McCoy, and Terry LeVeque, for their less obvious graphic and editorial assistance; and to the students at the School of Landscape Architecture, S.U.N.Y. College of Environmental Science and Forestry at Syracuse, who have contributed to this effort.

The book would not have happened without an interdisciplinary wetlands evaluation project which was led by Joe Larson at the University of Massachusetts, Amherst. Thanks also go to my original faculty advisors, including Julius Fabos and Walt Cudnohufsky, and to the other student and faculty members of the original wetlands research team, including Frank Golet, Tirith Gupta, Dick Heeley, Ward Motts, John Foster, and Chris Greene.

Thanks go to John Sinton at Stockton State College, who critically reviewed the first manuscript submitted to the publishers, and to Sarah Remon, who typed and retyped many of the chapter drafts. My sincere appreciation is due to Allanheld, Osmun for their patience throughout the long duration needed to develop this book. My appreciation is also due to other publishers who have given me permission to republish key graphics and text. These publishers include American Water Resources Association; Dowden, Hutchinson, and Ross; American Society of Civil Engineers; John Wiley & Sons; the Landscape Research Group; and the Ecological Society of America.

# Introduction

The purpose of this book is to present the reader with an array of information and techniques about the assessment of the visual-cultural values cf wetlands. Visual-cultural values include the enjoyment derived from wetlands by people in terms of scenery, recreation, and nature education. In recent years wetlands have become more valued for amenity resources as well as their ecological functions.

This book is divided into five parts. Part I is an introduction to policy and visual-cultural assessment of wetlands in the United States and Britain. It contains overviews of state-of-the-art techniques for assessing visual, recreational, and educational values of wetlands.

Part II examines how people actually perceive visual-cultural aspects of wetlands. These studies were done in Louisiana, Massachusetts, and West Virginia and illustrate methods of perceptual visual-cultural assessments at a statewide scale, a town scale, and an individual wetland, respectively. This collective work by Michael S. Lee, James F. Palmer, and William E. Hammitt shows which variables are important for assessing visual-cultural values.

Part III presents chapters by Molly Mooney and Rowan A. Rowntree on field-expedient methods for describing the physical landscape attributes of wetlands and their surroundings. These two approaches were developed as part of wetland studies for New York State freshwater wetlands along Lake Ontario and a California salt marsh, respectively.

Part IV contains two chapters on wetland evaluation. One includes a method developed by Smardon and Fabos of valuation of visual-cultural attributes of wetlands that use both perceptual studies, such as those in Part II, and physical landscape description techniques, such as those in Part III. The valuation methodology developed for northeastern wetlands includes both nonmonetary and monetary valuation techniques. This section also includes a summary of visual impact assessment methods by Smardon and specific techniques for assessing visual impact of introduced activities that would change the visual character of wetlands.

Part V suggests a framework for decision-making to determine which technique or group of techniques are needed and feasible for practical application in different decision-making contexts.

# PART I

# Overview

# 1 State of the Art in Assessing Visual-Cultural Values

### RICHARD C. SMARDON

## Introduction

Throughout the United States, land-use decisions affecting wetlands are being made without considering many important wetland values. As a result, many valuable wetland areas are rapidly disappearing (Niering, 1970). Aesthetic, educational, and recreational values in particular have been ignored because of the negative mythology that previously were attached to wetlands. This book discusses how these ignored visual-cultural values can be identified and assessed.

Visual-cultural values are the finite natural resources available for human use and perception within or associated with wetland areas. Human uses that treat wetlands as a visual-cultural resource include activities such as canoeing, hiking, and outdoor classes in natural history. In this book, visual-cultural wetland values, which are defined by human individuals or groups, will be explored as they relate to both freshwater and saltwater wetlands. Although heavy emphasis will be placed on visual perception and the visual quality of wetlands and their landscape contexts, educational and recreational uses and values will also be discussed.

## Perspective

The author's philosophical perspective is that visual or aesthetic, recreational, and educational values of wetlands are highly interdependent and strongly correlated (Smardon, 1973). Aesthetic perceptions are intertwined with other cultural perceptions. To a canoeist, for instance, a wetland area may have recreational value based on its location along a large stream, scenic value derived from the vistas and features seen while canoeing, and educational value for the wildlife and plants seen and identified.

Knowledge or information about the ecological functions of wetlands alters and transforms traditional values and beliefs into a new aesthetic that is ecologically derived. S. C. Pepper (1937), an aesthetic philosopher, proposes that knowledge of the context and meaning of an object can intensify the emotional aspect of aesthetic appreciation of that object. Continuing this line of reasoning from an ecologist's perspective, Pierre Dansereau (1973) suggests that knowledge of ecological and cultural processes will enhance aesthetic appreciation of the landscape. Thus to individuals who have ecological or informational perspectives, the once-abused backwaters are gradually being perceived as gems in the landscape. Landscapes formerly alien or hostile to human habitation are, in the true wilderness tradition, now becoming appreciated through "ecological aesthetics."

The first corollary to the ecological-aesthetics perspective is that different natural landscape regions, such as the Great Plains, the southwestern canyon lands, and coastal areas, as well as more restricted landscape units, such as wetlands and alpine areas, have different visual-cultural values based on their different physical attributes. The second corollary is that people with different cultural values are likely to perceive and value landscapes differently. Thus landscapes differ not only in their physical attributes, but in the ways that they are valued by people with different cultural backgrounds.

### Toward an Evaluative Framework

For the purpose of inventorying or evaluating visual-cultural values, wetlands cannot be separated from their landscape contexts. A wetland situated adjacent to a steep bluff, for instance, will have different scenic, recreational, and educational values than a wetland surrounded by low-lying landforms. In previous publications (Smardon, 1972, 1975) and in Chapter 9, the author outlines an evaluatory framework for assessing visual-cultural values related to individual wetlands, to wetlands and their landscape contexts, or to wetland complexes. This evaluation system assesses wetlands for *exceptional* values first, and then rates *nonexceptional* wetlands by other criteria. For example, a wetland is considered exceptional if it (1) is an outstanding wetland natural area (such as an endangered-species habitat); (2) has general landscape values (for instance, is a scarce wetland type within a region); or (3) has wetland-system value (for example, if one of several significant wetlands are interconnected by rivers and lakes). Detailed criteria for evaluating outstanding wetland areas, general landscape values, and wetland-system values are given in Smardon (1972, 1975) and in Chapter 9.

What are the values of nonexceptional wetlands? Nonexceptional wetlands are the most susceptible to development or modifica-

tion. Individual wetland areas and their immediate landscape contexts provide for many recreational and educational uses, and visual perception and the quality of the wetland are intertwined with them. Primary recreational uses of wetlands are fishing, hunting, bird watching, and nature study; other recreational uses include hiking, photography, canoeing, boating, and ice skating. Recreational uses of areas adjoining wetlands could include camping, picnicking, and using trails and roads for walking, cycling, horseback riding, cross-country skiing, and pleasure driving. More controversial recreational uses of wetlands might include swamp buggying, snowmobiling, air boating, motor boating, and driving other all-terrain vehicles. Many recreational food-gathering activities, such as clamming on mudflats and berry picking in wetland transitional areas, occur within or adjacent to wetland areas. Educational uses of wetlands include nature classrooms and scientific laboratories.

Beside the natural attributes of wetlands, man-made attributes or cultural variables should be evaluated in relation to visual, educational, and recreational use. Cultural or "extrinsic" variables may be defined as "man-made changes, adaptions, and additions to the natural resources" (Lewis, 1970). Man-made effects can both add to and detract from the natural resource value. Among cultural enhancement variables are:

1. *Educational proximity:* the nearness of elementary schools, high schools, and colleges to a wetland area.

2. *Physical accessibility:* the degree of access to a wetland by trail or road, and accessibility within the wetland by boat, trail, or road.

3. *Ambient quality:* the physical condition of the wetland as indicated by the degree of water pollution, air pollution, noise levels, and presence or absence of visual misfits or incompatible land uses.

The visual-cultural values and attributes of wetlands are identified here in a very general way. Many of these values and attributes are detailed in research on specific wetlands (Smardon, 1972, 1975), but they are generally applicable to wetlands in different ecological contexts throughout the United States and other parts of the world.

## Literature

Sparse literature is available on visual, recreational, and educational values of inland or coastal wetlands. However, four articles discuss visual-cultural values of inland wetlands in some depth (Hammitt, 1978; Lee, 1977; Rodgers, 1970; and Smardon, 1972). Only one article (Rowntree, 1976) discusses visual-cultural values of coastal wetlands in any detail. A few studies assess the scenic quality of wetlands along with other landscape types (Cherem and Traweek, 1977; Palmer, 1978). Marginal treatment of visual values of wetlands can be found in Errington (1957), Haslam (1973), Litton et al. (1972), Niering (1967), and Steinitz et al. (1978). Sources covering wetland recreational values include Cheek and Field (1977), Errington (1957), Haslam (1973), Larson and Foster (1955), and Shaw and Fredine (1956). Sources treating educational values include Niering (1970), Odum (1971), Randall and Brainerd (n.d.), Wharton (1970), and U.S.D.I., Fish and Wildlife Service (1962).

There is also much peripheral material on visual perception of landscapes, landscape assessment, and recreation. The most closely related research is in river recreation. Two recent proceedings contain much of the relevant work in this area (U.S. Forest Service, 1977; Louisiana State University, 1977), and the author has assembled most of the references dealing with visual aspects in a recent paper (Smardon, 1977). Litton et al. (1974) have written a book entitled *Water and the Landscape,* but most of the treatment is not specific to wetlands.

Little work deals directly with evaluation (nonmonetary) or valuation (monetary) of visual-cultural wetland values for environmental decision-making. Lee (1977), Smardon (1972, 1975), and Smardon and Fabos (1976) propose models using rating and ranking systems for evaluating visual-cultural values. Steinitz et al. (1978) have developed fairly sophisticated models for simulating visual impacts from alternative policies for preserving the North River and adjacent tidal wetlands in Massachusetts. Gosselink et al. (1973), Gupta and Foster (1975), and Krutilla and Fisher (1976), propose economic valuation techniques for wetlands. Only Gupta and Foster (1975) consider visual-cultural values, based on the evaluative model of Smardon (1972).

Detailed review of the literature reveals a number of findings about the role that wetlands play in providing visual-cultural values. These findings will be discussed as they pertain to (1) wetlands in comparison with other landscapes, (2) specific types of wetlands (in comparison with each other), (3) wetlands and their immediate surroundings, (4) the micro-landscape within wetlands, and (5) the dynamic aspects of wetlands.

### Wetlands vs. Other Landscapes

Tidal marshes, bogs, and freshwater marshes rate fairly high in landscape quality in comparison to other landscape types. Palmer (1978) and Chapter 5 found that photographs of wooded upland and marsh in Dennis, Massachusetts, were preferred over photographs of several other landscape types in the area. Scores for the various landscape types were figured from the means of rank-order sorting of photographs from 1 to 7, with 1 being the most preferred and 7 being the least preferred. Wooded upland and marsh received a score of 2.91, as compared to beach and water with 2.99, suburban development with 3.47, developed open land with 3.52, commercial development with 5.32, and dense residential development with 5.27. In another selected-preference evaluation, Steinitz et al. (1978) found that "meadows" (presumably tidal meadows) were placed in the "most positive" category. In Michigan, Cherem and Traweek (1977) used the novel method of letting hikers photograph the scenes they most preferred or disliked along a trail. The most preferred scene, photographed by 50 percent of the trail hikers, was a freshwater marsh. Finally, Hammitt (1978) and Chapter 6 studied landscape preferences using black-and-white photographs and Likert preference-rating scales, which ranged from 1 (not at all) to 5 (very much). In his study, photographs of bogs were rated considerably higher (3.33–4.58) than river landscapes (2.66–4.13) and seminatural environment (2.52–3.97) in the north central United States.

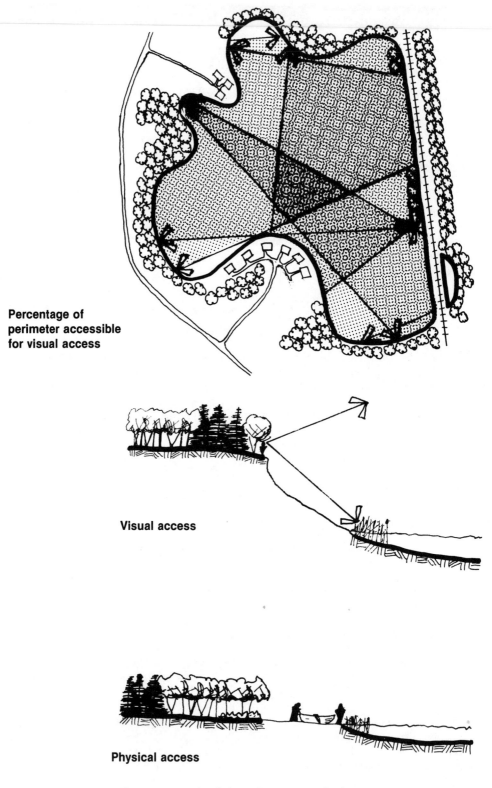

**Percentage of perimeter accessible for visual access**

**Visual access**

**Physical access**

**Figure 1.1.** Visual and physical access to wetlands.

Thus many wetland landscape types, especially open salt- and freshwater marshes and bogs, tend to rate highly in scenic quality in a landscape continuum.

The high scenic quality of wetlands is not paralleled by high recreational use. Cheek and Field (1977), comparing recreational use of different environments, found fewer types of recreational activities and less activity overall associated with swamp and marsh environments, as opposed to river, lake, ocean, forest/mountain, range/farm, and town/city environments. Based on actual usage, the most significant cluster of recreational activities associated with marsh/swamp environments were nature-study and food-gathering activities. These included visiting interpretative centers and displays, studying nature and observing wildlife, taking photographs, gathering natural food, and collecting objects. According to this study, other recreational activities seem to be much less associated with wetlands than with other environments. This could partially be explained by the difficulty of gaining physical access to or into wetlands.

## Wetlands vs. Other Wetlands

Little empirical work has been done on human preferences for one wetland type over another. However, from the fieldwork involved in Smardon's 1972 work, the average recreationist would prefer relatively open freshwater wetlands such as fresh meadows, shallow or deep freshwater marshes, bog mats, or low shrub swamps to thickly vegetated shrub swamps and wooded swamps without visual clearance under the woody canopy. The natural restrictions on visual and physical access (see Figure 1.1) within the latter types of wetlands may reduce their use, and value, for visual and recreational purposes. However, most wetlands are a composite of different vegetational types, and even densely vegetated areas lacking easy physical or visual access may come to be valued as people learn about other desirable characteristics of shrub and wooded wetlands.

A few other studies indicate the value of visually open wetlands. Palmer (1978) and Chapter 5 found through preference testing that people in Dennis, Massachusetts, preferred open saltwater marsh in the marsh/wooded

upland perceptual landscape classification type. Litton et al. (1972) noted that the "spaciousness" or openness of saltwater marshes in Tomales Bay, California, was an important attribute of the coastal landscape there.

Most people assume that the larger the wetland, the higher the visual-cultural value. This is not necessarily the case. Small wetlands (below twenty acres) may have high visual and educational values. Litton et al. (1972) pointed out that the small areas of saltwater marsh and meadow in Tomales Bay provided a greater sense of "openness" in the landscape than would be expected from their absolute size. Similar findings were made for freshwater wetlands (Smardon, 1972) and saltwater marshes (Steinitz et al., 1978) in New England. From an educational perspective, one of the most important qualities of wetlands is the diversity of different attributes that can be seen or experienced per unit area (Smardon, 1972). Thus an extremely small wetland with many different species or communities of plants and wildlife may have high educational value. Larger wetlands will have a higher recreational carrying capacity in terms of minimizing (or spreading out) ecological damage from a given amount of recreational use and in terms of allowing different types of recreational users within the same wetland area without conflict (Smardon, 1972). Larger wetland areas may in some cases support more wildlife or a greater variety of wildlife for consumptive or nonconsumptive recreational use.

## Wetlands and Their Immediate Surroundings

The enframing element that creates spatial enclosure and edge contrast bordering a wetland is important to the wetland's scenic and recreational quality. In the wetlands study in Massachusetts (Smardon, 1972, 1975), it was found that landforms and contrasting upland vegetation surrounding the wetland were both important in defining a sharp visual image and a feeling of enclosed space (see Figures 1.2, 1.3, 1.4). In the Louisiana River swamp study (Lee, 1977) and in Chapter 4, canopylike woody vegetation took on the major role of definition and enclosure and made the wetland environment attractive, as determined by professional judgment and preference testing. Strong but

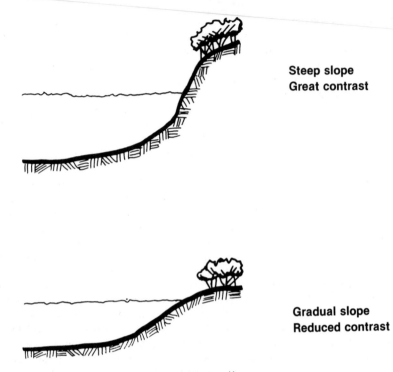

**Steep slope**
**Great contrast**

**Gradual slope**
**Reduced contrast**

**Figure 1.2.** Landform contrast.

varied landform edges or vegetative edges also create ideal spatial-sequential experiences for boating or hiking through a wetland area, as pointed out by Lee (1977) and More et al. (1977).

Fabos et al. (1975) found through preference testing that the most visually compatible land uses adjoining wetlands in the Northeast are open water, forest, and agricultural land. Fabos et al. (1975) and Palmer (1978) found that people in general prefer natural or agricultural land uses adjacent to wetland areas, although limited-intensity recreational or residential uses may be aesthetically acceptable. Wetlands adjacent to rivers, small lakes, ponds, and saltwater bays or inlets are optimum environments from a recreational and educational as well as visual perspective.

### Wetlands and the Micro-Landscape Within

When viewed in the context of the larger landscape, as in a photograph or from a car window, a wetland may be highly valued for providing openness and contrast in the landscape (Litton et al., 1972; Palmer, 1978; Rodgers, 1970; Smardon, 1972, 1975). As the view shifts to the micro-landscape within the wetland, the perceptual scale shifts, and along with it the values attached to the features of the wetland. Hammitt's (1978) empirical work in Chapter 6 on northern bogs indicates that people like to experience a mixture of open bog mat and wooded screens, which provide "mystery" or intrigue about areas yet to be explored. Hammitt's valuable work suggests that siting and design of boardwalks, channels, or other access enhancements should take advantage of varied spatial experiences and use both restricted and open views of wetland areas. The importance of sequential variance is suggested by More et al. (1977) and Rodgers (1970).

One of the most striking aspects of both freshwater and saltwater marshes is the textual contrast and the patterns formed by open water and aquatic vegetation. Niering (1967) and Rowntree (1976) noted the aesthetic quality of the "uniform bands" of vegetation in saltwater marshes. In his own work, the author has consistently been impressed with the complexity and richness of emergent aquatic-vegetative patterns, in wetlands and the interspersion, in

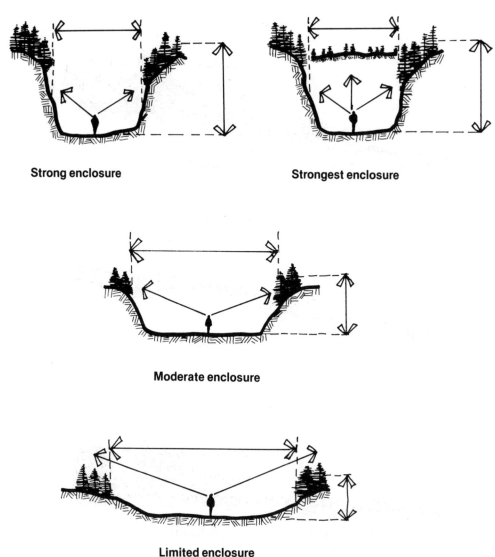

**Strong enclosure**

**Strongest enclosure**

**Moderate enclosure**

**Limited enclosure**

**Figure 1.3.** Wetland enclosure.

ideal proportions of vegetation and open-water areas (Smardon, 1972, 1975). The striking surface patterns and textures of wetlands are often highly transient and easily altered by changes in water level, vegetation robustness, color, or light conditions. Nevertheless, the water/vegetation surface patterns are clearly a unique attribute of both fresh- and saltwater wetlands (see Figures 1.5, 1.6).

Man-made elements in the wetland microlandscape, such as a boardwalk on a bog mat, may also be accepted as compatible with the natural area (Hammitt, 1978). If sensitively sited and designed, a boardwalk may even promote visual, recreational, and educational values by providing access to an otherwise restricted and extremely delicate area.

### Dynamic Aspects of Wetlands

Some of the dynamic aspects of wetlands include seasonal changes and their effects on wetland vegetation (Rodgers, 1970; Smardon, 1972). For example, skunk cabbage often

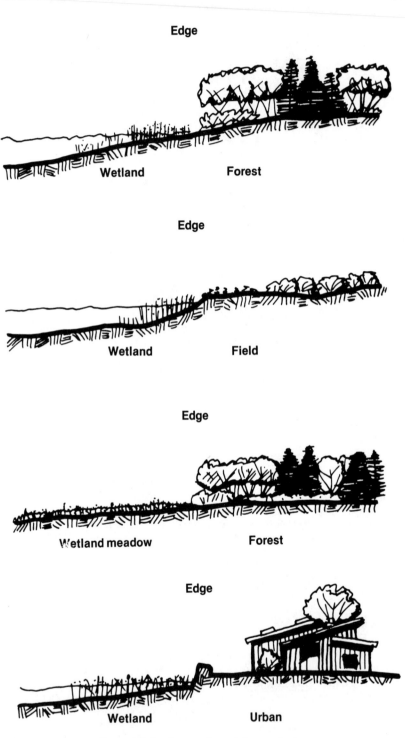

**Figure 1.4.** Land-use and vegetative contrast.

12

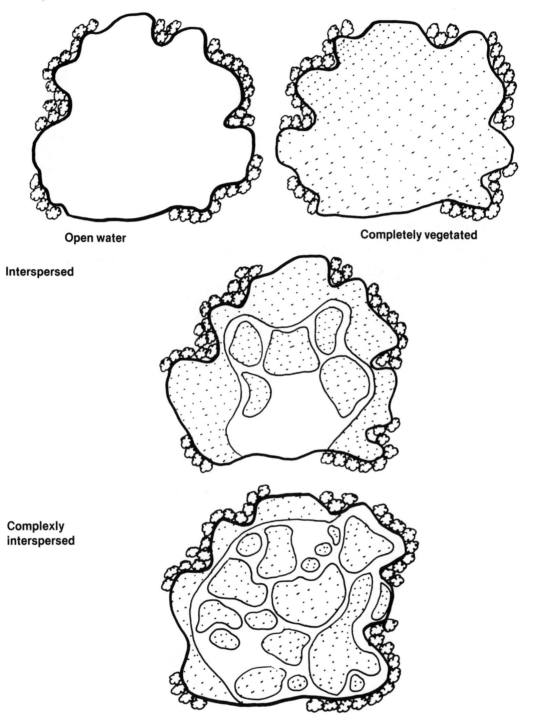

**Figure 1.5.** Vegetative/water interspersion patterns.

**Figure 1.6.** Vegetative/water interspersion patterns.

dominates the floor of northeastern wooded swamps in early spring; red maple, with its early fall color, visually dominates the wetland wooded environment in the fall. Early blooming, early greening, and fall color also contribute to the contrast between many northern wetlands and surrounding upland areas.

Probably some of the most important aspects of wetlands in terms of visual-cultural values are those that are the hardest to assess. Rowntree (1976) in Chapter 8 notes the dynamic visual aspects of salt marshes, especially the tidal flow itself and its manifestation in the morphology of the vegetative community. Even more dynamic is wetland wildlife, glimpses of which range from an occasional moose in northern bogs or the American alligator in the Everglades to huge flocks of migrating waterfowl in wetlands along major flyways. Wildlife inevitably steals the show from its habitat. Ironically, little, if any, empirical perceptual or behavioral work exists on the aesthetic aspects of wildlife in wetland environments—the raison d'être behind popular demand for preservation of wetland en-

vironments. In view of the increasing emphasis on passive recreation and nonconsumptive values of wildlife, this is truly an overlooked research area.

## Summary

Land-use allocation decisions are being made without adequate consideration of visual-cultural and other values of wetlands. From the perspective of ecological aesthetics, it is clear that wetlands are visually and educationally rich environments. Restrictions on recreational access also keep wetlands from being altered or developed for more intensive uses.

Many wetlands are outstanding natural areas harboring unique or rare natural phenomena. Individual wetlands also give visual contrast and diversity to the larger landscape. Wetland systems serve to structure development or provide needed solitude for wilderness or semi-wilderness experiences for urban dwellers. Assessments of composite visual, recreational, and educational values of nonexceptional wetlands have different evaluative and perceptual frameworks. For all perceptual and experiential modes and at all geographical scales, wetlands have high visual and educational values relative to other types of landscape.

These values can be projected over time to show their relative worth by an economic proxy accounting method (Gupta and Foster, 1975; Smardon, 1975) as shown in Chapter 9. Wetlands can also be rated according to visual, recreational, and educational preferences, as measured with visual stimuli, such as photographs, and various scales, such as Likert's rating scale (Hammitt, 1978) in Chapter 6 and the semantic differential or rank ordering (Lee, 1978) in Chapter 4.

# References

Cheek, N. H., Jr., and Field, D. R. 1977. Aquatic resources and behavior. *Leisure Sciences* 1 (1):67–83.

Cherem, J. C., and Traweek, D. E. 1977. Visitor employed photography: A tool for interpretative planning on river environments. In *Proceedings Symposium River Recreation Management and Research*. USDA, Forest Service Gen. Tech. Rep. NC–28, North Central Forest Experiment Station, St. Paul, Minn. Pp. 236–44.

Dansereau, P. 1975. *Inscape and landscape: The human perception of environment*. New York: Columbia University Press. 118 pp.

Errington, P. L. 1957. *Of men and marshes*. Ames: The Iowa State University Press. 150 pp.

Fabos, J. Gy.; Hendrix, W. G.; and Greene, C. T. 1975. Visual and cultural components of the landscape resource assessment model of the METLAND study. In E. H. Zube, R. O. Brush, and J. Gy. Fabos, eds. *Landscape assessment: Value, perceptions, and resources*. Stroudsburg, Pa.: Dowden, Hutchinson and Ross. Pp. 319–43.

Gosselink, J. G.; Odum, E. P.; and Pope, R. M. 1973. *The value of tidal marsh*. Gainesville: Urban and Regional Development Center, University of Florida. 32 pp.

Gupta, T. R., and Foster, J. H. 1975. Economic criteria for freshwater wetland policy in Massachusetts. *American Journal of Agricultural Economics* 57 (1):692–97.

Hammitt, W. E. 1978. Visual and user preference for a bog environment. Ph.D. dissertation, School of Forestry, University of Michigan, Ann Arbor. 159 pp.

Haslam, S. M. 1973. The management of British wetlands 1. Economic and amenity use. *Journal of Environmental Management* 1:303–20.

Krutilla, J. V., and Fisher, A. C. 1975. Chap. 9, Allocations of prairie wetlands. In *The economics of natural environments: Studies in the valuation of commodity and amenity resources*. Baltimore: The Johns Hopkins University Press. Pp. 219–32.

Larson, J. S., and Foster, C.H.W. 1955. Massachusetts marshes . . . and their owners. Boston: Wildlife Conservation, Inc., mimeo.

Lee, M. S. 1977. Visual quality assessment of Louisiana river landscapes: A methodological study. Master's thesis, Department of Landscape Architecture, Louisiana State University, Baton Rouge. 183 pp.

Lewis, P. H., Jr., ed. 1970. Appendix B: Aesthetic and cultural values. In *Upper Mississippi River comprehensive basin study*. Chicago: Upper Mississippi River Comprehensive Basin Study Coordinating Committee 1:1–489.

Litton, R. B., Jr.; Laurie, M.; and Wakeman, N. 1972. The landscape as a visual resource. In R. Corwin, ed., *Tomales Bay Study Compendium of Reports*. Washington, D.C.: Conservation Foundation. Pp. 25–53.

Litton, R. B., Jr.; Tetlow, R. J.,; Sorensen, J.; and Beatty, R. A. 1974. *Water and landscape: An aesthetic overview of the role of water in the landscape*. Port Washington, N.Y.: Water Information, Inc. 314 pp.

Louisiana State University. 1977. *Pre-Symposium Compilation of Papers Scenic Rivers Symposium*, June 17–19, Baton Rouge. 157 pp.

More, T. A.; Brush, R. O.; and Wagar, J. A. 1977. Variation and recreation quality in river management. In *Proceedings Symposium River Recreation Management and Research*. USDA, Forest Service Gen. Tech. Rep. NC–28, North Central Forest Station, St. Paul, Minn. Pp. 329–33.

Niering, W. A. 1967. The dilemma of the coastal wetlands: Conflict of local national and world priorities. In P. Dansereau, ed. *The fitness of man's environment*. Washington, D.C.: Smithsonian Annual II, Smithsonian Institution. Pp. 143–56.

———. 1970. The ecology of wetlands in urban areas. In B. F. Thomas, ed. *Preserving our freshwater wetlands*. New London: Connecticut Arboretum, Connecticut College. Pp. 12–19.

Odum, E. P. 1971. *Fundamentals of ecology*. 3rd ed. Philadelphia: W. B. Saunders. 574 pp.

Palmer, J. F. 1978. Citizen assessment of the coastal visual resource. In: Vol. 2, *Coastal Zone '78 Symposium on Technical, Environmental, Socioeconomic and Regulatory Aspects of Coastal Zone Management*, March 14–16, San Francisco. New York: American Society of Civil Engineers. Pp. 1019–37.

Pepper, S. C. 1937. *Aesthetic quality: A contextualistic theory of beauty*. New York: Charles Scribner's Sons. 255 pp.

Randall, W. E., and Brainerd, J. W., n.d. *Educational values of wetlands in Massachusetts*. Boston: Massachusetts Wetlands Commission Fact Sheet 5, Wildlife Conservation, Inc.

Rodgers, W. E. 1970. Design criteria for the visual enhancement of water resources formed or altered during the construction of major highways. M.L.A. thesis, Department of Landscape Architecture and

Regional Planning, University of Massachusetts, Amherst. 113 pp.

Rowntree, R. A. 1976. Visual attributes of the estuary: An emphasis on dynamics. In D. B. Harper and J. D. Warbach, eds. *Visual Quality of the Coastal Zone, Proceedings of a Conference/Workshop* May 29–30, 1975. Sea Grant Project, School of Landscape Architecture, SUNY College of Environmental Science and Forestry, Syracuse, N.Y. Pp. 51–65.

Shaw, S. P., and Fredine, C. G. 1956. *Wetlands of the United States: Their extent and their value to waterfowl and other wildlife.* USDI, Fish and Wildlife Cir. 39. Washington, D.C.: U.S. Government Printing Office. 67 pp.

Smardon, R. C. 1972. Assessing visual-cultural values of inland wetlands in Massachusetts. M.L.A. thesis, Department of Landscape Architecture and Regional Planning, University of Massachusetts, Amherst. 295 pp.

_____. 1975. Assessing visual-cultural values of inland wetlands in Massachusetts. In E. H. Zube, R. O. Brush, and J. Gy. Fabos, eds. *Landscape assessment: Value, perceptions, and resources.* Stroudsburg, Pa.: Dowden, Hutchinson and Ross. Pp. 289–318.

_____. 1977. Research strategy for assessing visual impact from management and land development activities on wild and scenic rivers. In *Pre-Symposim Compilation of Papers Scenic Rivers Symposium,* June 17–19, 1977, Louisiana State University, Baton Rouge. Pp. 79–85.

_____. 1973. Visual-cultural values of wetlands. In J. S. Larson, ed. *A guide to important characteristics and values of fresh-water wetlands in the Northeast.* Water Resources Research Center Pub. No. 31, University of Massachusetts, Amherst. Pp. 9–11.

Smardon, R.C., and Fabos, J. Gy. 1976. Visual-cultural sub-model. In J. S. Larson, ed. *Models for assessment of fresh-water wetlands.* Water Resources Research Center, Pub. No. 32, University of Massachusetts, Amherst. Pp. 35–51.

Steinitz, C.; Brown, H. J.; Wilkins, H.; Sinton, D.; Gillespie, D.; Kilner, S.; and Klinefelter, P. 1978. *Simulating alternative policies for implementing the Massachusetts Scenic and Recreational Rivers Act: The North River demonstration project.* Landscape Architecture Research Office, Graduate School of Design, Harvard University, Cambridge. 103 pp.

USDA, Forest Service. 1977. *Proceedings Symposium River Recreation Management and Research,* January 24–27, Minneapolis. USDA Forest Service Gen. Tech. Rep. NC–28, North Central Forest Experiment Station, St. Paul, Minn. 455 pp.

USDI, Fish and Wildlife Service. 1962. The value of wetlands to modern society. In *Proceedings of the MAR Conference,* November 12–16. IUCN Pub. (new series) 3. Washington, D.C.: U.S. Government Printing Office.

Wharton, C. H. 1970. *The southern river swamp—a multi-use environment.* Bureau of Business and Economic Research School of Business Administration, Georgia State University, Atlanta.

Parts of this chapter appeared in "Visual-Cultural Values of Wetlands" in *Wetland Functions and Values: The State of Our Understanding* (Minneapolis, Minn.: American Water Resources Association, 1979). Reprinted by permission.

# 2 Wetland Policy and Visual-Cultural Values in the United States

## RICHARD C. SMARDON

## Introduction

The purpose of this chapter is to review and examine wetland laws and policy as they specifically affect visual-cultural values within the United States. The value of wetlands were documented in a multidiscipline symposium held at Lake Beuna Vista, Florida, in 1977 (Greeson, Clark, and Clark, 1978). The definition of visual-cultural values with their attendant uses is heralded in a U.S. interagency task force report (Council on Environmental Quality, 1978). Wetland visual-cultural values are defined in the same way as in Chapter 1. Law and policy affecting how wetland land-use decisions are made occur within federal, state, and local governments. Pertinent laws, programs, and policies at all three levels will be briefly reviewed, but only in regard to visual-cultural values. A review of such laws and programs is comprehensively treated in Kusler (1978). The author will briefly review pertinent federal and state laws, programs, and policy guidance as well as critical court cases at the state level.

Policy implications will be reviewed at the end of the chapter.

## Federal Programs Affecting Wetlands

Community wetland programs are encouraged by a number of federal programs. Some of the best known include the Coastal Zone Management Act of 1972, the National Flood Insurance Act of 1968, and the Rivers and Harbors Act of 1899. Each will be examined briefly.

1. *The Coastal Zone Management Act of 1972.*[1] The Coastal Zone Management Act of 1972 applies to all states bordering on the oceans or the Great Lakes. To qualify for federal grants-in-aid for administration of a coastal zone program, a state must adapt land-use regulatory and purchase powers for coastal zone areas and either directly regulate uses or establish standards for local regulation of these uses. The Act also authorizes federal grants-in-aid for pur-

chase of estuarine sanctuaries, although these provisions have not been funded. States are required to inventory coastal zone areas of "particular concern." These have been defined by administrative guidelines to include wetland areas.

All coastal states have established coastal zone programs, although only one has been approved by the Department of Commerce as meeting administrative standards. Emphasis upon the identification and protection of coastal wetlands is a principal focus of many programs, including those of Maine, Massachusetts, Rhode Island, Connecticut, New York, North Carolina, Florida, California, Oregon, and Washington.

Many states have emphasized local and regional rather than state implementation of coastal zone policies including wetland protection, although the state retains the power to regulate directly coastal areas in the event that local units fail to adopt and administer regulations meeting state standards. States taking this approach include Maine, Oregon, Wisconsin, Minnesota, Virginia, and Washington. Local incentives for wetland regulation under state coastal zone programs include (1) local autonomy in administration and enforcement of regulations that would otherwise be implemented at state level, (2) state and federal data gathering and technical assistance, and (3) in a few states, state grants-in-aid. In addition, a community may gain a measure of control over federal projects in the coastal zone by adopting a program that is approved by the state and, in turn, by the Department of Commerce, since the Coastal Zone Management Act requires that federal projects comply with approved state coastal zone programs. Part of the purpose of the act is "to encourage states to achieve wise use of the land and water resources of the coastal zone, giving full consideration to ecological, cultural, historic, and aesthetic values [emphasis added]."[2]

2. *Corps of Engineers Permit Procedures.* A permit is required from the U.S. Army Corps of Engineers for most fills and dredging of U.S. waters pursuant to the Rivers and Harbors Act of 1899[3] and the Federal Water Pollution Control Act Amendments of 1972.[4] Under a judicially broadened definition of Corps jurisdiction, a Corps permit will soon be required for fills and dredging in lakes larger than five acres, rivers to the point of headwaters (the point at which flow is five cubic feet per second), coastal areas to the high-water mark, and associated wetlands. Permits will not be issued unless proposed uses are consistent with state coastal zone programs and local regulations. These requirements give community wetland protection programs a strong veto power over Corps permits.

In addition to the Corps' general guidelines, the Environmental Protection Agency (EPA) has published "Guidelines for Specification of Disposal Sites for Dredged or Fill Material" under section 404 of the Water Pollution Control Act Amendments of 1972.[5] Within Subpart G, Human Use Characteristics of These Guidelines, EPA has included sections on recreation, aesthetics, and amenities. These provisions are quoted in full here to show the breadth and depth of the considerations included in these guideline regulations.

**230.62 Recreation:**

Recreation encompasses activities undertaken for amusement and relaxation. Water related outdoor recreation requires the use, but not necessarily the consumptive use, of natural aquatic sites and resources, including wetlands.

(a) Values. Much of our outdoor recreation is water-dependent. A host of activities, including fishing, swimming, boating, water-skiing, racing, clamming, camping, beachcombing, picnicking, waterfowl hunting, *wildlife photography, bird watching and scenic enjoyment, take place on, in, or adjacent to the water.* In many parts of the country, space and resources for aquatic recreation are in great demand. Water quality is a vital factor in determining the capacity of an area to support the various water oriented outdoor recreation activities.

(b) Possible loss of values. *One of the more important direct impacts of dredged or fill disposal is on aesthetics;* more serious impacts impair or destroy the resources which support recreation activities. Among the water quality parameters of importance to recreation that can be impacted by the disposal of dredged or fill material are turbidity, suspended particulates, temperature, dissolved oxygen, dissolved materials, toxic materials, pathogenic organisms, degradation of habitat, *and the aesthetic qualities of sight, taste, odor and color.* Changes in the levels of these parameters can adversely modify or destroy water use for several or all of the recreation activities enjoyed in any given area.

(c) Guidelines to minimize impacts. In addition to the consideration of alternatives in 230.10(a), Guidelines to minimize impacts as described in 230.10(d), and water dependency in 230.10(e), and the specific measures described in Subparts E and F, where appropriate, specific measures to minimize impacts on recreational resources include, but are not limited to:

(1) Selecting discharge sites removed from areas of recognized recreational value.

(2) Selecting time periods of discharge that do not coincide with seasons or periods of high recreational use.

(3) Use of procedures and methods as described in 230.31(c) and 230.32(c) to minimize and contain the amounts of suspended particulates and dissolved contaminants, including nutrients, pathogens, and other contaminants released to the water column.

(d) Special determinations. In addition to the determination required by 230.20, and the special determinations required by Subparts E and F, where appropriate, special determinations where recreational areas may be affected by the discharge of dredged or fill material include whether the discharge will:

(1) Change or affect the suitability of an area of high recreational value to provide recreational opportunities.

## 230.63 Aesthetics:

*Aesthetics, associated with the aquatic ecosystem, including wetlands, consist of the perception of beauty by one or a combination of the senses of sight, hearing, touch and smell. Aesthetics of aquatic ecosystems apply to the quality of life enjoyed by the general public as distinct from the value of property realized by owners as a result of access to such systems (see 230.64).*

(a) Values. *The aesthetic values of aquatic areas are usually the enjoyment and appreciation derived from the natural characteristics of a particular area. Aesthetic values may include such parameters as the visual distinctiveness of the elements present, which may result from prominence, contrasts due to irregularity in form, line, color, and pattern; the diversity of elements present including topographic expression, shoreline complexity, landmarks, vegetative pattern diversity, waterform expression, and wildlife visibility; and the compositional harmony or unity of the overall area. . . .*

(b) Possible loss of values. *The discharge of dredged or fill material can mar the beauty of natural aquatic ecosystems by degrading the water quality, creating distracting disposal sites, inducing nonconforming developments, encouraging human access, and by destroying vital elements that contribute to the com-* *positional harmony or unity, visual distinctiveness, or diversity of an area.*

(c) Guidelines to minimize impacts. In addition to the consideration of alternatives in 230.10(a), Guidelines to minimize impacts as described in 230.10(d), water dependency in 230.10(e), and specific measures described in Subparts D, E and F, where appropriate, specific measures to minimize impacts on aesthetic values include, but are not limited to:

(1) *Selecting discharge sites and following discharge procedures that will prevent or minimize any potential damage to the aesthetically pleasing features of the aquatic site, particularly with respect to water quality.*

(2) Following procedures that will restore the disturbed area to its natural condition.

(d) Special determination. In addition to the determinations required by 230.20 and the special determinations required by Subparts E and F, where appropriate, *special determinations where aesthetic values in aquatic areas may be affected by the discharge of dredged or fill material include whether the discharge will change or affect the elements of an aquatic or wetland area which contribute to its aesthetic appeal.*

## 230.64 Amenities

*Amenities derived from a natural aquatic ecosystem, including wetlands, include any environmental feature, trait, or character that contributes to the attractiveness of real estate, or to the successful operation of a business serving the public on its premises. Aquatic resources which are unowned or publicly owned may provide amenities to privately owned property in the vicinity.*

(a) Values. *Persons or institutions claiming amenities of the unowned or publicly owned aquatic ecosystem have monetary investments in property, a portion of which can be realized only because of the existence of unowned but accessible aquatic amenities. The added property value attributable to natural amenities varies with the quality, use and accessibility of aquatic and wetland areas.*

(b) Possible loss of values. *The discharge of dredged or fill material can adversely affect the particular features, traits, or characters of an aquatic area which make it valuable as an amenity to property owners. Dredge or fill activities which degrade water quality, disrupt natural substrata and vegetational characteristics, deny access to the amenities, or result in changes in odor, air quality, or noise levels may reduce the value of an aquatic area as an amenity to private property.*

(c) Guidelines to minimize impacts. In addition to the consideration alternatives 230.10(a), the

Guidelines to minimize impacts as described in 230.10(d), water dependency in 230.10(e), and specific measures described in Subparts E and F, where appropriate, specific measures to minimize impacts on amenities include, but are not limited to:

(1) *Selecting discharge sites which are of lesser value to nearby property owners as natural aquatic or wetland amenities.*

(2) *Timing the discharge* to avoid interference during seasons or periods when the availability and accessibility of aquatic or wetland amenities are most important.

(3) Following *discharge procedures that do not disturb features of the aquatic ecosystem which contribute to the value of an aquatic amenity.*

(d) Special determination. In addition to the determinations required by 230.20 and the special determinations required by Subparts E and F, where appropriate, *special determinations where aquatic amenities may be affected by discharges of dredged or fill material include whether the discharge will change or affect any feature of an aquatic area which contributes* to its value as an amenity to property owners. [emphasis added].[6]

Note that EPA has written guidelines treating three distinct classes of visual-cultural values: recreational, aesthetic, and amenities. There are a number of interesting points in the characterization of these values. First, recreational values include those recreational activities that "take place on, in, or adjacent to the water,"[7] thus including the adjacent upland as contributing to the enjoyment of the value. Second, aesthetics includes "perception of beauty by one or more of a combination of the senses of sight, hearing, touch and smell,"[8] thus not delimiting aesthetics to visual only. Note also that the "enjoyment and appreciation [are] derived from natural characteristics of a particular area."[9] Many of these "characteristics" are documented and described in the following chapters. Third, and finally, note the special treatment of the amenity values, which in contrast to values enjoyed by the general public are "derived from a natural aquatic ecosystem, including wetlands, include any environmental feature, trait, or character that contributes to the attractiveness of real estate, or to the successful operation of a business serving the public on its premises,"[10] thus recognizing the economic attributes of aesthetic values through their contribution to property values and operation of certain amenity-dependent businesses.

In addition to recognizing these three distinctive classes of visual-cultural values, the EPA guideline regulations even specify a procedure for "site appearance determinations," which include photographic documentation of the site in question. The following passage is taken from EPA's guideline regulations and specifies procedures for visually documenting site conditions:

**230.20**

(g) Proposed disposal site appearance determinations. A determination shall be made of the appearance of the proposed disposal site and appropriate parts of the surrounding environment prior to the initiation of a discharge activity. Photographic determinations are preferable to narrative descriptions, provided they are accompanied by pertinent data such as exact location of photographer and direction of exposure, time of year and day and weather conditions affecting film exposure, the kind of camera, lens, etc. used, and the photograph clearly depicts those aspects of the aquatic environment and wetlands that will be impacted or modified by the discharge activity.

Comment: The appearance of the proposed disposal site and its surroundings prior to any discharge activity is relevant to the findings required in 230.10 and 230.11. Sufficiently detailed information concerning the appearance of the disposal site before discharge occurs will aid in predicting the impact of the discharge, assessing the adequacy of measures to minimize impacts, monitoring compliance with the permit, and restoring the site where appropriate.

(h) Special determinations. A determination shall be made of whether the material to be discharged will disrupt any special disposal site characteristics, taking into consideration the resource values, possible loss of these resources, and these Guidelines, as well as special determinations described in Subparts E through G of the proposed disposal site.[11]

This specific procedure was suggested by the author to EPA to ensure adequate records of the site before an activity had taken place, and to be used as visual information for assessing the adequacy of mitigation procedures and whether they had in fact taken place.

## State Programs Affecting Wetlands

State programs pertaining to wetlands include coastal wetlands acts, inland wetlands acts, coastal management acts, critical-area acts, navigable water acts, shoreline and lake management acts, open-space acts, and land-use planning acts.

Specific state statutes that mention aesthetic enjoyment of wetlands, scenic values of wetlands, or preservation of natural landscape character include coastal wetlands acts for Delaware,[12] Maryland,[13] New York,[14] Rhode Island,[15] and Virginia[16]; inland wetlands and navigable waterways acts for New Hampshire,[17] Vermont,[18] and Wisconsin[19]; state critical-area legislation for Alabama,[20] Arkansas,[21] Minnesota,[22] and Virginia[23]; coastal Management Acts for New Jersey,[24] Rhode Island,[25] and Texas[26]; shoreline and lake management acts for Maine,[27] Michigan,[28] and Washington[29]; an open-space act for Pennsylvania[30]; and a land-use planning act for Vermont.[31]

Specific state statutes that mention recreational values or enjoyment include coastal wetlands acts for Delaware,[32] Mississippi,[33] and New Jersey[34]; an inland lakes act for Michigan[35]; and a freshwater wetlands and a coastal management act for Rhode Island.[36] The critical-area acts for Minnesota[37] and Alabama[38] include cultural and historical values of wetlands. New York State's Tidal Wetlands Act[39] is the most comprehensive by including the educational and research values of wetlands as well as recreational and aesthetic values.

## Local Regulation of Wetlands

Local regulation of wetland activities is required by state wetland protection acts in Virginia, Massachusetts, Connecticut, and New York. The Wisconsin and Washington State shoreland zoning programs and the Florida critical-area program, which has been interpreted to apply to Big Cypress and Green Swamps, also require local controls. More than 1,000 local communities have adopted wetland protection regulations in these states. A larger number of other communities have adopted land-use regulations for wetland areas pursuant to coastal-zone or flood-plain regulatory efforts, or broader land-use zoning or subdivisions control programs.

As noted earlier, local adoption of wetland regulations has been encouraged not only by state wetland acts but also by the requirements of the National Flood Insurance Program, which requires local regulation of the 100-year frequency flood plain area in order to qualify for federally subsidized flood insurance. More than 14,000 communities have adopted or indicated an intent to adopt flood-plain regulations to qualify for this program. Other federal incentives to wetland protection by localities include the Coastal Zone Act of 1972 and the Corps of Engineers' 404 permit requirements.

Strong local as well as state and federal incentives exist for regulation of wetland areas. These include the achievement of common land- and water-use planning objectives, such as reasonable minimization of natural hazards, provision for open space and recreation areas, prevention of drainage and flood problems, prevention of septic tanks in unsuitable areas, allocation of lands throughout a community to their most appropriate uses, and protection of water supplies. Rarely are sufficient funds available at the local level to purchase more than a small portion of community wetlands to serve these objectives. In addition, it is often politically unacceptable to remove totally large acreages of land from the tax roles and all productive uses. For this reason, several types of land-use regulation are commonly adopted to restrict land uses with the most severe impact upon wetlands while permitting continued private use of lands.

## Regulatory Approaches and Techniques

The two main regulatory approaches applied to wetland areas are (1) complete prohibition of all fills, dredging, and structural uses, and (2) application of performance standards to uses that reduce flood losses, reduce impact upon wildlife, and serve a wide range of other objectives. The second approach is more common, although a considerable number of communities have adopted restrictive controls.

Explicit wetland protection provisions are typically incorporated in several types of local regulations:

1. Local wetland zoning regulations. These most common kinds of wetland protection are adopted as a primary or overlay zone within a broader comprehensive zoning ordinance or,

alternatively, as a separate wetland ordinance. The regulations may be based upon a special wetland regulatory statute, coastal zone, shoreland, or scenic and wild river statute, or broader zoning authority. Zoning regulations consist of a map showing wetland boundaries and a text listing prohibited and permitted uses and establishing general standards for special permit uses. Usually a zoning board of adjustment, planning board, or special board (e.g., a conservation commission) is authorized to evaluate applications for special permits within wetland areas.

2. Special wetland protection bylaws or ordinances. These may be adopted pursuant to special wetland protection statutes (e.g., a Massachusetts statute authorizes local units of government to regulate directly or comment upon wetland uses), statutes authorizing local control of grading and filling, tree cutting, and other activities, or to home rule powers. Typically, they contain a text setting forth prohibited, permitted, and special permit uses. Wetlands may be defined by description or with a map reference.

In addition to these two principal types of wetland regulations, control of wetland development may be achieved through several other types of special and general ordinances and bylaws. Rarely do any of these measures include specific provisions for consideration of visual-cultural or heritage values.

## Critical Court Cases

What is most interesting and significant in the implementation of local government wetland regulation is a number of court cases that have generated from disputes about appropriate decision-making by local units of government. These court cases can be generalized into two distinct directions on the basis of the judges' findings.

One direction is an environmentally conservative trend of courts to find in wetland regulation cases landowners who were deprived of their property rights by local governmental bodies when they tried to restrict their uses of the wetlands. Such was the basic trend in the cases of *Turnpike Realty Co.* v. *Town of*

*Dedham*[40] and *MacGibbon* v. *Board of Appeals of Duxbury*[41] in Massachusetts and in *State of Maine* v. *R. B. Johnson*.[42] In these cases, the court tended to diminish the importance of the natural functions of wetlands; it stressed individual property rights of wetlands owners or questioned procedural practices of local wetland regulation bodies in their restrictive actions.

On the other hand are the environmentally liberal cases that advance the doctrine of public trust applied to wetland areas: That is, certain environments like wetlands, beaches, shorelands, and river bottoms either have certain publicly held values and functions and/or the state holds title to certain of these areas or subareas under former precedent. These cases are characterized by *Muench* v. *Public Service Commission*,[43] *Just* v. *Marinette County*,[44] and, recently, *State* v. *Ashmore*.[45]

*Just* v. *Marinette County* in Wisconsin is the most interesting of the three in its articulation of the public-trust doctrine. First, the court states the context for the case and notes the changing sense of value of wetlands in general.

This case causes us to re-examine the concepts of public benefit in contrast to public harm and rescope of an owner's right to use his property. In the instant case we have a restriction on the use of a citizen's property, not to secure a benefit from the public, but to prevent a harm from the change in the natural character of the citizen's property. . . . What makes this case different from most condemnation or police power zoning cases is the interrelationship of the wetlands, the swamps and the natural environment of shorelands to the purity of the water and to such natural resources as navigation, fishing, and scenic beauty. Swamps and wetlands were once considered wasteland, undesirable, and not picturesque; but as the people became more sophisticated, an appreciation was acquired that swamps and wetlands serve a vital role in nature, are part of the balance of nature and are essential to the purity of the water in our lakes and streams. Swamps and wetlands are a necessary part of the ecological creation and now, even to the uninitiated, possess their own beauty in nature.[46]

Next, the court states what the owners rights are and what is and is not a reasonable use of the area in question:

An owner of land has no absolute and unlimited right to change the essential natural character of his land so as to use it for a purpose for which it was un-suited in its natural state and which injures the rights of others.

The exercise of the police power in zoning must be reasonable and we think it is not an unreasonable exercise of that power to prevent harm to public right by limiting the use of private property to its natural use.[47]

The changing of wetlands and swamps to the damage of the general public by upsetting the natural environment and the natural relationship is not a reasonable use of that land which is protected from police power regulation.[48]

The court acknowledges the precedence of its decision, but it presents a balancing test to weigh the interests in any given situation.

We realize no case in Wisconsin has yet dealt with shoreland regulations and there are several cases in other states which seem to hold such regulations unconstitutional; but nothing this court has said or held in prior cases indicates that destroying the natural character of a swamp or a wetland so as to make that location available for human habitation is a reasonable use of that land when the new use, although of a more economical value to the owner, causes a harm to the general public.[49]

The balancing test is to weigh the magnitude of the personal economic loss to the particular landowner against the magnitude of the harm to the general public, which is usually the infringement or elimination of the natural functions and character of the wetland. Finally, the court cites the case of Muench v. Public Service Commission[50] in Wisconsin in articulating the public-trust mandate for the state and including protection of recreation and scenic beauty in that mandate.

The active public trust duty of the State of Wisconsin in respect to navigable waters requires the state not only promote navigation but also protect those waters for fishing, recreation and scenic beauty.[51]

## Policy Implications

From the author's perspective, it seems inevitable that the liberal environmental view of decision-making concerning the fate of U.S. wetlands will prevail in certain states and gradually spread to others. Just as zoning upheld merely on aesthetic considerations has gradu-

ally been accepted in some jurisdictions, so will aesthetic considerations in wetland management. This can be seen in the differences in the breadth and scope of values that were not recognized in the early Massachusetts wetlands statute in contrast to the newer New York State statute. And it can be seen in the difference between the earlier Corps of Engineers' Section 404 wetland-permit considerations and the new EPA guideline regulations for Section 404. It also can be seen to some degree in the court decisions just described. Of course there should be procedural safeguards against highly discretionary or arbitrary decision-making that may harm personal property rights. However, as we come to know more about the natural functions and values of wetlands to the individual property owner and the public, the public trust must be given its proper consideration and weight.

## Notes

1. 16 U.S.C., section 1451 et seq., Coastal Zone Management Act of 1972.
2. Ibid.
3. 33 U.S.C. 403, River and Harbor Act of 1899.
4. 33 U.S.C. 1088 et seq., Water Pollution Control Amendments of 1972.
5. 33 U.S.C. 404.
6. 40 CFR 230, Federal Register, Vol. 44, No. 182, pp. 54248–49.
7. Ibid.
8. Ibid.
9. Ibid.
10. Ibid.
11. Ibid., p. 54235.
12. Coastal Wetlands, Delaware Code, Title 7, Section 6602.
13. Coastal Wetlands, Maryland Annotated Code, Title 9, Section 9–102.
14. Tidal Wetlands, New York State Environmental Conservation Law, Section 25–0101.
15. Coastal Wetlands, Rhode Island General Laws, Title 46, Chap. 23, Section 1.
16. Coastal Wetlands, Virginia Code Annotated 62.1–13.1 et seq.
17. Coastal and Inland Wetlands, New Hampshire Revised Statutes Annotated 483–A:1–b.
18. Navigable Waters, Shorelands, Vermont Statutes Annotated, Title 10, Section 1421.
19. Shoreland Areas, Wisconsin Statutes Annotated 144.26.
20. Coastal Areas, Alabama Code Title 9, Chap. 7, Section 2.
21. Environmental Quality Act, Arkansas Statutes Annotated, Chap. 9, Section 1401.
22. Comprehensive Critical Areas Act, Minnesota Statutes Annotated, Section 1166.02.

23. Critical Environmental Areas, Virginia Code Annotated, Sections 10–187 to 10–196.

24. Coastal Wetlands, New Jersey Statutes Annotated, Title 13, Chap. 9A–1.

25. Coastal Wetlands, Rhode Island General Laws, Title 46, Chap. 23, Section 1.

26. Coastal Act, Texas Statutes Annotated, Article 33.001.

27. Shorelands, Maine Revised Statutes, Title 12, Section 4811.

28. Shoreland Protection, Michigan Comprehensive Laws Annotated, Section 281.957.

29. Shoreline Areas, Revised Code of Washington Annotated, Title 90.58.

30. Open Space, Pennsylvania Statutes Annotated, Title 16, Section 11941.

31. Large-Scale Development Site Review Act, Vermont Statutes Annotated, Title 10, Sections 6001–89.

32. Coastal Zone, Delaware Code, Title 7, Section 7004.

33. Coastal Wetlands, Mississippi Code Annotated 49.27–1.

34. Coastal Areas, New Jersey Statutes Annotated, Title 13, Chap. 19.

35. Inland Lakes, Michigan Comprehensive Laws Annotated 281.951.

36. Coastal Wetlands, Rhode Island General Laws, Sections 2–1–13 et. seq., and Coastal Areas, Sections 46–23–1 to 46–23–16.

37. Comprehensive Critical Areas Act, Minnesota Statutes Annotated, Section 1166.02.

38. State Critical Area, Alabama Code, Title 9, Chap. 7, Section 1.

39. Tidal Wetlands, New York State Environmental Conservation Law, Section 25–0101.

40. *Turnpike Realty Co.* v. *Town of Dedham*, 362 Mass. 221, 284 N.E. 2d 891, 3 ELR 20221 (1972).

41. *MacGibbon* v. *Board of Appeals of Duxbury*, 347 Mass. 690 (1964), 356 Mass. 635, 255 N.E. 2nd 349 (1970).

42. *State of Maine* v. *R. B. Johnson*, 265 A 2d 711.

43. *Muench* v. *Public Service Commission*, 55 N.W. 2nd 40.

44. *Just* v. *Marinette County*, 56 Wis. 2d 7 201 N.W. 2nd 761, 3 ELR 20167 (1972).

45. *State* v. *Ashmore*, 6 ELR 20430 (Ga. Sup. Ct. Feb. 24, 1976).

46. *Just* v. *Marinette County*, 201 N.W. 2nd 761 at 10.

47. Ibid. at 11, 12.

48. Ibid., at 13.

49. Ibid.

50. *Muench* v. *Public Service Commission*, 55 N.W. 2nd 40 at 14, 15.

51. *Just* v. *Marinette County*, 201 N.W. 2nd 761 at 14–15.

# References

Council on Environmental Quality. 1978. *Our nation's wetlands: An interagency task force report.* Washington, D.C.: U.S. Government Printing Office. 70 pp., illus.

Greeson, P. E.; Clark, J. R.; and Clark, J. E. 1978. *Wetland functions and values: The state of our understanding.* Minneapolis: American Water Resources Association. 674 pp.

Kusler, J. A. 1978. *Strengthening state wetland regulations.* Washington, D.C.: USDI, Office of Biological Services, Fish and Wildlife Service, FWS/OBS–78/98. 147 pp.

# 3 An Evaluation of Wetland Policy in England and Wales

## EDMUND C. PENNING-ROWSELL

## Introduction

Landscape assessment and related research in Britain has always been controversial. Much British landscape research in the 1960s and 1970s focused on attempts to derive universally applicable field-survey or map-based assessment and evaluation systems (Lowenthal, 1978; Penning-Rowsell, 1981a). Many of these approaches have now lost favor with both researchers and land-use planners. The assessment systems devised have been seen as either insufficiently sensitive to local needs, particular problems, and special landscapes, or as of questionable validity. As a result, there has been a move away from qualitative assessments of landscapes toward attempts at quantitative character assessment—in which the components of the landscape are recorded without aesthetic judgments (Welsh Office, 1980)—and toward a greater understanding of the public's attachment to valued landscapes (Dunn, 1976; Penning-Rowsell et al., 1977; Shoard, 1978).

Linking visual and cultural aspects of landscape has not been common in Britain. Economic historians such as Beresford (1954) and Hoskins (1955) have stressed cultural aspects of landscape evolution, and geographers such as Lowenthal and Prince (1964, 1965) and Appleton (1975) have clearly identified the cultural associations involved in landscape appreciation. Planners have taken a more pragmatic approach, with simplistic attempts to measure the aesthetic value of conserved landscapes (Clark, 1968; Fines, 1968), although landscape architects such as Fairbrother (1972) and Laurie (Robinson et al., 1976) have certainly not ignored the fundamentally cultural context of landscape perception and appreciation.

The visual aspects of wetland areas in Britain have received remarkably little attention. In contrast, the cultural aspects have been extensively studied. The main thrust of such study has come from geographers and historians in attempts to illuminate the cultural history of areas that through technological innovation and the resulting agricultural development have changed markedly over the centuries. Many studies have documented the early draining of English marshlands (Darby, 1956; Parker and Pye, 1976; Williams, 1970), and few areas of the British landscape have received greater attention so far as their cultural landscape attributes are concerned.

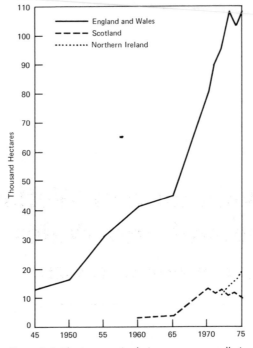

**Figure 3.1.** The increase in drainage area annually in Britain (Hollis, 1979).

Nevertheless, wetland areas are receiving greater attention from those concerned with landscape and nature conservation. The land-drainage program promoted by the Ministry of Agriculture, Fisheries, and Food has been an outstanding success; in virtually every year since 1945, an increased total area has been drained in order to promote higher agricultural productivity (Figure 3.1). As a result, many of the major wetland areas, such as the East Anglian Fens, the Somerset Levels, and the Pevensey Levels, have been partially drained. Minor wetland areas have been drained completely; thus the specialist fauna and flora that are characteristic of these habitats have become considerably rarer. Such trends have produced major conflicts between those concerned with nature conservation and those responsible for agricultural development, as the former attempt to limit the successes of the latter. The conflict is compounded by the lack of systematic data on the nature and extent of wetland habitats and landscapes. Little is known about the significance of wetland landscapes in comparison with other more widely known areas, such as national parks or Areas of Outstanding Natural Beauty. Further research is badly needed on the attributes of major wetland landscapes to complement the existing volumes on their cultural history.

## The Legal and Policy Framework in England and Wales

The legal framework surrounding the designation and use of wetlands is highly complex. Several major government agencies in Britain have responsibilities in the field, and their policies often conflict. Research into wetlands is similarly fragmented and sparse.

The main threat to current wetland landscapes comes from the pressures for agricultural intensification. The significant legislation in this area is the Land Drainage Act of 1930 and 1976. The historical background of this legislation shows a period of extreme agricultural depression in the 1920s, when much land capable of food production went out of use. The government intervened to set up, within an overall system of agricultural support, special Catchment Boards to oversee the drainage of most of England and Wales. Government grants were made available to these Boards and to individual farmers to drain their land. As Figure

3.1 shows, this process of farm drainage has continued unabated ever since, encouraged by a reduction of 50 percent in the real costs of drainage works (Cole, 1976; Parker and Penning-Rowsell, 1980) through the mechanization of the necessary ditch and dike clearance (George, 1976), with hydraulic machinery replacing the traditional draglines.

The current organizations responsible for this drainage work are the land-drainage committees of the regional water authorities, set up under the Water Act of 1973 (Parker and Penning-Rowsell, 1980). Because of the traditional rationale of land drainage in improving farming productivity, the central government's Ministry of Agriculture, Fisheries, and Food has a crucial role in the drainage field. Regional water authorities receive grants for land drainage of up to 85 percent of the capital costs of a scheme, and farmers also receive half of any capital costs they incur in their drainage work.

These grants are provided by the Ministry of Agriculture, Fisheries, and Food so long as the benefits of a scheme outweigh its costs. The cost-benefit exercise is vetted by Ministry officials who also review the schemes to ensure that certain design standards are met (Penning-Rowsell and Chatterton, 1977). However, the Ministry does not assess the overall environmental impact of the schemes, which has been shown to be considerable (Hill, 1976), nor are any visual design standards established for the scheme construction itself or for the resulting landscape of the drainage area. Notes issued by the Ministry's Agricultural Development and Advisory Service (1974–77) give no guidelines on the visual impacts of drainage or on the potential effect of drainage on culturally important landscape elements such as buildings, ancient dikes, roadways, or field boundaries.

The land-drainage policy of the Ministry of Agriculture, Fisheries, and Food is part of a wider agricultural program to increase the level of British food self-sufficiency and so reduce the adverse balance of trade payments between Britain and the rest of the world. In addition to this economic rationale, there is a long-standing policy that greater self-sufficiency adds to the strategic strength of Britain, which has customarily depended upon importing approximately half of all its food. Therefore, increasing home food production has been considered in the national interest (Ministry of Agriculture, Fisheries, and Food et al., 1979), and the maintenance of a strong and profitable home farming industry has been the resulting policy. Such a policy is supported by the government view that "the landscape which people are understandably keen to preserve would quickly deteriorate without a flourishing agriculture' (ibid., p. 19).

The maintenance of this flourishing state is assisted largely through grants and subsidies or taxation policies, since within the Common Agricultural Policy framework of the European Economic Community the British government views the prices for certain agricultural products as already too high to use increased prices as a means of retaining profitable farming. Therefore, there are strong arguments within the government for the maintenance of the land-drainage program, which must necessarily reduce the area of British wetlands. In theory, every ministry has the obligation under Section II of the Countryside Act of 1968 to "have regard to" conserving the natural beauty and amenity of the countryside. Also, under the Water Act of 1973, a similar and more extensive duty is placed on water authorities to protect wildlife and other natural features. However, these statutory duties for having regard to conservation and landscape considerations are vague and have been ignored on many occasions in the past. Very little systematic study by land-use and water planners is undertaken into the environmental effects of their decisions, and even less consideration appears to be given to the visual influence of a declining wetland resource.

The main agency for wetland conservation in Britain is the Nature Conservancy Council, but also of major significance are the numerous local and national amenity and conservation societies operating on a volunteer basis. The Nature Conservancy Council designates Sites of Special Scientific Interest (SSSI) and National Nature Reserves under a policy of protecting wildlife in "key areas" of conservation interest (Nature Conservancy Council, 1974). In many instances, these policies lack teeth in that SSSI status does not prevent farmers from plowing the land so designated or of draining wetlands, since the ultimate land-use control rests with the landowner.

In National Nature Reserves there are greater powers, and many are owned by the Nature

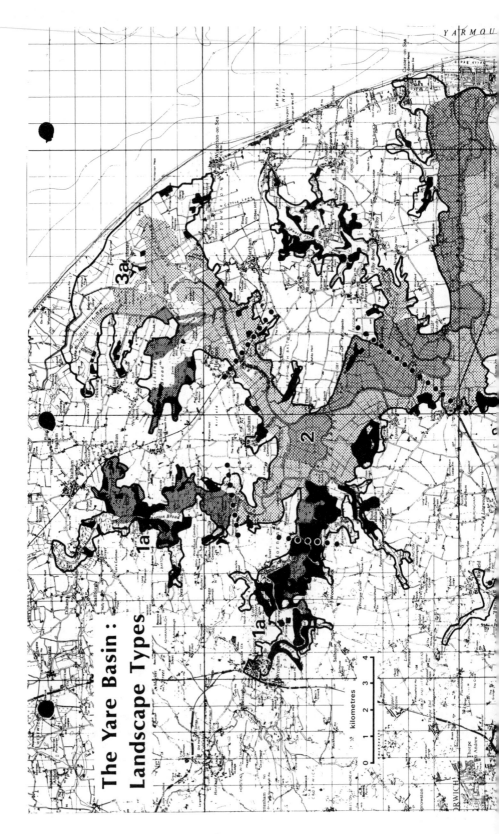

The Yare Basin :
Landscape Types

3a

1a

1a

2

kilometres
0 1 2 3 4

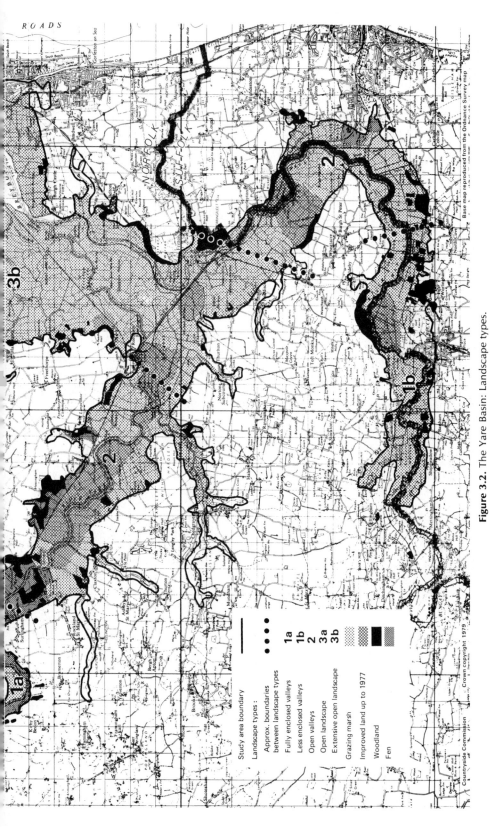

**Figure 3.2.** The Yare Basin: Landscape types.

Study area boundary

Landscape types :

Approx. boundaries between landscape types

Fully enclosed valleys — 1a
Less enclosed valleys — 1b
Open valleys — 2
Open landscape — 3a
Extensive open landscape — 3b

Grazing marsh

Improved land up to 1977

Woodland

Fen

Countryside Commission © Crown copyright 1979    Base map reproduced from the Ordnance Survey map

29

Conservancy Council, but such reserves cover only 0.6 percent of Britain (Davidson and Wibberley, 1977). Local amenity societies and the Royal Society for the Protection of Birds both own and manage nature reserves, including key wetland sites, but their power and influence is limited despite substantial growth in membership over the last decade. The most powerful of these organizations are concerned with wildlife conservation, particularly birds, but the Council for the Protection of Rural England and the National Trust—with memberships of 30,000 and 1 million, respectively—have a keen concern for landscape conservation (Penning-Rowsell, 1981b).

This brief analysis of the legal, financial, and political aspects of wetland conservation shows that the power clearly lies with the Ministry of Agriculture, Fisheries, and Food in its ability to pay grants to water authorities and landowners. These grants undoubtedly provide a strong incentive to landowners to improve the productivity of their wetlands. Statutory provisions for environmental and visual impact studies are nonexistent, although there are obligations and agreements between the Ministry and the Nature Conservancy Council for the former to consult the latter when grants are sought for draining SSSIs (George, 1976). Nevertheless, grants have been given in these circumstances, for draining part of the Somerset Levels, when the Ministry felt that agricultural productivity outweighed environmental and landscape considerations. However, no systematic study has been undertaken of the nature of British wetlands that could be used as a guide for such considerations; and there are many areas outside existing designations where landscape change is rapid and nature conservation value is being lost through drainage and other factors promoting land-use change.

## Wetland Assessments: Methodology and Issues

Two examples of wetland landscape and environmental assessments reveal the problems and potentialities of such attempts to gauge the value of these complex environments. In both cases, the information on the visual, cultural, and nature conservation value of the wetland areas was collected to counterbalance the more tangible economic evidence favoring agricultural intensification.

The first case includes a systematic study of the landscape of the Yare Basin (commonly known as the Norfolk Broads) and comprises an analysis of both the visual and the cultural landscape elements of this important wetland area (Land Use Consultants, 1978) (Figure 3.2). The second example details a public inquiry into drainage proposals for a significant wetland area at Amberley Wild Brooks in Sussex. Here, no such systematic study was undertaken, but evidence from a wide range of agencies and individuals gives useful insight into the visual and nature conservation values of the area. Both cases illustrate the many methodological and conceptual difficulties of assessing the significance of wetland landscapes.

### The Yare Basin Landscape Study

Research by Land Use Consultants (1978) was commissioned by the Countryside Commission (a government agency within the Department of the Environment) to assess the landscape of the Yare Basin and the changes that might result from a flood-control scheme proposed by the Anglian Water Authority. The scheme is designed to prevent flooding from the sea, which is increasingly likely as aging flood-control banks become less capable of withstanding tidal surges.

The Yare Basin (Figure 3.2) comprises the valleys of the rivers Bure, Yare, and Waveney and their tributaries. The area includes navigable waterways, open broads (lakes), reed fens, fen woodlands, reclaimed grazing marshland, and some cultivated arable land. In the west and north, the rivers are narrow, but they open out gradually toward the sea and join in the central area to form a large expanse of open marshland. Much of the valley flood plain lies below the level of the rivers and has to be drained by pumping.

In the eleventh century A.D. and before, the area was a vast reed swamp and unreclaimed marsh that had been deforested. Peat digging was practiced extensively in the twelfth century A.D. and the open Broads are now believed to be peat excavations that were flooded in the thirteenth and fourteenth centuries A.D. For centuries vast expanses of marshland remained, but inroads were gradually made, and with the use of wind pumps and subsequently steam pumps the majority of the area was drained to form the existing grazing marshes. Much of the area is still prone to winter flooding, which keeps agricultural productivity at a low level and largely prevents arable cultivation.

Some 2,800 hectares remain undrained, predominantly in the north in the vicinity of the Broads. These have remained as open water and reed swamp, although natural vegetational colonization has resulted in a complex mosaic including fen carr and fen woodland. For many years traditional management for the production of reeds, sedge, and alder poles restricted the development of natural woodland; but decline in the management system has meant that woodland has increased and open water has been lost to reed and sedge beds. The agricultural use of the open marshland has slowly intensified, but it remains based on livestock production from summer grazing. The area is subject to intense recreational pressure; in 1971, 260,000 holidays were spent in the Broadland area (Broads Consortium Committee, 1971).

The assessment methodology adopted by Land Use Consultants involved four distinct stages (Figure 3.3), designed to produce an evaluation of the impact of the flood-control scheme on the character-defining landscape elements of the area. Six major groups of elements were defined, comprising aspects of landform, sky, water, vegetation, animals, and human artifacts.

The significant aspects of *landform* identified were the flatness of the valley bottoms, the open, extensive plain of the central marshland, and the slight but important elevation of the surrounding low hills, which provide important visual contrast to the generally low-lying landscape. In such areas the *sky* assumes great importance and occupies a major part of any view. Variations in light and cloud forms throughout the day were considered important, exaggerated by the flatness of the plains and the areas of open water, "creating many subtle effects of shadow, highlight and reflection" (Land

Use Consultants, 1978, p. 4).* The presence of *water* throughout the area, and therefore throughout the landscape, was seen to bring strong associations with the wetland nature of the area. In particular, the open waters of the Broads themselves are dominant, with a preponderance of "edge" effects where they meet the adjoining reed fen and woodland, "which must largely be responsible for their popularity with holiday-makers" (ibid.). In the southern area the rivers are prominent, with their elevated river banks, and the drainage dikes in the surrounding marshland break up the continuous expanse of grazing land.

The *vegetation* of the area has four important elements: woodland, trees, reed beds, and open grazing. In the upper reaches of the northern rivers the landscape is enclosed, mainly by fen woodland that has colonized the reed swamp. Elsewhere, the landscapes are open, but woodland is still an important element in the form of small but frequent areas of carr woodland on the peat soils that fringe large parts of the river valleys. Here there is an appearance of dense woodland, even though the areas in question are generally small, owing to the contrast with the open marshland and flat valley bottoms. Similarly, the incidence of trees outside the woodland areas is low; but where there are lines or clumps planted in association with dikes or rivers, they provide "important incidents in the open landscape" (ibid., p. 5). The tree species in both open valleys and woodland areas have strong wetland associations, being usually willow, alder, or poplar.

*Reed beds* form important margins to the open water of the Broads and fringe the rivers and fen woodland of the northern areas. The tall reeds emphasize the lines of the drainage dikes, and "apart from their visual significance to the landscape, these areas [of reeds] are important as habitats for birds, and in their contribution of sound through continuous movement of reeds in the winds" (ibid., p. 5). Away from the woodlands and the reedbeds, which in area are quite small, the *open marshes* are "the most characteristic feature of the landscape" (ibid., p. 5). Their visual appearance depends on their

---

*This section describing those landscape elements identified as important by Land Use Consultants (1978) draws heavily upon its report. Quotations are followed by page references (4), but other sections here paraphrase the text and are intended to show which landscape elements were identified for particular attention.

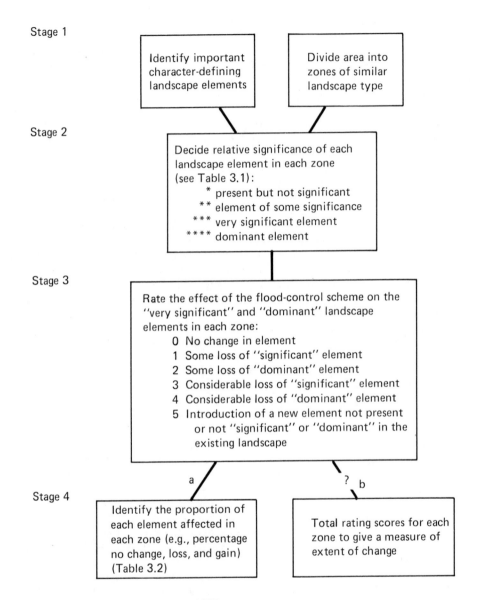

Stage 1

Identify important character-defining landscape elements

Divide area into zones of similar landscape type

Stage 2

Decide relative significance of each landscape element in each zone (see Table 3.1):
* present but not significant
** element of some significance
*** very significant element
**** dominant element

Stage 3

Rate the effect of the flood-control scheme on the "very significant" and "dominant" landscape elements in each zone:
0 No change in element
1 Some loss of "significant" element
2 Some loss of "dominant" element
3 Considerable loss of "significant" element
4 Considerable loss of "dominant" element
5 Introduction of a new element not present or not "significant" or "dominant" in the existing landscape

a

? b

Stage 4

Identify the proportion of each element affected in each zone (e.g., percentage no change, loss, and gain) (Table 3.2)

Total rating scores for each zone to give a measure of extent of change

*Source:* Land Use Consultants, 1979.

**Figure 3.3.** Stages in the assessment of the Yare Basin landscape (compiled from methodology used by Land Use Consultants, 1978).

state of agricultural management, but generally the rough, tussocky mixture of rush, thistle, and other "weed" species give a strong image of the wetland character of the area. When these areas are drained and converted to arable cropping or ley grassland, "the link with the wetland environment is lost" (ibid., p. 5).

The *animals* grazing on the marshland provide important interest within the extensive vistas of permanent grass through their movement, numbers, and contrast in color. Movement and interest is also provided by birds and wildfowl, which are present in large numbers throughout the area. Land Use Consultants appears doubtful whether these are "strictly definable as a landscape element," although it suggests that the wildlife of the area is an important part of the whole environment: "The attractiveness of the area is just as much dependent on its natural flora and fauna and physical features as is the scientific interest" (ibid., p. 6).

Special consideration is given to *human artifacts*. Of greatest significance are those features that through their elevation about the surrounding flat areas form prominent landmarks within the sea of grazing. Ancient windmills, church towers, steam-pump chimneys, and traditional gates are singled out for favorable mention, while electricity pylons and holiday-industry developments are seen as intrusive elements. Where elevated above the general flatness, both roads and railways are prominent, especially where they are raised to cross rivers or dikes. "Traditionally, boats have been an important part of the landscape. The sailing wherries (barges) form the unique spectacle for the land-based observer of disembodied sails passing across meadows, with the water invisible below" (ibid., p. 6). The large number of holiday boats in the area feature strongly in its landscape character.

From such analyses Land Use Consultants identifies the major landscape elements and their significance within the different landscape zones (Table 3.1; Figures 3.2 and 3.3). This significance is judged intuitively on a four-point rating scale (Figure 3.3), and those elements that are judged as "very significant" or "dominant" are then rated on a further scale to identify the effect of the flood-control scheme. As can be seen from the scale in Figure 3.3 (Stage 3),

primary importance is accorded to new features of the landscape as a result of this scheme, such as new agricultural buildings, further electricity supply lines, pumping stations, and arable cultivation. A final stage in the methodology enumerates those landscape elements that would experience no change, those that would be lost, and those that would be gained within each landscape zone (Table 3.2). While the approach adopted by Land Use Consultants does not total the rated scores (Figure 3.3, Stage 4b), this is implicit in the scoring methodology and gives a measure of the extent of landscape change within the different areas based on the ratings of the different visual features listed in Table 3.1.

The method of landscape assessment is notable in recognizing the significance of human artifacts to the landscape character and quality of the area. As such, this survey follows a long tradition of assessments of the Broadland area, from the Hobhouse Report (1947) and the Broadland Study and Plan (Broadland Consortium, 1971). Artists and writers have also recognized the significance of human artifacts within the landscape, and Land Use Consultants uses this material to complement its quantitative assessment. However, the sources of information on which the assessments are made of the importance of features to the landscape are not unambiguous; few of the policy papers of local and national planning agencies are explicit about the exact nature of the landscape character on which great value is placed, although "there is every indication that the typical open marshland landscape . . . forms a major part of the image of the Broads" (ibid., p. 21). Also, surveys of residents and visitors indicate that only between 6 percent and 18 percent considered the scenery to be a major attraction. Nevertheless, the researchers attached great importance to the apparent consensus across a wide range of information, including their own survey, that the existing features of the landscape were highly valued and that agricultural intensification would have an adverse effect on the visual and cultural attributes of the Yare Basin.

The assessment methodology, however, can easily be criticized. How decisions were made labeling some elements as "very significant" and

**Table 3.1  Major Character-Defining Landscape Elements and Their Significance in the Main Landscape Zones of the Yare Basin, Britain**

| Landscape Element | Landscape Types | | | | |
|---|---|---|---|---|---|
| | 1A<br>Fully enclosed valley | 1B<br>Less-enclosed valley | 2<br>Open valley | 3A<br>Open | 3B<br>Extensive, open |
| *Physical Elements* | | | | | |
| Sky | ** | ** | *** | **** | **** |
| Flat flood plain | * | ** | *** | **** | **** |
| Enclosing uplands | ** | **** | *** | ** | * |
| Open broads | **** | — | — | *** | * |
| Cuts and drainage dikes | ** | *** | *** | **** | **** |
| Elevated river banks | * | *** | **** | * | **** |
| *Natural Elements* | | | | | |
| Fen woodland | **** | — | ** | — | — |
| Fringing Carr woodland | * | **** | **** | ** | * |
| Reed fen | **** | * | ** | *** | — |
| Reed beds, fringing river | ** | ** | **** | * | *** |
| Vegetation in dikes | * | *** | *** | **** | *** |
| Trees on marshland | * | **** | ** | **** | *** |
| Hedgerow trees on upland | * | *** | **** | * | * |
| Grazing marshes | * | **** | *** | *** | **** |
| Arable and ley fields | * | * | ** | * | ** |
| Grazing animals | * | ** | *** | *** | **** |
| Wildfowl and other birds | **** | ** | *** | *** | *** |
| *Human Artifacts* | | | | | |
| Traditional gates to dike crossings | * | ** | *** | ** | **** |
| Farm buildings on marsh | — | * | * | — | — |
| Farm buildings on upland | * | * | *** | * | * |
| Pumping stations | * | ** | ** | ** | *** |
| Farm access roads | — | ** | ** | * | * |
| Fencing | * | * | * | * | * |
| Villages | **** | ** | *** | * | * |
| Pubs by river | *** | * | ** | * | * |
| Holiday and recreation centers | **** | * | *** | ** | * |
| Roads | ** | ** | * | * | ** |
| Railways | * | * | ** | — | *** |
| Boats | **** | * | *** | *** | ** |
| Bridges | ** | ** | * | — | * |
| Ferries | * | — | * | — | — |
| Churches on upland | * | ** | *** | *** | * |
| Wind pumps | ** | — | *** | **** | **** |
| Pylons | — | *** | — | — | *** |
| Low power lines | * | ** | *** | ** | *** |

Key:   * = present but not significant element.
　　　 ** = element of some significance.
　　　 *** = very significant element.
　　　 **** = dominant element.

*Source:* Land Use Consultants, *A landscape assessment of the Yare Basin flood control study proposals* (Countryside Commission Working Paper 13). Cheltenham, England, 1978.

some as "of some significance" is not clear. Why do all new features in the landscape receive high adverse scores? Indeed, why within their methodology is there a scoring system at all? The analysis that leads through to Table 3.2 gives all landscape elements equal weight, which must falsify their "true" relative significance. Nevertheless, such criticism is at least partially unfair; the report does not pretend that landscape is absolute and measurable in any easy way, and indeed the most credible "assessments" within the overall evaluation come from the surveys of people who know the area intimately, from the analysis of features commonly recorded by artists and writers, and from the continuity of agreement within planning reports about the uniqueness of the landscapes of the area. However, such criticisms would be valid if the area were unknown; who then would be able to extol its virtues? In these circumstances, then, perhaps just such a simple evaluation technique might be useful in identifying the potential threats to an important wetland, although it is not easy to see how a list of significant landscape features, such as those presented in Table 3.1, could then be devised for use in the assessment methodology.

### The Amberley Wild Brooks Inquiry

Controversy concerning drainage proposals for the Yare Basin has continued (O'Riordan, 1981) with the search for some compromise between drainage, nature conservation, and landscape protection. This search has involved establishing a special Broads Authority to plan the future use of the area in recognition of the national importance of this major wetland scenic resource. On a smaller scale, a similar conflict occurred between landscape and drainage interests over the future of a small but valuable wetland site in southern England, well away from the major traditional centers of drainage in the fenland countries of East Anglia.

In March 1978 a public inquiry was held in Arundel, Sussex, to look into a proposal by the Southern Water Authority to install a pumped drainage scheme that would improve the agricultural productivity of the 365-hectare wetland area on the River Arun known as Amberley Wild Brooks. This inquiry was signifi-

cant in that it was the first public examination of a land-drainage scheme under the new Land Drainage Act of 1976, which in itself was the first legislation providing for public inquiries into drainage schemes. The Brooks form part of an Area of Outstanding Natural Beauty, designated by the Countryside Commission, and comprise a shallow, flat area surrounded by the chalk hills of the South Downs. The land use is mixed, with areas of marsh, bog, and fen together with rough grazing supporting beef cattle during summer months. The area is completely flooded during most winters and is waterlogged for many months each year. The drainage proposal was designed to prevent flooding more than once every five years and so permit increased stocking of the grazing areas and some limited extension of arable cropping (Parker and Penning-Rowsell, 1980; Penning-Rowsell, 1978; Penning-Rowsell and Chatterton, 1977). Within Britain, inland wetlands of the size of Amberley Wild Brooks are rare, and by Smardon's criteria (1975, 1979), the wetland would be considered an exceptional natural area with general landscape values (Smardon, 1979). In addition, there are species of dragonflies that are known to breed only in the acid peat bog area of the Brooks, and the area is of international importance as a site for wildfowl, including the Bewick swan, shovelers, and ruff, and of national importance for pintail, teal, and snipe.

The drainage proposal generated considerable opposition. Those opposing the scheme included the local planning departments, national statutory agencies (among them the Nature Conservancy Council), and many local and national amenity societies. By far, the majority of the evidence produced to oppose the scheme concerned the Brooks' value as a wildlife sanctuary; but in many cases, opponents also referred to the visual value of the area and its value for education and natural history study. These references reveal attitudes to wetland landscapes and the value placed by the public on wetland resources.

The local county planning department considered that "whatever the merits of the drainage scheme to agriculture, they would not outweigh the qualities of landscape and value to nature conservation which made the Amberley

**Table 3.2  Significance of Changes of the Major Landscape Elements within the Main Landscape Zones of the Yare Basin, Britain**

| | Landscape Zones | | | | |
|---|---|---|---|---|---|
| | 1A | 1B | 2 | 3A | 3B |
| | Fully<br>enclosed | Less-<br>enclosed | Open | Open | Extensive<br>open |
| Measure of Change | valley | valley | valley | | |
| 1. New elements introduced<br>or becoming significant | 0 | 38 | 21 | 28 | 26 |
| 2. "Significant" or "dominant"<br>elements suffering<br>considerable loss | 0 | 38 | 33 | 33 | 42 |
| 3. "Significant" or "dominant"<br>elements remaining<br>unchanged | 100 | 14 | 42 | 39 | 31 |

*Note:*  Figures are percentages and show the proportion of landscape elements listed in Table 3.1 that are affected as shown.

*Source:*  Land Use Consultants, 1978.

Wild Brooks unique" (Ministry of Agriculture, Fisheries, and Food, 1978, p. 20)*. The changes to land use and field patterns, which would accompany agricultural "improvement", would affect adversely the scenic qualities in the extensive flat plain of the river valley. The landscape character of the flood plain is a foil to adjoining chalk downs, forming a special element in the Area of Outstanding Natural Beauty. The site comprises approximately 6 percent of the total flood-plain land in the County of Sussex, but it is a unique example of a relatively unchanged wetland habitat.

The Council for the Protection of Rural England maintained at the inquiry that the landscape would become "an ordinary piece of countryside with an insignificant mixture of field uses" (ibid., p. 22), as opposed to its current rich variety of land use, if the scheme were to go ahead. The Wild Brooks is a subtle landscape of particular charm among the attractions of Sussex, and it should be retained unspoiled for posterity. Increasing access facilities to the

Brooks would attract motorists and adversely affect the peace and tranquility of the landscape.

Local amenity societies stressed the nature-conservation value of the Brooks as well as their educational importance. Information on the numbers of visits by groups and individuals was presented to support this case; fourteen bird-watching societies had visited the Brooks 43 times in the last three years, with an average party size of twenty-five to thirty. Naturalists, botanists, entomologists, and natural-history societies also made visits; fourteen of these societies had visited the area 18 times in the previous three years. Educational parties from local schools, colleges, and universities also made a significant number of visits to study the flora and fauna. The Wild Brooks Society drew attention to the "splendid views over the Brooks to the downs [hills] above Amberley" (ibid., p. 32) and the "pleasant walks over the site."

The society opposed the scheme because "it would destroy the primary wetland value of the site with severe loss of wildfowl, flora and fauna,

---

*The subsequent sections describing the evidence put by opponents of the drainage scheme draw heavily upon the text of the Inspector's report to the Ministry of Agriculture, Fisheries and Food (1978). Where quotations are given the page numbers refer to this report.

making visits there much less enjoyable and changing the characteristics so much that amenity would be substantially reduced" (ibid., p. 32).

The inquiry inspector (adjudicator) recommended against the drainage scheme mainly because the cost-benefit analysis was not favorable (Parker and Penning-Rowsell, 1980). However, some useful comments were made about the visual and nature conservation value of the Brooks. The opponents of the scheme, in the inspector's view, had "clearly demonstrated that the Amberley Wild Brooks constitute a very important site in respect of unique natural history features, flora, fauna, birdlife and general amenity.* Amenity interests are bound up with the natural history to a considerable degree, but there are also pleasant walks and views which would become less attractive if the drainage works were carried out" (ibid., p. 39). In ratifying this recommendation, the Minister for Agriculture recognized the amenity and nature-conservation value of the Brooks and refused to grant aid for the drainage works.

One persistent theme running through this inquiry was the need for more detailed guidelines for balancing the requirements of agriculture and conservation. In the final decision, the Minister refused to establish an assessment system because he considered that "such guidance would not be of practical value because the factors affecting each individual site—that is, the farming, conservation and amenity requirements—and the weight to be given to them will be different in each case" (ibid.). Such a judgment would appear to favor assessments of wetlands in isolation, perhaps at public inquiries, rather than through an overall assessment scheme for British wetlands as a whole.

## Conclusions

The visual, cultural, and nature-conservation values of wetlands in England and Wales are becoming more clearly recognized as the resource diminishes. Further assessments of these resources are under way and new guidelines are being prepared for balancing agricultural and other interests. Two new

sources of information are important in this respect. First, regional water authorities are undertaking systematic surveys of their wetland areas at the request of the Ministry of Agriculture, Fisheries, and Food, as is their obligation under Section 24(5) of the Water Act of 1973. These surveys are intended to identify all areas of potential land drainage and set priorities for future drainage schemes (Ministry of Agriculture, Fisheries, and Food, 1974; Parker and Penning-Rowsell, 1980; Penning-Rowsell and Chatterton, 1976). Some water authorities have virtually completed these surveys (Severn Trent Water Authority, 1978; Wessex Water Authority, 1979) and they provide a complete analysis of wetland areas for the first time. Nevertheless, these assessments do not evaluate the visual or nature-conservation values of the wetland areas concerned, and the cost-benefit analyses provisionally undertaken simply judge the costs of drainage compared with the benefits of increased agricultural production. Clearly these assessments need to be complemented by a comparable survey of other significant wetland values.

The second source of information is helpful in this respect. The Water Space Amenity Commission (1978), an advisory organization responsible for assisting water authorities in the recreation and amenity field, has produced guidelines for land-drainage engineers that should promote a greater understanding of the effects of land drainage on wetland environments. Detailed advice is given for the complete range of wetland environments on how best to reconcile drainage with the maintenance of environmental and visual values. For example, the guidelines advocate that provision should be made in all capital schemes for replacing the trees, shrubs, and hedges removed during the drainage works, and where possible these should be augmented. Their siting "should enhance the landscape and where necessary screen and soften the effect of intrusive elements such as sluices, locks and gauging stations." An invaluable complementary data source is the complete review of the ecological importance of all sites of nature-conservation value in Britain, undertaken over a period of ten years by the Nature Conservancy Council

---

*In Britain, the words *amenity* and *landscape* are often used synonymously.

(Ratcliffe, 1977), which details and evaluates the wildlife value of many wetland sites in England and Wales. Together, these assessments should give those making land-use and land-drainage decisions more information on the values of the wetland sites.

There are limitations, however. The review undertaken by the Nature Conservancy Council makes no assessment of visual aspects of wetlands, since this is not the area of the council's concern. The Water Space Amenity Commission Guidelines fail to note criteria by which decisions *not* to drain wetland areas might be taken. The water authority surveys are narrow, concerned only with areas that potentially warrant drainage.

Moreover, many fundamental aspects of wetland areas are revealed by the Amberley Wild Brooks inquiry and the Yare Basin survey, and research directed at obtaining more information may simply fall into the trap of equating data with answers (Penning-Rowsell, 1981a). In both studies the opponents of the drainage and flood-protection schemes do not make explicit what constitutes unacceptable landscape change. For example, Land Use Consultants states: "It is unlikely that new planting will be acceptable along dykes, as this would impede maintenance . . . but lines of trees could perhaps be planted along new access roads. Regular lines of trees in the central area [of the Basin] would be a new element in the landscape, but would not necessarily be unacceptable" (Land Use Consultants, 1978, p. 17). New farm buildings, however, are considered unacceptable, although the old wind pumps and steam pumps — relics of a former farming system and technology — are highly prized. The conclusion from this example is that whatever is old is good and whatever is "unnatural" is bad. The "prairie" that forms the grazing land in the center of the Yare Basin is highly praised for its landscape character, yet elsewhere the removal of farm landscape features and thereby the creation of prairie landscapes is deplored or at least meets with disapproval (Westmacott and Worthington, 1974; Shoard, 1980). By what logic are grain towers ugly and windmills attractive? How should or how can assessment systems cope with attitudes that simply revere the past or what is familiar except by recording potential change? In essence, this is what Land Use Consultants has attempted, and it recognizes that there can be "no absolute statement of the acceptability, or otherwise, of the changes of the landscape. Ultimately a political judgment must be made by those charged with the responsibility for conserving and managing the countryside generally" (Land Use Consultants, 1978, p. 18).

Thus we return to those organizations and agencies that are responsible for wetlands policy and management. Protagonists of wetland conservation must understand the forces governing the agricultural intensification of these areas and other pressures for land-use change. The change of wetland resources through these forces must be located within the economic system governing environmental change and thus located as a consequence of political decisions. From such analyses the researcher can only conclude that to label the assessment of wetland resources as merely a technical problem requiring a technical answer is misguided and dangerous.

Obviously, more research is required, principally into the human reactions to landscapes in general and wetlands in particular so that landscape description and assessment systems and frameworks and other technical aids in decision-making are well founded upon knowledge of what people value in wetland environments. This area is a minefield of conceptual problems, not the least of which concerns the complex relationship between landscape familiarity and appreciation that renders all things old as wonderful and all things new as unacceptable. However, we know little about the bases and determinants of such attitudes. Nevertheless, until we have more detailed information on reactions to and perceptions of wetland landscapes, the defense of the most cherished landscape areas will continue to involve confrontation, and landscape protection will, as a last resort, be attainable only at inquiries, investigations, and in the courts of law.

# References

Agricultural Development and Advisory Service. 1974–77. *Getting down to drainage.* London: Ministry of Agriculture, Fisheries, and Food.

Appleton, J. 1975. *The experience of landscape.* London: Wiley.

Beresford, M. W. 1954. *The lost villages of England.* London: Lutterworth.

Broads Consortium Committee. 1971. *Broadland study and plan.* Norwich.

Clark, S.B.K. 1968. Landscape survey and analysis on a national basis. *Planning Outlook* 4:15–29.

Cole, G. 1976. Land drainage in England and Wales. *Journal of the Institution of Water Engineers and Scientists* 30(7):345–67.

Darby, H. C. 1956. *The draining of the Fens,* 2nd ed. Cambridge: Cambridge University Press.

Davidson, J., and Wibberley, G. 1977. *Planning and the rural environment.* Oxford: Pergamon Press.

Dunn, M. C. 1976. Landscape with photographs: Testing the preference approach to landscape evaluation. *Journal of Environmental Management* 4:15–26.

Fairbrother, N. 1972. *New lives, new landscapes.* London: Penguin Books.

Fines, K. D. 1968. Landscape evaluation: A research project in East Sussex. *Regional Studies* 2:41–55.

George, M. 1976. Is wildlife being drained away? *Conservation Review* 11:4–5.

Hill, A. R. 1976. The environmental impacts of agricultural land drainage. *Journal of Environmental Management* 4:251–74.

Hobhouse Report. 1947. Report of the National Parks Committee (England and Wales) Command Paper 7121. London: Her Majesty's Stationery Office.

Hollis, G. E. 1979. Agriculture and the hydrological regime: Recent research in the U.K. Paper presented to the International Institute for Applied Analysis conference, April 23–27, Smolenice, Soviet Union.

Hoskins, W. G. 1955. *The making of the English landscape.* London: Hodder and Stoughton.

Land Use Consultants. 1978. *A landscape assessment of the Yare Basin flood control study proposals.* Countryside Commission Working Paper 13. Cheltenham.

Lowenthal, D. 1978. Finding valued landscapes. *Progress in Human Geography* 2(3):373–418.

Lowenthal, D., and Prince, H. 1964. The English landscape. *Geographical Review* 54:309–46.

———. 1965. English landscape tastes. *Geographical Review* 55:186–222.

Ministry of Agriculture, Fisheries, and Food (MAFF). 1974. *Guidance notes for Water Authorities,* Water Act 1973, Section 24. London.

———. 1978. *Report on the public local inquiry into proposals by the Southern Water Authority for drainage of Amberley Wild Brooks.* London.

———. 1979. *Farming and the nation.* Command Paper 7458. London: Her Majesty's Stationery Office.

Nature Conservancy Council. 1974. *Conservation of nature.* Command Paper 7122. London: Her Majesty's Stationery Office.

O'Riordan, T. 1981. A case study in the politics of land drainage. *Disasters* 4(4):393–410.

Parker, A., and Pye, D. 1976. *The Fenland.* London: David and Charles.

Parker, D. J., and Penning-Rowsell, E. C. 1980. *Water planning in Britain.* London: Allen and Unwin.

Penning-Rowsell, E. C. 1978. *Proposed drainage scheme for Amberley Wild Brooks: Benefit assessment.* Enfield, London: Middlesex Polytechnic.

———. 1981a. Fluctuating fortunes in gauging landscape value. *Progress in Human Geography* 5(1):25–41.

———. 1981b. Land drainage policy and practice: Who speaks for the environment? *Ecos* 1(3):16–21.

Penning-Rowsell, E.C., and Chatterton, J. B. 1976. Constraints on environmental planning: The example of flood alleviation. *Area* 8(2):133–38.

———. 1977. *The benefits of flood alleviation: A manual of assessment techniques.* Farnborough, England: Saxon House Press.

Penning-Rowsell, E.C.; Gullett, G.H., Searle; G.H., and Witham, S. A. 1977. Public evaluation of landscape quality. *Middlesex Polytechnic Planning Research Group Report No. 13.*

Ratcliffe, D. A., 1977. *A nature conservation review.* 2 vols. Cambridge: Cambridge University Press.

Robinson, D. G.; Laurie, I. C.; Wager, J. F.; and Trail, A. L., eds. 1976. *Landscape evaluation.* Manchester: University of Manchester.

Severn Trent Water Authority. 1978. Land drainage survey: Section 24(5) Water Act 1973. Interim Report. Birmingham, England: Severn Trent Water Authority.

Shoard, M. 1978. The lure of the moors. Paper presented to the annual conference of the Institute of British Geographers, Hull.

———. 1980. *The theft of the countryside.* London: M. T. Smith Press.

Smardon, R. C. 1975. Assessing visual-cultural values of inland wetlands in Massachusetts. In E. H. Zube, R. O. Brush, and J. Gy. Fabos, eds., *Landscape assessment: value, perceptions and resources.* Stroudsburg, Pa.: Dowden, Hutchinson and Ross.

———. 1979. Visual-cultural values of wetlands. In *Wetland functions and values: The state of our understanding.* Minneapolis, Minn.: American Water Resources Association. Vp. 535–44.

Water Space Amenity Commission. 1978. *Conservation and land drainage guidelines: Draft for consultation.* London.

Welsh Office. 1980. *A landscape classification of Wales.* Cardiff.

Wessex Water Authority. 1979. *Somerset land drainage survey report.* Bridgwater, England.

Westmacott, R., and Worthington, T. 1974. *New agricultural landscapes.* Cheltenham, England: Countryside Commission for England and Wales.

Williams, M. 1970. *The draining of the Somerset Levels.* Cambridge: Cambridge University Press.

*Legislation cited:* Land Drainage Act of 1930, Land Drainage Act of 1976, Water Act of 1973, and Countryside Act of 1968.

# PART II

# Perception of Wetland Visual Values

# 4 Assessing Visual Preference for Louisiana River Landscapes

MICHAEL S. LEE

## Conceptual Approach

Visual preference in the landscape is related to a complex range of cultural, psychological, and environmental factors. Only recently have attempts been made to evaluate and examine visual preference to make it possible to incorporate this factor in the decision-making process. Previous attempts have focused on the examination of information or stimuli provided by the visual display. Such a process has long been used in the field of psychology. Recently, researchers have used this informational approach in an attempt to explain factors relevant to visual preference in the environment. This form of analysis is based on the theory that examination of the information presented in a scene can be used as a clue to the explanation of environmental preference.

Kevin Lynch (1960) in *The Image of the City* proposes the concept of imageability, which he defines as "that quality in a physical object which gives it a high probability of evoking a strong image in any given observer" (p. 9). Lynch attempts to build a theoretical model in his analysis of urban structure. This concept of imageability parallels many of the ideas perti-

nent to models related to the informational approach. The imageability of an object is dependent upon the visual information that is transmitted from the object to the individual. By examining imageability Lynch attempts to explain some of the factors contributing to human preference in the environment.

This concept relates strongly to the process of individual perception described by Wohlwill (1966) and Newby (1971). Wohlwill explains an individual's relationships with the environment in terms of levels of stimulation. Experiments with animals have demonstrated that living organisms develop differently under varying levels of sensory stimulation in the environment. Each individual develops what Wohlwill describes as an adaption level to the stimuli or information received from the environment. An individual's sensory experience in the environment is related to his ability to process this information based on individual experience or adaption level (Wohlwill, 1966, pp. 30–37).

Newby similarly describes human perception of the environment as incorporating "the interaction of man's senses into a system whereby he is able to adapt to a world of constantly changing environmental conditions" (Newby,

1971, p. 70). The isolation of the components involved in the processing of perceptual information is logically the key to understanding human informational processing. Newby identifies four variables as being important to the processing of the environmental stimulus: (1) order, (2) complexity, (3) edge, and (4) spatial definition (pp. 68–72).

Rachel Kaplan (1973, 1975) and Stephen Kaplan (1973, 1975), just as Lynch, Wohlwill, and Newby, attempt to explain the perceptual process in terms of informational processing. This theory suggests that examination of the information an environment provides can be used to isolate components relevant to individual preference.

The Kaplans identify two general variables that aid in the identification of factors important to visual preference. One variable concerns the order and structure apparent in the scene. These factors aid in the cognition and individual structuring of the visual display. The second set of variables are described as involvement or interest factors. A preferred environment is therefore one that people can organize perceptually and also become involved with (S. Kaplan, 1975, p. 94).

In contrast to the general theoretical framework provided by these informational studies are the more structured, statistically based experimental approaches. Through testing, researchers attempt to identify factors relevant to human visual preference and perception in the environment. These researchers often rely on adjective checklists and elaborate testing techniques to obtain results from respondent reactions to visual stimuli. A criticism of this approach is that often the information derived is difficult to apply to any method for the analysis of visual preference (R. Kaplan, 1975, pp. 119–20). This is because of the frequently fragmented nature of the results and the inability to produce any general principles or domains for preference evaluation (Levin, 1977, p. 1).

Despite this criticism, the informational and experimental approaches appear to complement each other in the creation of a model that attempts to analyze factors relevant to visual preference in the landscape. Through a detailed analysis of the fragmented results of the experimental approach, these factors or concepts identified as influencing visual preference in the landscape can be related to the theoretical structure proposed in the informational approach. The combination of these factors could provide a logical basis for the development of a model analyzing visual preference in the landscape. By using this approach, the model would combine statistically justifiable data with a sound theoretical model.

Specialized disciplines often fail to integrate pertinent information from other groups in preference studies. For example, designers often fail to realize that despite the "horror" of attempting to evaluate numerically and test factors relevant to environmental preference, significant behavioral findings should not be taken lightly. Too often designers have separated the significance of the art and the elements of design from the behavioral sciences. Similarly, scientists and technologists often have failed to recognize the relationships of science and technology to art and nature. Designers should not close their eyes to behavioral research, nor should the behaviorist fail to recognize the importance of the principles of design.

This study was an attempt to integrate information, ideas, and thoughts from several disciplines into a logical evaluative approach to the explanation of visual preference related to Louisiana river corridors. Despite this approach, many of the concepts indicated in this study may be of value in the evaluation of visual preference in other landscape types.

## Study Description

This study focuses on the visual preference values associated with the river-swamp environment of southern Louisiana. Visual preference in any environment is regionally based. A river experience in Louisiana is different visually from other regions. While visual preference values change regionally with the variations in landscape character, regionally based cultural influences also affect visual preference. Before examining these regional preference values, the Louisiana river-swamp phenomenon must be identified and defined.

The Oxford Dictionary states that the word *stream* is a universal term for flowing water. Thus a river can be considered as a type of stream. In the United States a river is thought of as a fairly large flowing body of water whose

**Figure 4.1.** The study area.

character is determined by the geology, topography, soils, and land use of the watershed (Patrick, 1972, p. 67). The visual impression created by a river landscape is therefore an expression of a region's geological past and the relationship between water and the internal structure of the land.

### Study Area

Louisiana is a part of the geologic region described as the Gulf Coastal Plain (Figure 4.1). Most of the plain is underlain by a series of sedimentary deposits dating from the Jurassic period to the present. The sediments along the existing coast of Louisiana, Mississippi, and Texas are estimated at from 20,000 to 30,000 feet thick (Eardly, 1962, p. 650). Variations from this character exist in northern Louisiana, where large domes and uplift areas create a significant change in the character of the Louisiana landscape.

In northwestern Louisiana a river may lie at the base of a 300-foot incline, which is a mountain by Louisiana standards. These hills are dominated by hardwood species, towering pines, and dense underbrush. Moving southward, the complexion of the landscape changes. The land gradually flattens and an abundance of freshwater marshes and channels crisscross the countryside. Here the only significant rises are natural ridges, or levees, along rivers and streams. In the southern region tupelo gum and cypress trees abound, creating a visual character significantly different from the northern Louisiana hill country.

The river current in the hill country varies little from other regions in the United States, yet it generally differs from that in southern Louisiana, where rivers seem to disobey hydrologic convention. Rivers, swamps, and channels appear to merge and crisscross the landscape. French colonists who explored this region reported mysterious bodies of water. This region of "sleeping or dead" water, exhibiting little discernible current, was identified as undesirable to explorers, since the vast maze of waterways could easily cause confusion and disorientation. Here the land is crisscrossed by a complex pattern of rivers, swamps, and bayous. The term *bayou* is defined by geographers as a watercourse that serves as a distributary or natural outlet of a river. Louisianians are less precise in their definition, applying the term to every form of watercourse, distributary or tributary, whether it begins or ends in a river, swamp, lake, or marsh (Fiebleman, 1973, pp. 20–21).

This analysis of the visual preference value associated with Louisiana rivers deals with a variety of waterway situations. The fine line between a river, a bayou, and in some cases a swamp is often difficult to distinguish. The scenes used here are primarily water corridors where a definable shoreline exists. The significant factor is that the geological and cultural history have a profound effect on the visual character and preference value attributed to the southern Louisiana river-swamp landscape. These influences create a landscape character that is unique and regionally based. It is this visual character that will be analyzed and described. Whether a waterway is described as a river, bayou, canal, or swamp is of little consequence.

This study pertains to the analysis of factors influencing visual preference of the southern Louisiana river landscape. A methodology is developed and tested analyzing factors relevant to visual preference. The logic used in the development of the evaluative system is based upon previous research in landscape assessment, environmental psychology, and landscape architecture.

## Respondents

The sample consisted of 101 students in landscape architecture at Louisiana State University. The students were tested over a three-day period. Students in landscape architecture were chosen because it was felt that the group could be considered a uniform sample as well as a source readily available for testing. This choice was influenced by the fact that often an individual's state of mind concerning visual preference is related to career motivation rather than to other factors, such as age and sex (Dearinger et al., 1973, p. 11).

## Stimuli

A questionnaire accompanied the respondent analysis of twenty Louisiana river landscape scenes. Some of the slides used in the evaluation were supplied by staff in the Department of Landscape Architecture at Louisiana State University. The remainder were supplied by the researcher. The 35-millimeter slides depicted a wide variety of characteristics of the river environment. All of the scenes were taken from a position on the waterway viewing toward the shoreline environment. The slides were based upon demonstrated variability in landform, waterform, and/or vegetative characteristics. This variability was sought in an attempt to analyze the validity of concepts identified in the visual preference model. This analysis was based upon respondent reaction to the visual stimuli (slides).

## Procedure

*Development of the model for visual preference:* A theory proposed by Stephen and Rachel Kaplan provided a basis for the structuring of the preferential model. The theory attempted to explain the perceptual process in terms of informational processing, suggesting that examination of the information an environment provides can be used to isolate components relevant to individual preference.

Four factors are identified as being important

**Table 4.1    The Evaluative Process**

Level 1:    Perceptual Influences

| Major Topic | Major Variable | Vegetation | Land | Water | Total scene |
|---|---|---|---|---|---|
| Legibility | Definition | X | X | X | |
| | Edge contrast | X | X | X | |
| Complexity | Diversity | X | X | X | |
| | Edge complexity | | | | X |
| Spatial definition | Enclosure | | | | X |
| | Depth | | | | X |
| Mystery | Mystery | | | | X |

Level 2:    Emotional Influences

| Distinctive elements | Visual distinction | | | | X |
|---|---|---|---|---|---|
| | Natural shoreline distinction | | | | X |
| Disturbance factors | Man-influenced shoreline distinction | | | | X |
| | Visual pollution | | | | X |

to visual preference in the environment, two informational variables and two involvement variables. Legibility and spatial definition are important informational variables; complexity and mystery are the two involvement variables.

*Legibility* involves the clarity or coherence of a scene, aiding in individual recognition of visual elements. *Spatial definition* primarily involves the arrangement of three-dimensional space within the visual array. It affects orientation and has a definite influence on individual perception and preference.

*Complexity* involves the number and relative distribution of landscape elements. *Mystery* concerns the promise of additional information and encourages an individual to enter a visual display in order to seek this additional visual data. As the complexity of a scene increases, the amount of visual information available to the viewer also increases. The effect of mystery upon the amount of visual information available is similar. The difference between the two concepts is that complexity requires more time and

analysis, whereas mystery promises additional information through a change in vantage point (S. Kaplan, 1975, p. 94).

Judith Levin (1977) attempted to test the validity of these concepts in application to analysis of riverscape preference. These four variables appeared to be of value in the prediction of preference for river landscapes.

In this study two important levels of evaluation are identified in the analysis of preference value for a scene. The first involves the identification of perceptual influences. The four variables serve as the general base for this level. The second involves the identification of emotional influences in the landscape, those that attract attention and can exist as positive or negative influences upon visual preference for river corridors. An analysis is conducted identifying distinctive or feature elements and disturbance factors appearing in the landscape. The next step was to relate these principles to the primary landscape components — land, water, and vegetation.

**Table 4.2 A Sample Rating Sheet**

Date ______________ Slide # ______________

River ______________ Evaluator ______________

| Variable | Dimension | Rating Dimension | Rating Scale 1 | 2 | 3 | 4 | 5 | Rating |
|---|---|---|---|---|---|---|---|---|
| Legibility | Definition | Vegetation | | | | | | |
| | | Water | | | | X | | 4 |
| | | Landform | X | | | | | 1 |
| | Contrast | Vegetation | | | | | X | 5 |
| | | Water | | X | | | | 2 |
| | | Landform | X | | | | | 1 |
| Complexity | Diversity | Vegetation | | X | | | | 2 |
| | | Water | | X | | | | 2 |
| | | Landform | | X | | | | 2 |
| | Edge complexity | Skyline | | | X | | | 3 |
| | | Shoreline | | | X | | | 3 |
| Spatial definition | | Enclosure | | | X | | | 3 |
| | | Depth | | | | | X | 5 |
| Mystery | | Mystery | | X | | | | 2 |
| Distinctive elements | | Distinction | | X | | | | 2 |
| | | Natural | | | X | | | 3 |
| Disturbance factors | Shoreline Disturbance | Man (inf.) | | | | | X | 5 |
| | | Pollution | | | | | X | 5 |
| | | (1) Total Points | | | | | | 50 |
| | | (2) Total Possible Points | | | | | | 95 |
| | | Assessment Ratio | | | | | | .588 |

*Note:* Total possible = number of factors rated X 5; Assessment ratio = (1) divided by (2).

The general evaluative process developed in this study is illustrated in Table 4.1. Each of the major topics discussed is further divided into a major variable or variables (not discussed in this section). The right-hand columns of the table gives the landscape dimension (landform, vegetation, water, or total scene) evaluated in the rating process: "X" indicates the landscape dimension rated under each of the variables. The evaluation of visual preference value of a scene may therefore involve the analysis of vegetation, land, water, or the total scene (composite visual factors) according to a specific rating-procedure variable. A total of seventeen factors are analyzed for each landscape scene.

A descriptive approach is used in the analysis of the criteria relating each evaluation to a descriptive rating scale. Preceding each rating scale is a brief review of the literature applicable to the rating topic to justify and clarify each procedure. The original study is written as a "cookbook" approach. It explains rating procedures and provides descriptive rating scales with the thought that by thoroughly studying the procedures and concepts, any interested individual could apply the proposed system of analysis.*

The rating scales were not created as a gauge to specific right or wrong answers, but to serve as a general indicator of preference. It was envi-

*A detailed discussion of all the rating criteria, processes, and weightings appears in Lee (1978).

sioned that the detail required by the 17 analyses would force rating dimensions to offset each other and allow combinations and the relationships between the dimensions to develop. Through this form of analysis the combinations of factors and these influences would dominate the model result rather than the influence of a single dimension. The determination of preference value in a scene requires a detailed analysis of the combination and relationships of preference factors. These combinations were hypothesized to be more significant in the prediction of preference than the analysis of a single dimension.

Through the analysis of factors relevant to visual preference, greater knowledge was gained in developing an understanding of the "substance of a view." After developing preference categories and applying these to the landscape components of land, vegetation, and water, an attempt was made at consolidating these separate analyses into a meaningful model for visual preference prediction. It was assumed that by analyzing these separate categories and combining them into a logical decision-making format, a tool would be produced that is significant in the prediction of visual preference for Louisiana river landscapes.

The importance of the study lies not in the specific rating criteria or the numerical scales used. The numerical values were mainly used for the comparison and testing of the concepts presented in the evaluative system. The importance of the study lies in the general approach and the concepts that served as a basis for the evaluation. Important also are the results and conclusions identified in the study of the Louisiana river landscapes. These general factors will involve most of the remaining discussion.

*Testing the Evaluative Model:* The evaluative model system was used in the analysis of twenty Louisiana river scenes. A form similar to that presented in Table 4.2 was used in the evaluation of the scenes. The table shows a sample rating. In the analysis seventeen factors were isolated as influencing preference in river landscapes. These factors or dimensions were then related to descriptive five-point scales in the analysis of the twenty scenes. These separate evaluations were then combined into a numerical average, termed an "assessment ratio." This ratio was hypothesized as indicating

the relative visual preference value for the Louisiana river landscape scene. The slides were then ranked from 1 to 20 (1 indicating the highest preference value, 20 indicating the least preference value) according to the assessment ratios determined by the evaluative-model format.

The same slides were shown to the students in landscape architecture. The students were asked to rate the slides according to the following scale:

7. extremely beautiful (breathtaking)
6. very beautiful
5. moderately beautiful (slightly above average)
4. average scene
3. moderately unattractive (slightly below average)
2. very unattractive
1. extremely unattractive (eyesore)

The students were shown the slides before they indicated the preference value. This was done so that the respondents could view the relative visual character of the scenes before determining their preference. The slides were mixed and shown in random order, and the students were given thirty seconds to evaluate each one from 1 to 7.

The values for each slide were totaled, then ranked, similar to the procedure used in the model evaluation, from 1 to 20 according to the totals. The rankings for the two procedures were statistically compared to determine if a significant correlation existed between them.

### Results

The results of the preference evaluations appear in Tables 4.3 and 4.4.

The ratings were analyzed and the scenes were ranked from 1 to 20. The analysis was conducted separately for both the model evaluation and the respondent evaluation. The rankings as indicated by both appear in Table 4.5.

The Kendall rank coefficient was used to analyze the degree of agreement between the two ranking procedures (Siegel, 1956, p. 213).

$$\tau = \frac{S}{\frac{1}{2}N(N-1)} = \frac{150}{\frac{1}{2}(20)(19)} = .7894$$

This value (.7894) represents the degree of correlation between the respondents' evalua-

**Table 4.3   Ranking of the Scenes in the Respondent's Evaluation**

| Slide # | Total | Rank | Slide # | Total | Rank |
|---------|-------|------|---------|-------|------|
| 1 | 451 | 14 | 11 | 420 | 15 |
| 2 | 576 | 3 | 12 | 410 | 13 |
| 3 | 405 | 16 | 13 | 500 | 9 |
| 4 | 498 | 11 | 14 | 499 | 10 |
| 5 | 476 | 12 | 15 | 318 | 18 |
| 6 | 590 | 2 | 16 | 611 | 1 |
| 7 | 510 | 7 | 17 | 323 | 17 |
| 8 | 296 | 19 | 18 | 543 | 5 |
| 9 | 509 | 8 | 19 | 523 | 6 |
| 10 | 561 | 4 | 20 | 169 | 20 |

*Note:* The higher the total, the higher the preference value of the scene.

**Table 4.4   Ranking of the Scenes in the Model Evaluation**

| Slide # | Ratio value | Rank | Slide # | Ratio value | Rank |
|---------|-------------|------|---------|-------------|------|
| 1 | .505 | 12 | 11 | .450 | 16 |
| 2 | .644 | 3 | 12 | .522 | 9 |
| 3 | .477 | 17 | 13 | .552 | 7 |
| 4 | .517 | 10 | 14 | .544 | 8 |
| 5 | .488 | 14 | 15 | .470 | 15 |
| 6 | .655 | 2 | 16 | .688 | 1 |
| 7 | .578 | 5 | 17 | .437 | 19 |
| 8 | .444 | 18 | 18 | .500 | 13 |
| 9 | .511 | 11 | 19 | .555 | 6 |
| 10 | .635 | 4 | 20 | .425 | 20 |

*Note:* The higher the ratio value, the higher the preference value of the scene.

**Table 4.5   Comparison of the Model Evaluation and the Respondent Evaluation**

| | Ranking of the twenty slides |
|---|---|
| Pr. #1 | 1  2  3  4  5  6  7   8   9  10  11  12  13  14  15  16  17  18  19  20 |
| Pr. #2 | 1  2  3  4  7  6  9  10  13  11   8  14   5  12  18  15  16  19  17  20 |

Pr. #1 = Model ranking.
Pr. #2 = Respondents' ranking.

tion and the model evaluation. If the 101 students are considered to be a random sample from some population, the significance of the association between the model evaluation and the respondents' evaluation can be tested by using the following formula (ibid., p. 221).

$$Z = \frac{\tau}{\sqrt{\dfrac{2(2N+5)}{9N(N-1)}}} \quad \frac{.7894}{\sqrt{\dfrac{2\,(2)(20)+5}{9\,(20)(20)-1}}} \quad \frac{.7894}{\sqrt{\dfrac{90}{3420}}} = 4.866$$

$$Z = 4.866$$

If it is hypothesized that there is no significant correlation between the rankings, a Z value of 4.866 has the probability of occurrence of p = .0000005896. Thus the null hypothesis (Ho) can be rejected at a significant level of .0000005896. The alternative hypothesis (Ha), that there is a highly significant correlation between the model and the respondent evaluation, can be accepted. If the null hypothesis (Ho) is really true, the probability of drawing a random sample producing the same result is .0000005896.

## Discussion of the Results

The statistical analysis indicates that a strong relationship exists between the model ranking and the respondent's analyses of the twenty Louisiana river scenes.

### Legibility

The top three scenes chosen according to the model format and also by the respondents rated very high in terms of vegetation legibility. Each of the three scenes rated high in terms of vegetation legibility because of the clear presentation of individual plant forms and internal vegetative structure (limbs, trunks). Visual penetration (ability to see into the shoreline environment) and physical access (ability to enter the shoreline environment) was not obstructed by tangled masses of vegetation. This concept is demonstrated to a degree in Figure 4.2 (ranked third in the model and respondent evaluation). The forms of the individual cypress trees are not totally obstructed; connections and limb structure are readily apparent. Also, the penetration of view further into the shoreline environment is not totally obstructed by dense vegetation.

The presence of a strong vegetation edge, par-

ticularly in conjunction with water, appears to be a characteristic related to visual preference in the Louisiana river landscape. All of the preferred scenes and the scenes in the middle ranks possessed dominant vegetation in conjunction with the water surface (this factor is also related to enclosure). Figure 4.3, ranked thirteenth by the model evaluation and fifth by the respondents, shows a channelized waterway. The model-based analysis ranked the scene thirteenth primarily because of the shoreline disturbance and the lack of shoreline complexity. The respondents did not seem to react as strongly to the channelization as the model evaluation predicted. The dominant edge contrast produced by the trees in conjunction with the water appear to subordinate the influence resulting from channelization of the waterway. It appears that despite the obvious human influence the landform vegetation and water characteristics seemed to negate the human impacts upon the visual preference value of the river scene.

### Complexity

The complexity of the water surface appears to have an influence on visual preference for the Louisiana river environment. Both scenes (Figures 4.4 and 4.5) demonstrate similar vegetation characteristics. Tangled vegetation dominates the middle-ground zone. This can be described as an illegible situation in terms of vegetation. Individual plant forms cannot be distinguished, and the mass of vegetation limits the view of the shoreline from the river. Physical as well as visual access to the shoreline environment is destroyed by vegetation. The primary difference in the scenes is the complexity of the water surface. Water appears to become a more distinct element as the complexity of the water surface increases, producing heightened visual interest. Figure 4.4, a low-ranking scene in terms of vegetation and landform characteristics, gains visual distinction because of the diversity of the water surface. Figure 4.5 displays a less complex scene relating to the water surface than does Figure 4.4 while depicting similar landform and vegetation characteristics. This concept is supported by the higher rating given to Figure 4.4 than to Figure 4.5 by both the model-based evaluation and the respondent evaluation.

The complexity of the skyline and shoreline

**Figure 4.2.** Legible vegetation.

**Figure 4.3.** A strong edge created through the contrast of dominant vegetation and water.

**Figure 4.4.** Highly complex in terms of water-surface variation.

**Figure 4.5.** Less complexity relating to the water surface than in Figure 4.4.

**Figure 4.6.** Skyline and shoreline complexity.

was evaluated for each of the twenty scenes. These analyses were made on the assumption that the more irregular the skyline and shoreline edges, the greater the visual interest in the scene. The three highest ranking scenes according to both the model evaluation and the respondent evaluation possessed irregular skyline edges. Figure 4.6 was rated first by both the model and the respondent evaluations, and it was also rated high in terms of skyline complexity. (Skyline complexity refers to an analysis of the irregularity of the junction between the land and/or vegetation and the sky.)

This relationship is strongly dependent upon vegetation in Louisiana. The skyline complexity in Figure 4.6 is influenced by the irregularity of the cypress trees and the height variation existing between the individual trees. This irregularity produced by form and height variation creates an irregular interface between the vegetation and the sky and thus produces a complex skyline edge.

Figure 4.6 also demonstrates a degree of shoreline complexity. (Shoreline complexity refers to an analysis of the irregularity of the junction between the land and/or vegetation and the water.) The structure of the shoreline is strongly related to the geological action upon the material that composes the river or stream basin. Generally, the more irregular or complex

shorelines form in regions where bedrock or glacial deposits occur as the river cuts its course through the landscape. In Louisiana rock outcroppings are rare, and ancient alluvium serves as the primary material of the river basins. In most cases Louisiana rivers appear to follow a meandering course.

Figure 4.6 is an exception. The irregularity of the shoreline is created not by rock formations, but by the large cypress trees extending out into the water surface. Vegetation is legible because individual plant forms and limb structure are visible.

### Spatial Configuration

All of the highly rated scenes have significant enclosing or space-defining elements (primarily trees). A lack of these elements appears to have a detrimental influence on individual preference. Figure 4.7, ranked poorly by both the model evaluation and the respondents, lacks enclosure and significant space-defining elements and thus is monotonous. It appears that individuals respond to space-defining elements. Such elements are important for orientation and the identification of significant scale relationships. A lack of such space-defining or modulating elements produces a negative effect upon visual preference.

**Figure 4.7.** Few space-defining elements.

### Mystery or Anticipation

Figure 4.8 demonstrates the mystery dimension. Here overhanging vegetation obscures but does not totally obstruct the view. The river course moves out of sight, creating anticipation. Despite this feeling of mystery, the legibility or clarity of the visual information is reduced. This indicates the interdependence existing between all of the preference variables used in the evaluation.

The discussion indicates that for a scene to be of superior visual quality it must maintain a mix or balance of dimensions. One dimension (in this case, mystery) cannot dominate the other dimensions. The highest ranking scene (see Figure 4.6) possesses a good mix of the vital dimensions (legibility, spatial definition, mystery, complexity). Figure 4.8 illustrates dominant mystery and spatial enclosure, but legibility and complexity were rated lower.

### Disturbance Factors

Shoreline disturbance may have a negative influence on visual preference of the Louisiana river environment, but further testing is necessary to determine to what degree. Figure 4.9 features an eroding shoreline. The disturbance, probably caused by fluctuation in the water level during periods of flooding, has initiated erosion and destroyed the shoreline character, as well as native vegetation. This disturbance was followed by the encroachment of weedy vegetation, which obscures the individual plant forms, producing an illegible situation. The cut bank also isolates the dominant native vegetation from the water surface, which limits potential contrast. Landform serves as the primary contrasting element relating to the flat water surface, yet despite this distinction, the erosion and the starkness produced by the barren soil surface may have further contributed to the negative visual reaction.

Figure 4.10, ranked poorly in the model evaluation and by the respondents, contains little complexity, enclosure, mystery, or distinction, yet it is quite legible. It is difficult to determine what primary factors produced the negative visual response.

In the channelized waterway scene (see Figure 4.3) negative impacts from channelization were subordinated by positive landscape characteristics (vegetation edge contrast, enclosure). Figure 4.10 exhibits little in terms of visual preference value because of the lack of contrast, complexity, spatial interest, and mystery or anticipation. It is difficult to determine whether the respondents reacted directly to the evidence of human presence or indirectly to the

**Figure 4.8.** Mystery resulting in heightened visual interest.

**Figure 4.9.** A shoreline disturbance caused by high water.

**Figure 4.10.** A shoreline disturbance initiated by human activity.

effects of this influence on natural shoreline character and the landscape characteristics.

Figures 4.9 and 4.10 could have produced a negative reaction because of photographic quality. Both scenes are somewhat overexposed and appear to be barren and devoid of color. Obviously in most cases this overexposure will produce a negative visual reaction. Despite the variation in the photographic quality of the two scenes, both rated the landscape characteristics poorly. It is interesting that despite the overexposure, the respondents placed no emphasis on photographic quality and a heavy emphasis on the landscape components. It is therefore not possible to determine the extent to which the photographic quality influenced the respondents' reactions versus their reaction to the landscape characteristics.

## Implications

### General Landscape Character

The geologic character of the southern Louisiana landscape has a profound influence in the creation of a region exhibiting unique visual character. This geologic structure has contributed to a region where the land appears to merge with water as numerous waterways crisscross the landscape. Rapid flowing water in

a Louisiana river is a unique occurrence and because of this scarcity seems to gain visual significance. Water in the Louisiana landscape is often muddy and nonreflective, since it is naturally high in sediments.

In southern Louisiana the river shoreline environment lacks the visual complexity found in other regions. Here intrusions and massive rock formations are rare. The ancient sediments that form the foundation of the Louisiana basin offer little resistance to the slowly moving waters. The characteristic meandering shorelines contrast significantly with the complex, irregular shorelines found in other regions in the United States.

This lack of shoreline and waterform complexity (lack of swift water and complex water-surface patterns) in southern Louisiana is a highly significant visual occurrence. But while it is significant in Louisiana, it would be of little visual significance in other landscape types.

The envelope of land that surrounds a waterway gains visual distinction as elevation change increases. Water as a characteristically flat surface gains visual significance as surrounding landforms become irregular and slopes steepen. The steeper the slope, the more opportunities there are for viewing the land and its surface features. In regions such as southern Louisiana observation comes primarily through level lines of sight, and much of the scene is hidden by obstructing objects. Topographic variability is important in increasing visual landform distinction, but vegetation obstructing or obscuring the view decreases it. Isolation of the landform through visual obstruction destroys the potential for visual interest existing in the characteristic relationship between landform and water (Litton et al., 1974, p. 69).

The lack of topographic change in Louisiana decreases the significance of landform and increases the impact of vegetation upon visual preference. In this region vegetation provides much of the visual stimulus that in areas of dominant topographic change are more dynamically provided by landform.

This visual preference for the Louisiana river landscape appears to be highly dependent upon the legibility, contrast, and complexity of vegetation. In regions of low relief vegetation becomes the primary formative element in visual display. In regions of significant topographic change the landform legibility, contrast, and complexity dimensions would gain importance relating to individual preference for the river environment, while the importance of vegetation would be diminished.

### The River-Shoreline Relationship

The influence of topography on visual preference is regional in nature. What is significant in a flat landscape may be incidental in mountainous terrain. Because of the scarcity of significant topographic change in Louisiana, enclosure is less dependent upon landform impact than it is on ground pattern created by vegetation. It is vegetation, not landform, that modulates space and provides significant scale orientation.

For a river user space and scale relationships provided by shoreline vegetation must be clearly definable from the viewer's position on the river. Openness or a large expanse of water with little vegetation may provide a momentary change in viewing sequence, but continuous exposure to this situation will become monotonous and disorient the observer.

The visual connection between the river and the shoreline is extremely important (Figure 4.11). The water provides excitement and change, while in Louisiana the shoreline vegeta-

tion provides important scale and spatial clues. In an expanse of water a viewer cannot receive this information from the shoreline environment. Any factor that would separate or block this important visual connection may produce a negative influence on visual preference for river corridors. Preference is not necessarily related to the degree of enclosure in a scene. What is important is the presence or absence of scale and space-modulating elements and the important visual connection between the water and shoreline environments (Figure 4.12).

### Legibility of Vegetation

The clarity or legibility of vegetation and the edge relationships it provides are extremely important to visual preference. In the Louisiana river landscape an individual must be able to see connections and the structure of vegetation. Preference studies indicate that individuals dislike "unkempt vegetation" (Levin, 1977, p. 35; R. Kaplan, 1976, p. 246; 1977, p. 287). This implies that the vegetation component is not legible, connections cannot be seen between parts, and forms are obscured as uncontrolled vegetation causes plant forms to merge and conflict (Figure 4.13). Tree trunks are hidden among a mass of vegetation and destroy the important visual connection between the vegetation and the land.

Preference studies show that legible vegetation need not exist totally without human intervention. Rabanowitz and Coughlin determined that people generally prefer landscapes that tend to be "parklike" in appearance; "mowed grass and scattered large shade trees seem to be determining factors" (Rabanowitz and Coughlin, 1970, p. 7). Analysis shows that people relate visual preference to anticipated use of an environment.

Visual as well as physical access is related to the visual preference of a river scene, particularly for a recreationist. For example, a climax forest with tall mature trees and little understory entices visual and physical exploration because it is accessible. Dense understory vegetation blocks the view from the river into the forest. In addition, if a river user wanted to leave the river to move into the shore environment, dense vegetation or a sharp stream embankment

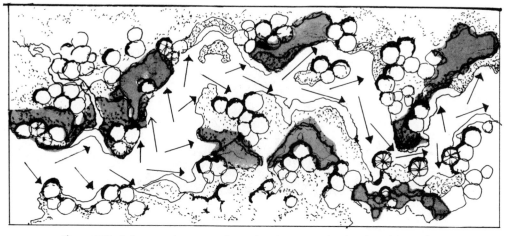

**Figure 4.11.** A river traveler constantly receives important visual and spatial cues from the shoreline environment.

would impede his entrance. A similar concept is indicated by Newby:

An environment must be accessible not only in physical terms, but also in psychological and visual terms; it must not deny but rather encourage participation, involvement and choice. Without such attributes, an environmental display becomes nothing more than reflection of everyday life, space with its monotonous and non-motivating character. This is a situation to be avoided. (Newby, 1971, p. 69)

Vegetation can partially obscure a view to the surrounding river environment. It may also indirectly create a sense of anticipation by limiting and modifying the amount of light entering a visual display. Alteration of light intensity can obscure vision by producing darkness or by modifying light patterns.

### Legibility versus Complexity

The legibility of vegetation is important to visual preference in the Louisiana river landscape. Preference testing indicates that legibility was important, but an important relationship exists between legibility and complexity.

Wohlwill (1966, pp. 29–38) describes the legibility of the outdoor environment in terms of an individual's ability to adapt or understand a visual experience. Each individual has an adaption level to environmental stimuli that is based upon the environment he or she experiences daily. Individuals derive pleasure in variations from this typical visual display or setting.

The horizontal scale in Figure 4.14 measures the amount of stimulation; the vertical scale illustrates the effect. Any variation from the adaption level produced by either an increase in stimulation (a more complex environment) or a decrease in stimulation (a less complex environment) produces an initial positive reaction. Any increase in the amount of stimulation produces excess information, which inhibits an individual's ability to process or perceive information, and the scene is no longer legible. This increased complexity in the environment produces a negative impact upon a perceptual experience; thus the environment becomes chaotic. While legibility encourages perceptual lingering, visual chaos produces stress and alienation (Newby, 1971, p. 70). A decrease in the amount of stimulation will also evoke a positive response, because of the increased legibility and simplicity in the environment. However, a point is reached where the decrease in stimulation results in monotony, producing a negative perceptual reaction.

This indicates that for a scene to evoke a positive visual response, it must be more than merely legible. A legible scene, clearly exhibiting strong identifiable relationships among parts, may also be monotonous. A degree of

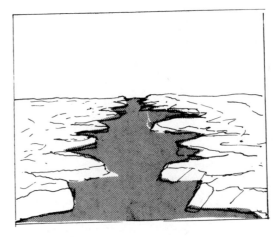

**Figure 4.12.** The more complex or irregular the shoreline, the greater the visual interest.

**Figure 4.13.** Legible versus illegible vegetation.

complexity or interest must exist for a visual display to evoke a positive viewer response. Visual complexity has a positive effect upon visual preference until the scene is no longer legible. At this point the visual display becomes chaotic, indicating a negative response.

Thus there is an optimal or ideal level of stimulus or complexity that each individual is capable of translating to meaningful information. Even though an optimal level of complexity exists, measuring this level is a more difficult problem.

## Summary

In this study the general concepts proposed in the informational theory were expanded, applying them to the landscape components of land, vegetation, and water and attempting to create a model that could predict human preference for Louisiana river landscapes. The importance of the interdependence between the evaluative factors become readily apparent. The strong interdependence indicates that a scene will not possess exceptional preference value with one or two of the characteristics (legibility, complexity, spatial definition, mystery, distinction, or disturbance) dominating. A high-ranking scene in visual preference, in most instances, will possess qualities relating to each factor. Thus the mixing and combination of factors and the resultant effect upon visual preference appears to be more significant than the effect of a single factor. To what extent each factor influences preference could not be concluded in this study. This concept indicates potential areas for future research.

## Utilization of the Study

The study is founded upon the assumption that a visual experience on a river consists of a series of views or sequential glimpses down a river corridor. If a system were developed to evaluate the visual preference for these views, a significant tool will be available for the evaluation and subsequent land-use planning in river corridors or any water-related landscape. The model could be used as the basis for establishing an inventory system for the analysis of rivers in Louisiana. Coupled with a photographic inventory, the model could be used that eventually would result in the establishment of a hierarchy of rivers or river sections based upon predicted preferential value.

A numerical value, or "assessment ratio," has been determined for each of the photographs or slides. A photographic inventory could be conducted on all rivers or river sections in a scenic river system. By evaluating each photograph numerically according to the seventeen rating criteria and by totaling these values, a hierarchy could be established based solely upon visual preference. Rivers or river stretches rating the highest might be preserved, while other use designations would be given according to the numerical results of the evaluation.

At a site scale of evaluation, the model could be used to identify key river stretches and distinctive river sections. Zones could be located relating to a hierarchy of uses based upon visual preferences. For example, a recreational activity may be located in a zone of low visual quality, while viewing or observation

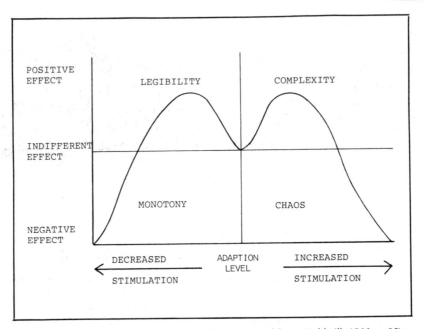

**Figure 4.14.** Discrepancy from adaptation level (adapted from Wohlwill, 1966, p. 35).

points may be established in key visual zones that have been set aside for protection. The detail of the photographic inventory indicates the detail of the analysis.

The model could also be used to locate key areas for recreation sites, bridges, or power-line crossings. An evaluation could be made on the impacts of proposed or existing activities on visual quality. A more detailed analysis of the inventory data would yield information on individual rating factors, such as complexity, spatial enclosure, legibility, and shoreline disturbance.

## Future Research

The need for extensive testing of the concepts discussed in this study should be stressed. Testing should be done, analyzing further each rating dimension used in the model evaluation. Each dimension should be tested examining the influence of the dimension upon visual preference. Once the significance of each rating dimension has been evaluated, the relationships among the dimensions should also be examined. Statistical tests should be run on the relative significance and behavior of each dimension as well as the relationship between

dimensions. Limitations in the scope of this study did not allow for extensive statistical analysis of the evaluative model. The preliminary indications are that the model has value in the assessment of visual preference for Louisiana river landscapes, but the use of the system for practical purposes should not be conducted until the model has been adequately tested and revised for utility, clarity, and accuracy.

Additional analysis should be conducted testing the concepts proposed to determine the correlation between landscape preference and visual-quality evaluation in the landscape. Such an analysis is needed in the development of visual assessment systems. Such systems would be of significant value in the land-use decision-making process.

## References

Dearinger, John A., and Woolwine, George M. 1973. Measuring the intangible values of natural streams, Pt. II Research Report No. 66, Water Resources Institute, University of Kentucky.

Eardly, A. J. 1962. *Structural geology of North America,* 2nd ed. New York: Harper and Row.

Fiebleman, Peter S., 1973. *The bayous.* American Wilderness Series. New York: Time-Life Books.

Kaplan, Rachael. 1975. Some methods and strategies in the prediction of preference. In E. H. Zube, R. O. Brush, and J. Gy. Fabos (Eds.), *Landscape assessment: Value, perceptions, and resources,* pp. 118–30. Stroudsburg, Pa.: Dowden, Hutchinson and Ross.

Kaplan, Stephen. 1973. Cognitive maps, human needs and the design environment. In W. F. E. Preiser, (Ed.), *Environmental design research.* Stroudsburg, Pa.: Dowden, Hutchinson and Ross.

———. 1975. An informal model for the prediction of preference. In E. H. Zube, R. O. Brush, and J. Gy. Fabos, (Eds.), *Landscape assessment: Value, perceptions, and resources.* pp. 92–102, Stroudsburg, Pa.: Dowden, Hutchinson and Ross.

Lee, Michael S. 1978. Visual quality assessment of Louisiana river landscapes. Master's thesis, Louisiana State University.

Levin, Judith E. 1977. Riverscape preference: on-site and photographic reactions. Master's thesis, University of Michigan.

Litton, R. Burton, Jr.; Tetlow, Robert J.; Sorensen, Jens; and Beatty, Russell A. 1974. *Water and landscape: an aesthetic overview of the role of water in the landscape.* Port Washington, N.Y.: Water Information Center, Inc.

Lynch, Kevin. 1960. *The image of the city.* Cambridge: Massachusetts Institute of Technology Press.

Newby, Floyd L. 1971. Understanding the visual resource. In E. H. Larson, (Ed), *The forest recreation symposium,* SUNY, College of Forestry, Syracuse, USDA, Forest Service, Northeast Forest Experiment Station.

Patrick, Ruth. 1972. Commentary on 'what is a river.' In Douglas H. K. Lee, E. Wendell Hewson, and Daniel A. Okun (Eds.), *River ecology and man.* New York: Academic Press.

Proshansky, Harold M.; Ittelson, William H.; Rivlin, Leanne G.; and Winkel, Gary H. 1974. *An introduction to environmental psychology.* City University of New York. New York: Holt, Rinehart and Winston.

Rabanowitz, Carla B., and Coughlin, Robert E. 1970. Analysis of landscape characteristics relevant to preference. Regional Science Research Institute, Discussion Paper No. 38.

Siegel, Sidney. 1956. *Nonparametric statistics for the behavioral sciences.* New York: McGraw-Hill.

Wohlwill, J. F. 1966. The physical environment: a problem for a psychology of stimulation. *Journal of Social Sciences* 22 (November): 29–38.

# 5 Assessment of Coastal Wetlands in Dennis, Massachusetts

**JAMES F. PALMER**

## Introduction

Throughout the 1960s it became increasingly apparent that local citizens and governments were losing the ability to protect those qualities of the environment that they held most dear. This trend is most pronounced in areas rich in natural resources and cultural heritage, such as the nation's coastal zone, where everyone seems to want to live, even if only for a few days each year. Our increased national affluence has made this a real possibility for an overwhelming proportion of the population. The result is that the small coastal communities that had thrived on a moderate level of tourism are now overrun and foundering. Growth in many of these communities is outstripping all expectations as wetlands are filled and new development destroys scenic views. The blight of tourism is slowly diminishing those qualities that were once most highly prized.

Local citizens are left feeling helpless in the wake of this unchecked growth. This sense of helplessness is particularly acute when they try to protect the visual resources that have intense emotional associations yet are difficult to describe systematically. The case study presented here illustrates how a group of citizens from the town of Dennis on Cape Cod sought to inventory and evaluate their local visual resources. This effort is part of a larger resource analysis conducted by citizens of Dennis with technical assistance from the Massachusetts Natural Resource Planning Program administered by the Soil Conservation Service (Chandler, 1976).*

The objectives of the visual resource survey are:

*The data used in this report were collected by members of the Dennis Comprehensive Planning Committee with technical assistance from Geoffrey Chandler as part of the Massachusetts Natural Resource Planning Program. This planning program has been developed by the Soil Conservation Service to offer the methods and technical assistance for communities systematically to collect, evaluate, and utilize information concerning their natural resources.

Particular thanks are due to Constance Bechard and Mary Hood Hagler for the information they provided about their town.

1. Involve a large number of people in the planning process and increase their awareness of the community's visual resources
2. Find the community's special image of its land and preserve this image for future residents
3. Determine which local landscapes are preferred by local citizens
4. Provide communities with useful information on landscape quality for practical planning purposes (Soil Conservation Service, 1977)

To meet these objectives, two types of information concerning local perceptions of the Dennis landscape were collected. The first type is used to classify landscape views based on their perceived similarity; the second provides a rating of the scenic value of these same landscape views.

## Procedure

Preparation for the visual resource inventory began in the spring of 1976 with the appointment of a committee of concerned citizens. In order to develop a sample of landscape views, each member of the committee indicated on a local street map views that he or she considered representative of the range of views in Dennis. Each of these views was photographed in color using a 35-millimeter wide-angle lens. The 5-by-7-inch prints of these scenes were borderless with a mat finish and mounted on thin cardboard. The committee then selected the 56 photographs that it felt most accurately portrayed the range of landscapes in Dennis.

The cooperation of a random sample of registered voters was then sought to evaluate the visual quality of these 56 landscape views. A total of 96 citizens contributed judgments of landscape quality by sorting the photographs according to one of two different sets of instructions. In the first set the participants were told:

Each of these photographs represents a landscape view found in Dennis. For the purposes of this study, the "landscape" may be thought of as all the various elements that you see in the photograph.

Please sort these photographs into piles containing other landscapes which you feel are similar. We request that each pile you form have three or more landscapes each. You may make as many piles as you like.

In addition, for each pile the participants were asked to:

describe in a few words or phrases those characteristics that best represent the similarities of the landscapes in the group.

The second set of instructions asked the participants to:

Sort the 56 photographs into 7 piles according to the scenic value of the landscape in the photos. In pile #1, place 3 landscapes which you think have the highest scenic value. In pile #7, place 3 landscapes which you think have the lowest scenic value. From the remaining 50 landscapes, place the 7 with the highest scenic value in pile #2, and the 7 with the lowest scenic value in pile #6. From the remaining 36 landscapes, place the 11 with the highest scenic value in pile #3, and the 11 with the lowest scenic value in pile #5. Place the remaining 14 landscapes in pile #4.

Each respondent was then randomly selected to answer one of two additional sets of questions investigating the different factors that contribute to the scenic value of the landscape. In one case they were instructed to:

describe in either a few words or phrases those factors which add the most to the scenic value of pile #1. . . . Identify those factors which detract the most from the scenic value of pile #7. . . . Describe those factors which make the scenic value of pile #4 mediocre.

In the other case respondents were provided with a checklist of 56 factors that were thought to influence scenic value. The respondents were asked to:

identify three landscape factors that add to the scenic value of each of the three photographs in pile #1. . . . Next identify three landscape factors that detract from the scenic value of each of the three landscapes you placed in pile #7. . . . Now take the first six photographs from pile #4 and for each of these landscapes identify three factors each which add and detract from the scenic value of these landscapes.

The participants' recorded responses were later analyzed by the local citizens' committee and a technical assistant.

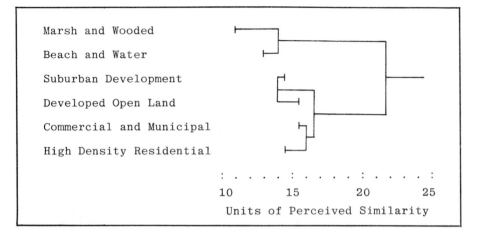

**Figure 5.1.** Perceived similarity among the landscape types in Dennis, Massachusetts.

## Results

While the citizens who participated in the visual resource survey were selected randomly from the current list of registered voters, it is not possible to test their representativeness of the total population in Dennis. The town has grown so fast in the past decade that local census data are outdated and current population characteristics are unknown. However, the participants do represent a full range of ages, occupations, sex, residential neighborhoods, and lengths of residence. In addition, there are no significant differences among the groups of participants who performed the three different sorting tasks. Possibly the most important test of representativeness is that the town folk seem to accept the validity of the results and are comfortable with its representation of their point of view.

## Conceptual Classification of Landscapes

A total of 27 citizens sorted the landscape views according to their similarity. Using a clustering procedure developed by Palmer and Zube (1976), the judgments of landscape similarity made by these citizens are aggregated into a conceptual classification of the different landscape types in Dennis. Six distinct types are identified: (1) marsh and wooded landscapes; (2) beach and water landscapes; (3) suburban development; (4) developed open lands; (5) commercial and municipal landscapes; and (6) high-density residential landscapes. A diagrammatic summary of the perceived similarity among these types is shown in Figure 5.1. A description of the essential characteristics of each landscape type is obtained through a systematic content analysis of the words and phrases that the participants used to characterize their piles of similar landscapes.

### Marsh and Wooded Landscapes

These are perceived to be the most "natural" scenes in Dennis. "They are the open spaces we want to protect and keep for birds and men alike." Evoking a sense of "peacefulness" and "beauty," this type is closely identified with the "Cape Cod landscape." As illustrated in Figure 5.2, a wide variety of wetland types are represented, ranging from coastal marshes to shrub swamp. The identifying characteristic as perceived by the participants is the comparatively lush vegetation pattern, which varies from low-lying "marshland" to higher "woodlands." Those wooded areas represented by the landscape sample are included in this class.

It is interesting to speculate that the more wooded scenes might have been placed in a class of their own if suitable photographic representations had been available. However, in the Cape's gently undulating topography, it is

**Figure 5.2.** Marsh and wooded landscapes of high scenic value (*top*) and low scenic value (*bottom*).

**Figure 5.3.** Beach and water landscapes of high scenic value (*top*) and low scenic value (*bottom*).

nearly impossible to photograph the woods because of the trees in the way. Support for this possibility comes from a study of Connecticut River Valley landscapes, in which open meadows enclosed by woods were found to be conceptually different from forested hills (ibid.). If a separate Woodlands Landscape class did exist, this past research indicates that it would be closely related to Marsh Landscapes.

### Beach and Water Landscapes

The interface of "beaches and sand dunes" with "saltwater" is the dominant conceptual characteristic of this type, as exemplified by Figure 5.3. Therefore, a tidal salt marsh is perceived as part of this class when the tide is in and among the marsh landscapes when the tide is out.

These scenes are generally "unspoiled" and "void of human habitation"; appropriate human presence is manifested through a recreational attraction such as "swimming and fishing." The participants in this survey are sensitive to the use of certain areas in this landscape type by "tourists," while others are "for the year-round resident who wants to get away from the tourists." These scenes are "attractive" in their more natural state but are beset by the pressures of "capitalistic endeavor," which invariably creates a sense "that is not very appealing to the eye." This degradation through private exploitation becomes more significant because of the important role this landscape type plays in the local perception of the Cape's regional identity.

### Suburban Development

In describing suburban development, the role played by natural elements, the presence of water, or aspects of landform are rarely mentioned. These are "low-density residential areas" and "quiet country lanes" that pass "through the countryside without houses directly on the roads." This is the "hometown Cape" in which the "locals" live. Participants frequently distinguish the more traditional older developments from the newer, more modern forms within this type. For instance, in grouping photos one participant separates "single-family dwellings in developments" from "quiet country roads with vintage houses." Figure 5.4 illustrates

a residence and a highway that are both from this landscape type.

### Developed Open Land

Developed open land is illustrated in a small group of scenes depicting open land associated with some form of development (Figure 5.5). Included in this group are a cemetery, a power line right-of-way, a golf course, and a churchyard. Their distinguishing characteristic is that they are perceived as "developed areas that exhibit compatability with the environment." Participants commonly associate them with one of the other developed landscape types—sometimes with the suburban development because they are "historic" and conceptually part of the "hometown Cape," and other times with the commercial and municipal landscapes because of their "public service" character.

### Commercial and Municipal Landscapes

Different types of nonresidential developed areas are gathered together within this conceptual class, which is illustrated in Figure 5.6. Among those mentioned are a shopping center, school, industrial area, commercial establishment, police station, church, and various other service structures. As a class, descriptions of landform, cover types, or water are totally absent. This is Dennis at its worst in the eyes of the local residents. One resident exclaims, "Horrid! They should be forced to restore and start over." However, most respondents seem less belligerent, and many are even resigned to the inevitability and probable growth of this kind of landscape. As one respondent notes, "These are the necessary evils of civilization." This congested and objectionable landscape is definitely not considered part of the regional image of Cape Cod and could be found in Anywhere, USA.

### High-Density Residential Landscapes

High-density residential landscapes, exemplified in Figure 5.7, are perceived as the places where the "off-Cape" population stays. Interestingly, they are not called "homes" but "rental units," a type of commercial venture. Termed "claptraps" and "schlock residential" areas, they

**Figure 5.4.** Suburban developments of high scenic value (*top*) and low scenic value (*bottom*).

**Figure 5.5.** Developed open land of high scenic value (*top*) and low scenic value (*bottom*).

**Figure 5.6.** Commercial and municipal landscapes of high scenic value (*top*) and low scenic value (*bottom*).

**Figure 5.7.** High-density residential landscapes of high scenic value (*top*) and low scenic value (*bottom*).

are a scenic blight in the eyes of the local residents. There is some resignation that they are "necessary," but there is also substantial concern that they are rapidly encroaching upon the most valuable areas of the Cape. One respondent observes acutely: "Here's some near epitome of the gross overpopulation of an area. Everyone wants a piece of the beauty and bit by bit the beauty is removed." In this case the beauty comes from the beach and water landscapes, which have special qualities that are conspicuously absent from the suburban landscapes where the respondents live.

## Judgments of Scenic Value

Two groups of citizens were asked to sort the landscape views according to scenic value: 37 were asked to use their own words or phrases to describe the qualities that added or detracted from the scenes; 32 were given a landscape-factor checklist as a means of providing similar information. The scenic resource value for a particular landscape view is the mean rating it received from the respondents. The scenic resource values for all landscape views as judged by both groups are compared using t-tests. In only two instances are the judgments significantly different (p < .05), therefore the scenic resource values used below are calculated from the ratings by all 69 respondents.

A clear pattern emerges from the content analysis of the words and phrases respondents used to describe the factors that contribute to the landscape's scenic value. The most scenic landscapes are overwhelmingly perceived as "natural" and even as "wild" by some. The presence of water and the dominance of "green" vegetation is mentioned only in connection with these highly valued scenes. Respondents seem to favor a pastoral notion of what is scenic, characterizing it as "well kept" and "spacious" with "distant prospects," the way Cape Cod "should look." There are no "gross man-made additions," and where buildings appear in the scene they are "distant" and "fit in on the Cape." There also seems to be a compositional value seen in the "interplay of land and water, colors and shapes."

The least scenic landscapes are perceived as "cluttered" and "unimaginative" views dominated by misfit features: "signs," "overhead wires," "broken asphalt," "supermarkets," "concrete mixing plant," and the like. These are "lifeless" and "artificial" scenes "without trees and bushes."

Those scenes that are given moderate ratings are primarily characterized as being "ordinary" and "anywhere," not just Cape Cod. Misfit features also characterize this group, but they are less dominant than in the least scenic landscapes.

## The Scenic Value of Landscape Types

The usefulness of the visual resource survey in Dennis becomes more apparent when the scenic value for each landscape type is compared with the other types. An analysis of variance ($F = 642.4$, $df = 5, 3789, 3794$, $p < .001$) indicates more significant differences in scenic value among rather than within the landscape types. The differences in scenic value between landscape types are investigated further using t-tests, shown in Table 5.1. In most cases significant differences are found. However, no significance is found between those pairs of landscape types that are shown in Figure 5.1 as being conceptually most similar. For instance, the marsh and wooded landscapes and the beach and water landscapes are perceived as being very similar and thus do not have significantly different scenic values. However, they are both perceived as quite dissimilar from the high-density residential landscapes, which have a significantly poorer scenic value.

The results of the landscape-factor checklist are summarized in Tables 5.2 and 5.3 according to landscape type and give some indication of what factors influence scenic value for each type. The pattern that emerges from these tables corroborates the prior content analysis of what contributes to scenic value. A romantic notion of the most scenic prevails, while misfit characteristics dominate the least scenic landscapes. This pattern can also be seen by comparing the examples in Figures 5.2 through 5.7 of high and low scenic value for each landscape type.

A more careful examination of Tables 5.2 and 5.3 provides several additional insights. For instance, both the beach and water and marsh and wooded landscapes are valued for their "naturalness." However, the marshes are

**Table 5.1  T-tests Comparing Mean Scenic Value for Each Landscape Type**

| Landscape Type | n[b] | x̄ | T-value[a] | | | | |
|---|---|---|---|---|---|---|---|
| | | | Beach | Marsh | Suburban | Open Land | Commercial |
| Beach and water | 759 | 2.99 | | | | | |
| Wooded upland and marsh | 552 | 2.91 | 1.10n.s. | | | | |
| Suburban development | 759 | 3.47 | −8.04*** | −8.80*** | | | |
| Developed open land | 276 | 3.52 | −5.85*** | −6.50*** | −.54n.s. | | |
| Commercial | 828 | 5.32 | −39.78*** | −38.92*** | −33.36*** | −20.62*** | |
| High-density residential | 621 | 5.27 | −37.78*** | −37.09*** | −31.38*** | −19.74*** | .98n.s. |

[a] The t-values reported here are for independent groups with unequal variances; therefore the values are an approximation.
[b] This value is the total number of ratings made by 69 respondents of all the scenes within a landscape type.

*Significance:* n.s. $p \geq .05$, *** $p < .001$


**Table 5.2  Landscape Factors That Add to the Scenic Value of Each Landscape Type**

| Rank[a] | Landscape Types | | | | | |
|---|---|---|---|---|---|---|
| | Beach and water | Marsh and wooded | Suburban development | Developed open land | Commercial and municipal | High-density residential |
| **Highest:** | | | | | | |
| 1. | Naturalness | Serenity | Serenity | Serenity | Building color | Building design |
| 2. | Water | Vastness | Local character | | Building design | Walls and fences |
| 3. | Shoreline | Naturalness | | | Natural color | |
| **Moderate:** | | | | | | |
| 1. | Water | Naturalness | Vegetation | Serenity | | |
| 2. | Depth of view | Natural color | Natural color | Naturalness | | |
| 3. | Natural color | | Naturalness | | | |
| 4. | | | Depth of view | | | |

[a] Landscapes with the highest scenic value were in pile #1. Those with moderate scenic value were in pile #4.

*Note:* The landscape-factor checklist was completed by 28 respondents.

**Table 5.3   Landscape Factors that Detract from the Scenic Value of Each Landscape Type**

| | Landscape Types | | | | | |
|---|---|---|---|---|---|---|
| Rank[a] | Beach and water | Marsh and wooded | Suburban development | Developed open land | Commercial and municipal | High-density residential |
| **Lowest:** | | | | | | |
| 1. | | | | | Overhead wire | Bare earth |
| 2. | | | | | Barrenness | Barrenness |
| 3. | | | | | Cars and trucks | Building design |
| 4. | | | | | | Overhead wire |
| 5. | | | | | | Building material |
| 6. | | | | | | Building setback |
| **Moderate:** | | | | | | |
| 1. | Horizon line | Horizon line | Roads | Overhead wire | Overhead wire | Building color |
| 2. | Building design | Barrenness | Pavement | Roads | Cars and trucks | Building material |
| 3. | Overhead wire | Natural color | Cars and trucks | | | Straight line |
| 4. | Flatness | | | | | |

[a] Landscapes with the lowest scenic value were in pile #7. Those with moderate scenic value were in pile #4.

*Note:*   The landscape-factor checklist was completed by 28 respondents.

primarily valued for their emotional associations—their serenity, vastness, and uniqueness. In contrast, those aspects of a beach that contribute to its quality are physical—the water, sand, and shoreline.

Another interesting implication of these tables is that vegetation and natural materials play an important role in the scenic value of the less densely developed areas. Where roads, overhead wires, and the like are not effectively screened, scenic value drops. In contrast, building characteristics such as materials, design, color, and setback become important in the more densely developed landscape types. In these situations the buildings are so concentrated or massive that they cannot be completely screened. All that one expects is the mitigation of a barren appearance through appropriate landscaping.

## Discussion

Sometimes it is awkward to be a landscape planner committed to the development of systematic methods for consideration of the landscape as a visual resource. The public often responds with skepticism. It is a measure of success that the results of a visual resource survey seem so obvious. Yet few critics would ever give prior support to the possibility that there is substantial agreement regarding the landscape types perceived in an area as well as what contributes to their scenic value.

In Dennis there seems to be a reasonable acceptance of the results of the visual resource survey, probably because of the large degree of local control and participation throughout the entire process. This survey is one of the reasons why Dennis was named the All-American City for 1978. When bestowing the award, the National Municipal League of Cities and Towns stated that it was particularly impressed by the example Dennis provided other towns for (1) citizen participation, (2) comprehensive planning, and (3) conservation acquisition and historic preservation. The visual resource survey contributed to each of these areas.

One important ramification of the visual resource survey is its utility as a powerful tool for education. It has brought "visual quality" out

of the closet and made it a respectable topic in local planning. It is now clearer to the local decision-makers that there are ways to describe landscape appearances systematically. Even more important, there is much more substantial agreement among town residents than anyone ever expected. In addition to being used at town meetings, photographs are being shown to students in the public schools to make them more aware of their local visual resource.

A second ramification of the survey is its influence on the new zoning bylaws for the town of Dennis. While all the changes in the old zoning bylaws are founded on other aspects of the comprehensive Natural Resource Planning Program survey, they also have a visual basis that is recognized by the local citizens. For instance, the study's results suggest that the presence of any structure in the foreground becomes so dominant in an otherwise beach and water or marsh and wooded landscape that the pastoral image is destroyed. The possibility of this visual incompatibility is given some credence by the single landscape view that did not clearly belong to any landscape type—a scene viewed across a salt marsh toward a densely developed residential area. Other areas where beach cottages composed the foreground were obviously judged high-density residential landscapes. Therefore, future commercial and high-density residential developments will be concentrated in those areas already identified with these landscape types. Through zoning, a serious attempt is being made to halt the sprawl of these landscapes and to encourage their infilling. An attempt is also being made to protect the integrity of undeveloped natural areas. Those areas near coastal beaches and marshes are rezoned from a minimum residence lot size of 20,000 square feet to a minimum of 60,000 square feet. These areas have the greatest scenic value and are least able visually to absorb development. The remaining natural landscapes are rezoned to a minimum lot size of 40,000 square feet. All areas that are already considered suburban development remain at the previous minimum lot size of 20,000 square feet.

The third ramification of the survey is the town's commitment to acquire publicly those areas that are visually most valuable. In 1979 the citizens of Dennis purchased 25 acres of prime marshland and 200 acres of beachfront. These are added to the town's already extensive public-conservation and recreation areas.

# References

Chandler, Geoffrey B. 1976. *Natural and visual resources, Dennis, Massachusetts.* Dennis: Dennis Conservation Commission and Planning Board.

Palmer, James F., and Zube, Ervin H. 1976 "Numerical and perceptual landscape classification." In E. H. Zube, ed., *Studies in landscape perception.* Amherst: Institute for Man and Environment, University of Massachusetts.

USDA, Soil Conservation Service. 1977 "A Natural Resources Planning Program Handbook" (draft). Amherst, Mass., 1977.

An earlier version of this paper was presented at the Coastal Zone 78 symposium held in San Francisco between March 14 and 16, 1978. It appeared as "Citizen Assessment of the Coastal Visual Resource" in *Coastal Zone 78* (New York: American Society of Civil Engineers, 1978), pp. 1019–37. Reprinted with permission.

# 6 Assessing Visual Preference and Familiarity for a Bog Environment

## WILLIAM E. HAMMITT

## Conceptual Approach

Perception of the visual environment necessarily depends on previous experiences and the memory of such encounters. Familiarity or past experiences with an environment or environments similar to it can greatly influence how it is perceived (Appleton, 1975; Arnheim, 1969; Kaplan, 1973). Therefore, visual preference for certain environments or aspects of environments depends largely on the visual resources perceived in that environment and the associated information processed with that encounter and past encounters.

The design of the present study and the interpretation of the results are based on a particular theoretical approach which assumes that people are information-processing organisms of their environment. Various environments or components of environments contain different information and are preferred on the basis of the information they offer. Simply stated, the theory proposes that humans, as evolutionarily successful organisms, are efficient at processing environmental information, and that humans are constantly building mental models of the environment they experience. Through environmental encounters, humans are exposed to considerable environmental information, which is processed and incorporated to varying degrees into mental representation of the external environment. The mental models that one develops from environmental encounters are, in turn, instrumental in how one interprets future environmental encounters. As stated by Kaplan and Kaplan (1978, p. 43),

the cognitive map (or mental model) provides a link between the human thought process and the physical environment. The way an individual experiences and reacts to a given environment begins to be understandable in the context of an experience-based internal structure that corresponds, at least in certain respects, to the environment in question.

Also basic to the conceptual framework of this study is the belief that humans are primarily "visual" processors of environmental informa-

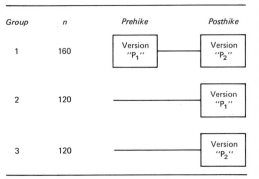

| Group | n | Prehike | Posthike |
|-------|-----|---------|----------|
| 1 | 160 | Version "P₁" | Version "P₂" |
| 2 | 120 | | Version "P₁" |
| 3 | 120 | | Version "P₂" |

**Figure 6.1.** Research paradigm for sampling bog visitors.

tion. While the perception of natural environments is a complex process, involving all of our senses, our past experiences and their lasting traces in memory, it is vision that people depend on most for relating to the environment. Sight is of crucial importance and probably influences human response to environments more directly and with greater salience than do our other senses (Welsh, 1966). Even when the other senses are involved in processing information, they are usually associated with a visual image, either called up from memory or existing in the physical environment. When processing visual information, humans group into classes or categories (Bruner, 1957) or schemata (Attneave, 1957) those visual images that they encounter most frequently, find intriguing, and gravitate toward for various reasons.

Even though humans are primarily "visual" processing organisms – and much of this information is coded in memory – the visual information is not recorded as a "picture." Kaplan (1978, p. 56) points out that

while the [cognitive model concept] may be equated in a very rough way with the idea that a person has a "picture of the environment" in his head, the information is far more schematic and incomplete than "picture" implies, to say nothing of the fact that this "picture" will in general never have been seen all at once.

The mental "picture" is an approximation of reality, an approximation that will vary according to individual experience level.

If, indeed, humans do formulate mental models of their environment, based primarily on visual encounters, then one could hypothesize that on-site experiences in natural environments could be important in cognitive model development of such environments. In addition, since much of the on-site information is processed visually, the use of photographs might be a logical approach for abstracting what visitors do perceive and record mentally during on-site encounters. Determination of those visual scenes most preferred and those that become most familiar could benefit resource planners and managers involved in providing visual resource experiences.

## Study Description

### Study Area

Visual preference and familiarity for photographs of a bog environment were investigated at the Cranberry Glades Botanical Area, Monongahela National Forest, West Virginia. Cranberry Glades contains four bogs, of which visitors have access to two by way of a loop-designed boardwalk trail. The boardwalk is 2,800 feet (853 meters) long and requires about a thirty-minute hike. Annual visitation (Memorial Day through Labor Day) totals approximately 26,000 visitors. The boardwalk was the actual location within the study area of the survey.

### Respondents

The sample consisted of 400 on-site visitors. One individual per party was interviewed, with 20 visitors per day being surveyed over a twenty-day period during July and August 1977. Participants were at least eighteen years of age and were representative of the public visiting the boardwalk trail during the study period.

### Stimuli

Two versions of a photo questionnaire (designated P₁ and P₂), each comprised of twenty-four black-and-white bog scenes, were used to obtain visitor response. Sixteen of the photographs were duplicated between the two questionnare versions for purposes of examining a particular aspect of familiarity. Photographs for the questionnaire included

1  2  3  4  5                              no  ?  yes    1  2  3  4  5                              no  ?  yes

**Figure 6.2.** Examples from the photo questionnaire demonstrate the rating procedure for preference and familiarity.

some taken by visitors, some furnished by the interpretive staff of Cranberry Glades, and the remainder provided by the researcher. Visitor photographs were obtained by furnishing fifteen visitors to the bog with instamatic cameras prior to the actual survey and having them photograph bog scenes and features as they hiked along the boardwalk trail. From the three sources of photographs (visitor, interpreter, and researcher), a representative set was selected for inclusion in the questionnaire. Criteria used for selecting representative photographs were frequently photographed scenes in the case of visitor produced photos and scenes of distant, intermediate, and immediate aspects of the bog. Criteria used to eliminate photos were people included in photos and close-ups of individual flowers, plants, or objects. Six bog scenes from Michigan and a bog adjacent to the study area were also included for testing a portion of the familiarity component of the study.

In addition to the visual images, a brief portion of the photo questionnaire consisted of written items concerning reasons for visiting the bog and number of previous visits to the study area and other bog environments.

### Procedure

Some visitors were asked to view and rate the bog photos just prior to hiking the bog boardwalk trail and then again after the hike (Figure 6.1, Group 1). Other visitors were shown the photo questionnaire only upon completing the hike (Groups 2 and 3). In both cases visitors were asked to indicate visual preference (on a 5-point Likert scale, ranging from 1 = preferred not at all to 5 = preferred very much) for each photographed scene. Preference was defined as "how much you like a scene for whatever reason." Respondents were instructed to preview quickly the bog photographs to get a general feeling for what the photos were about and then to indicate their preference for the twenty-four photos directly on the questionnaire by circling one of the five rating numbers below each photo.

Only at the end of the hike was information obtained about visitors' feeling of how familiar various photographs seemed (Groups 1 and 3). Familiarity was defined as the visitor's recall of having viewed a scene during the hiking experience. A three-choice option (yes = familiar, no = not familiar, ? = not sure) was provided for recording familiarity. As for the preference ratings, respondents were instructed to indicate familiarity for each photograph by simply circling one of the three choices located below each photo (see Figure 6.2). The written portion of the photo questionnaire was also completed only after the hike.

All respondents were sampled at the boardwalk trailhead, which served as both the beginning and ending point of the loop-designed trail. Thus all visitors were intercepted during the sample periods.

## Bog Preference and Dimensions

Visual preference for the bog environment was analyzed from two approaches. First, to determine which individual scenes people preferred

**Figure 6.3.** Results of preference ratings. *Top:* two most preferred bog scenes. *Bottom:* two least preferred bog scenes.

most to see, mean photograph ratings were examined. Then, using the preference rating data, the bog scenes were factor and cluster analyzed to determine the underlying patterns or commonalities among the scenes. The dimensions of bog scenes were then interpreted from both a descriptive and an information-processing viewpoint (Kaplan, 1975) to suggest environmental preference predictors operating in the various dimensions.

### Preference for Bog Photographs

Mean preference ratings for the bog scenes ranged from a low of 3.33 to a high of 4.58. The overall mean for the twenty-four photographs was 3.90. Thus the scores were skewed toward the upper end of the scale, indicating a high preference for the bog. Results from other studies using similar methodologies indicate that the bog was rated considerably higher. Levin (1977) received on-site preference ratings (1–5 scale) for river landscapes in the range of 2.66 to 4.13. Gallagher (1977), in a study of a seminatural environment, obtained means in the range of 2.52 to 3.97.

A comparative examination of the most and least preferred photos revealed an obvious difference in habitat preference within the bog ecosystem (Figure 6.3). Scenes of the "bog forest" were most preferred, while scenes of the open "bog mat" were least preferred. Another pattern, related to the habitat zones, was the close, closed appearance of the preferred bog forest scenes as compared to the more distant, open character of the least preferred bog mat scenes. These results suggest that bog visitors should have the opportunity to experience many habitats of the bog ecosystem rather than only the ecologically interesting bog mat area. This has particular significance for the location of boardwalks by resource managers.

### Identifying Dimensions

The use of ratings of individual scenes to predict preference has its limitations. First, it is impractical to interpret a very large data set. Second, there is the question of just how valuable it is to the resource manager to know the preference for individual scenes. Only in limited situations can one design or manage an area to provide a particular scene. It is much more practical to search for underlying patterns among the scenes. Yet to rely on the mean preference rating as the basis for such grouping has its problems too. Groups of scenes based on high or low preference ratings can lead to a mixture of different patterns of scenes in each group that are sometimes difficult to explain.

Another approach to reducing the data set to meaningful and manageable groups is based on cluster-analytic procedures. These involve any of a number of mathematical techniques that group items (or scenes) in terms of patterns of relationships in the respondents' ratings. Using only the preference ratings, the resulting groups of items reveal similarities in the way the scenes were viewed by the respondents. R. Kaplan (1975) discusses criteria for selecting particular procedures and the role of the researcher in interpreting the results.

Because the bases for the groupings in dimensional procedures are necessarily related to the algorithms involved, two different techniques were used to add stability to the groupings generated. In both instances the preference ratings of the $P_2$ questionnaire respondents (n = 274) were used. The Guttman-Lingoes Smallest Space Analysis (SSA–III) (Lingoes, 1972), a nonmetric-factor analytic procedure, produced four dimensions of bog scenes. All twenty-four photographs had factor loadings greater than the determined minimum value of 0.40. Stability of the dimensions was reinforced by the findings of the second clustering techniques, ICLUST (Kulik, Revelle, and Kulik, 1970). ICLUST, a metric, hierarchical cluster procedure, also produced four dimensions. The two techniques produced essentially equivalent dimensions. Even though a few photos were placed in different dimensions by the two analyses, the central theme of each dimension did not change. The strength of associations and ordering of the scenes within the dimensions of both techniques were also quite similar, especially for the higher loading (SSA–III) or centrally arrayed (ICLUST). Since both techniques yielded similar dimensions of bog scenes, only the SSA–III results will be used for interpretation.

## Bog Dimensions

The four dimensions of bog scenes and their factor loadings are summarized in Table 6.1. Each dimension was assigned a name, based on the general content theme that characterized it. The patterns of scenes characteristic of each dimension were consistent, and they make intuitive sense. Because it is impractical to include all the photos comprising each dimension, a brief description of the dimensions will be given, as well as one exemplary scene from each dimension. Although the dimensions to be described were based on the preference ratings of photographs, it should be reemphasized that while rating photos respondents were, in practicality, responding at the same time to the actual bog environment they had just hiked. Thus the visual preference dimensions indicate those

**Table 6.1   Preference Dimensions, Based on Visitor Ratings of Bog Photographs**

|  | Factor Loadings |
|---|---|
| Dimension 1: | .6630 |
| "Bog Mat" | .6521 |
|  | .6459 |
| $\overline{X}$ = 3.69 | .6453 |
|  | .5885 |
|  | .5062 |
| Dimension 2: | .6737 |
| "Boardwalk" | .6695 |
|  | .5580 |
| $\overline{X}$ = 4.12 | .4707 |
| Dimension 3: | .6328 |
| "Feature" | .5381 |
|  | .5363 |
| $\overline{X}$ = 3.99 | .4991 |
|  | .4555 |
|  | .4267 |
| Dimension 4: | .6902 |
| "Edge" | .6861 |
|  | .6407 |
| $\overline{X}$ = 3.77 | .6189 |
|  | .5701 |
|  | .4650 |
|  | .4389 |

**Figure 6.4.** Example of one characteristic scene from each of the four dimensions of bog scenes, determined by factor analysis. Photo A, top left; **Photo B,** top right; Photo C, bottom left; Photo D, bottom right.

aspects of the bog that the visitors potentially experienced and preferred.

*Bog Mat:* This grouping of photographs included six-scenes characterized by the open, expansive view of the vegetative bog mat. The scenes appeared as having even, uniform, grasslike texture in the foreground that was surrounded by a distant fringe of trees or mountains. The scenes lacked any visual barriers to entry and had few distinct features or edges of immediate vegetation. Visitors rated this aspect of the bog the least preferred (Figure 6.4, Photo A).

*Boardwalk:* The most preferred dimension was dominated by scenes of the trail boardwalk. An additional component to these scenes was the type of habitat the boardwalk passed through. Boardwalk scenes in the forest were consistently preferred over those in the bog mat. The boardwalk seems to be an important component of the bog experience, especially if it affords entry into areas that appear otherwise difficult, yet desirable, to penetrate both in the physical and visual sense. Particularly preferred

were those situations where the boardwalk made a bend in the trail within dense vegetation, thus producing a visual barrier as to what occurs farther ahead on the trail (Fig. 6.4, Photo B). Such scenes encourage the viewer to become visually involved, to walk around the corner to explore for the hidden view. An essential element of the hidden visual information component is the availability of dense vegetation, landform, or some example of visual barrier to block the viewer's vision of what lies around the corner. For example, in the open bog mat area bends in the trail failed to receive higher preference than straight segments of trail because of the lack of visual barriers present.

*Feature:* A third grouping of scenes involved distinct landscape features and minihabitats of the bog. An isolated clump of ferns (Fig. 6.4, Photo C), an odd-shaped tree, and a dense colony of rhododendron were typical examples. The unique features and the isolated minihabitats are different from frequent, repetitious elements along the trail, and they are noticed for their differentness. The features present an element of novelty and identifiability to the visual experience. They are distinctive objects or places that are easily recognized, that represent "change," and serve as landmarks in the sequence of bog events perceived. The element of change, especially when it is distinctive, attracts attention. As the unknown becomes known, and as the stream of perceived environmental stimuli becomes repetitious, it is change that often attracts attention and offers new involvement. The desire to walk around all sides of an unusually shaped birch tree is underlaid with the promise of different and additional information upon further observation. Features within the bog landscape rate high in visual involvement, coherence, and legibility and were preferred second to the boardwalk dimension.

*Edge:* The final dimension was characterized by an abundance of jagged edge where two or more habitat types of vegetation met. All scenes contained an element of the bog forest, shrub, and mat habitats (Fig. 6.4, Photo D). Scenes in this dimension contained little unity and focus. Their legibility is weak in that it is difficult to identify a dominant pattern that makes the scenes easily readable. The great mixture of irregular textures where the vegetational units interface offers complexity but little coherence and predictability for the viewer. There are few coherent items or sharp boundaries to focus on. All this leads to a low "sense of place" and orientation. Preference for these scenes ranked third, only somewhat higher than for the bog mat dimension.

"Sense of place" may be an important cognitive issue when dealing with the repetitious but nonlegible jagged edge of bogs. Bogs are notorious environments for getting disoriented in and lost in. The problem seems to lie in not being able to recognize or relocate the point at which one entered the bog mat from the shrubby bog edge. The problem is easily solved by using a handkerchief as a landmark to indicate the entry point. Lack of focus is obviously at issue.

Because visitors rated all aspects of the bog environment fairly high, the dimension means do not vary by a great amount. Nevertheless, when compared, the means proved to be significantly different (Table 6.2). It might be argued that the statistical significance was simply a function of the large sample size. The dimensions, however, are meaningfully different thematically and help identify distinct aspects of the bog for visual-management purposes.

## Familiarity as a Component of Visual Preference

Familiarity gained through prior information and past experiences can be vital to how humans will react to an environmental scene, and it often leads to increased preference. At the same time, it can also lead to decreased preference.

While familiarity can have varying effects on preference, it is also true that preference for an environmental scene has the potential to influence the degree of familiarity for that scene. One often tends to remember the most beautiful, the highly preferred, and in certain situations the ugly, the least preferred. In this section two aspects of familiarity are investigated: (1) the influence of various types of familiarity (i.e., the on-site experience, prior photographic information, and previous number of visits) on visual preference for the bog environment, and (2) the degree of familiarity resulting from the on-site recreational encounter.

### Influence of Familiarity on Visual Preference

*On-Site Experience:* To determine the influence of the on-site experience, mean preference scores were compared between prehike ($P_1$) respondents and posthike ($P_2$)

**Table 6.2   Comparison of Preference Means for the Four Photographic Dimensions**

| Dimension | Mean | t-value | Significance |
|---|---|---|---|
| Bog Mat | 3.69 | | |
| | | 2.08 | .05 |
| Edge | 3.77 | | |
| | | 5.38 | .001 |
| Feature | 3.99 | | |
| | | 2.98 | .005 |
| Boardwalk | 4.12 | | |

Based on proximate pairs of dimensions. Nonadjacent pairs were all significant at p ≤ .001.

**Table 6.3** Mean Preference Ratings and Rank Position of Photographs Viewed Before or After Bog Hike

| $P_1$ | $P_1$ | Significance | Before | After |
|------|------|------|------|------|
| Before | After | | | |
| 4.65 | 4.80 | .05 | 1 | 1 |
| 4.44 | 4.60 | | 2 | 2 |
| 4.41 | 4.59 | | 3 | 3 |
| 4.36 | 4.37 | | 4 | 6 |
| 4.29 | 4.49 | | 5 | 4 |
| 4.19 | 4.32 | | 6 | 7 |
| 4.17 | 4.31 | | 7 | 8 |
| 4.10 | 4.45 | .01 | 8 | 5 |
| 3.95 | 4.08 | | 9 | 10 |
| 3.79 | 4.06 | .05 | 10 | 12 |
| 3.75 | 4.07 | .01 | 11 | 11 |
| 3.71 | 3.95 | .05 | 12 | 13 |
| 3.67 | 3.69 | | 13 | 23 |
| 3.62 | 4.11 | .001 | 14 | 9 |
| 3.55 | 3.91 | .01 | 15 | 15 |
| 3.47 | 3.66 | | 16 | 24 |
| 3.46 | 3.82 | .01 | 17 | 20 |
| 3.44 | 3.85 | .01 | 18 | 19 |
| 3.40 | 3.83 | .001 | 19 | 18 |
| 3.38 | 3.84 | .001 | 20 | 17 |
| 3.28 | 3.95 | .001 | 21 | 14 |
| 3.24 | 3.88 | .001 | 22 | 16 |
| 3.08 | 3.78 | .001 | 23 | 22 |
| 2.98 | 3.75 | .001 | 24 | 21 |

$\bar{X} = 3.95$  $\bar{X} = 4.28$

*Note:* Paradigm of comparison: $\boxed{P_1}$ – $P_2$; – $\boxed{P_1}$; – $P_2$

significant increases ($p < .05$). One might speculate that the lower ratings "before" the hike occurred because the photographs did not represent the actual on-site visual environment: that is, a picture cannot represent the real thing. There is support to suggest that this was not the situation. First, the "before" rating scores for photographs, even though lower than the "after" ratings, were still fairly high ($X = 3.95$). This would suggest that visitors could interpret the photos and had no problem in relating to the scenes. Second, when the mean scores for the "before" and "after" visitors were ranked from high to low (Table 6.3), there was little shift in position of preference between when the photos were viewed. The rank correlation value (rho) was .86, indicating a high degree of association. Thus variation in *pattern* of preference response for the bog scenes changed little. The same scenes were liked, but they were liked even more after the hike. This would again suggest that visitors had little difficulty in interpreting and responding to the photographs before the on-site hike. Third, evidence from other studies that have compared preference ratings of photographs with preference ratings of the actual on-site environment have shown high correlations (Daniel and Boster, 1976; Levin, 1977; Shafer and Richards, 1974). Thus the change in visitor response as a result of familiarity gained through the on-site experience appears to be the result of the information and rewards derived from the experience.

*Prior Photographic Information:* The influence of prior photographic information as a type of familiarity was determined by comparing preference scores of the sixteen duplicate photographs (between questionnaire versions) for visitors who saw the photos before the hike versus those who did not. In Figure 6.1 this involves comparing the posthike scores of Group 1 versus Groups 2 and 3. Data for Groups 2 and 3 were combined for the analysis since their means were similar.

The effect of having seen the photographs before the hike was opposite of what one might hypothesize. Instead of increasing visitor preference, the prior viewing appeared to have "preconditioned" the on-site experience, or ratings that followed, in a negative way (Table 6.4). The prior information group's ratings were lowest for all but one photo. The precondition-

respondents (see Figure 6.1, Groups 1 and 2). The prehike group rated the photographs "before" the hike, the posthike group only "after" the hike. For the posthike group the photographs were viewed in terms of an experienced event.

The on-site experience was quite influential on visitors (Table 6.3). All twenty-four photos received a higher mean preference score after the hike. Fifteen of the scenes had statistically

ing effect might be explained in several ways. Seeing the photographs before the on-site hike may have led visitors to anticipate an experience less gratifying, or different, than that experienced by those visitors who had no prior information. A more probable explanation is that having given relatively low initial ratings before the bog hike the visitors may have been preconditioned as to how high their after ratings would range.

The extent of preconditioning was fairly substantial (ten of the sixteen duplicate photos had significant differences (p ≤ .10). Yet there was little variation in the rank ordering of the preference ratings among the groups. Rank correlations between the various treatment groups for the sixteen duplicate photos showed the following rho values:

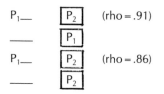

Thus the prior information (viewing and rating photographs) sensitized those visitors and decreased their magnitude of "after" preference, but it did not influence their order of preference among the bog scenes.

*Previous Number of Visits:* A third major area of familiarity considered was the previous number of times a visitor had been to the bog. Dimensions or clusters of photographs as determined by the nonmetric-factor analytic procedure were used for the comparison.

Number of previous visits was positively related to visual preference ratings (Figure 6.5). Preference increased at a steady rate for each of the four dimensions, with no sign of leveling off after three previous visits. The increment in preference with each level of prior visits was statistically significant at the .05 level or higher. The relationship of higher preference rating to number of visits is no doubt an interaction of an enhanced perception of environmental information by return visitors, as well as a greater appreciation of the setting by return visitors. The return visitor perceives different and additional information than the first time visitor because of past familiarity and cognitive structure for the

bog area. These findings suggest the importance of on-site experiences in aiding visitors to develop cognitive structures for perceiving environmental information and in determining environmental preference during on-site engagements (Hammitt, 1981).

### Influence of On-Site Experience on Familiarity

*On-Site Experience:* Visitors seemed to have little problem determining which scenes they had seen and which they had not. For some of the bog scenes as many as 90 percent of the participants indicated they were "familiar" with the scene. Thus visitors appeared to be quite cognizant of what they saw during the on-site bog experience. Far fewer participants used the "not

---

**Table 6.4  Influence of Prior Photographic Information on Mean Preference Ratings**

| Group 1 | Groups 2 and 3 |
|---------|----------------|
| 3.61 | 3.91[a] |
| 3.47 | 3.79[a] |
| 3.85 | 4.06[a] |
| 4.17 | 4.27 |
| 3.63 | 3.62 |
| 4.22 | 4.40[a] |
| 3.82 | 4.00[a] |
| 3.82 | 4.07[a] |
| 3.45 | 3.54 |
| 4.54 | 4.51 |
| 3.83 | 4.00[a] |
| 3.52 | 3.79[a] |
| 3.76 | 3.93 |
| 3.46 | 3.70[a] |
| 3.69 | 3.86[a] |
| 4.52 | 4.62 |

[a] Significant difference (p ≤ .10).

*Note:* Group one ($P_2$) of bog visitors had viewed the duplicate photographs before the hike; groups two ($P_1$) and three ($P_2$) had not.

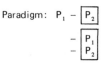

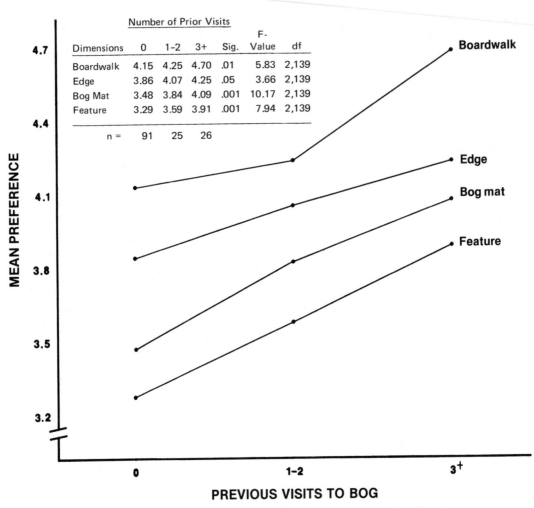

Figure 6.5. Influence of previous bog visits on mean preference ratings for dimensions of bog photographs.

sure" option than anticipated ($\overline{X}$ = 16 "pct"). The efficiency of participants' cognitive system for recognizing what they had seen was further demonstrated when visitors were able to recognize similar bog scenes from Michigan, or adjacent bogs near the study site, as having not been seen during the on-site hike.* Five of the six control or off-site photos were among the eight least familiar scenes.

Figure 6.6 shows most and least familiar scenes, based on the percentage of "familiar" scores. Some interesting patterns emerge when one examines the scenes for elements that aid and hinder familiarity. The most familiar or most remembered scenes are all characterized by two main bog components, boardwalk and distinct features. These scenes are distinctive and identifiable, and as a consequence, visitors

---

*Rating of the photos for preference and familiarity took place at the trailhead, in a forested area and out of sight of the photographed bog scenes. Participants were required to recall what they had seen; it was impossible for them to see the scenes during the interview process. Visitors rated the photos twenty minutes or more after the hike began.

**Figure 6.6.** Results of familiarity ratings. *Top*: two more familiar bog scenes, A and B. *Bottom*: two least familiar bog scenes, C and D.

were quite sure as to whether they had viewed the scenes. Photos A and B represent the dominance of the boardwalk as a visual component in the bog.

Familiarity for the features and the boardwalk correspond well with the findings of Lynch (1960), Devlin (1976), and R. Kaplan (1976). Lynch found that two of the major components in the "sketch maps" of city dwellers were landmarks (features) and paths (boardwalk). Both Lynch and Devlin found these two components to be among the initial elements that people incorporate into their cognitive models. Only with additional experiences over time were details added to one's model. In the study of way-finding skills Kaplan states, "a critical component of these skills must be the capacity to identify distinctive aspects of the environment. Landmarks are vital to cognitive map development; their identification is enhanced when one is sufficiently well acquainted with the setting to know what is distinctive." Of course, the uni-

queness, novelty, and even the function served by landmarks will have a bearing on how acquainted one must be with a setting to know what is distinctive. As will be discussed later, in the case of recognizing scenes that were seen during the bog hike, even a single experience seemed to be adequate.

The least familiar scenes tended to be those that lacked distinguishing features and/or were scenes that visitors in fact were unlikely to have seen during the hike. Photo C was of a bog environment in Michigan and thus fell into the latter category. Photo D was a distinct, novel, and memorable scene that the visitors did not see.

*Influence of Prior Information and Visits:* One might hypothesize that viewing photographic materials before an on-site experience, or having a familiarity with a setting through previous visits, would influence the ability to recall what had been seen during the on-site experience. The pre-post and control design of this study allows for investigating the first of these relation-

**Table 6.5   Influence of Prior Photographic Information on Familiarity Scores for Bog Scenes**

| "Familiar" scores | | Photographic rank | |
|---|---|---|---|
| Group | | Group | |
| 1 | 3 | 1 | 3 |
| 92.3 | 94.9 | 1 | 1 |
| 92.3 | 91.5 | 2 | 2 |
| 90.4 | 86.4 | 3 | 4 |
| 85.9 | 82.2 | 4 | 6 |
| 85.3 | 88.1 | 5 | 3 |
| 77.6 | 78.0 | 6 | 7 |
| 75.6 | 83.9 | 7 | 5 |
| 73.7 | 77.1 | 8 | 8 |
| 73.1 | 69.5 | 9 | 9 |
| 63.5 | 61.0 | 10 | 11 |
| 60.9 | 69.5 | 11 | 10 |
| 56.4 | 60.2 | 12 | 12 |
| 55.8 | 54.2 | 13 | 13 |
| 51.9 | 36.4 | 14 | 19 |
| 50.0 | 54.2 | 15 | 14 |
| 48.7 | 50.0 | 16 | 15 |
| 46.2 | 47.5 | 17 | 16 |
| 35.9 | 40.7 | 18 | 18 |
| 35.9 | 32.2 | 19 | 20 |
| 35.3 | 31.4 | 20 | 21 |
| 34.6 | 44.1 | 21 | 17 |
| 34.0 | 29.7 | 22 | 22 |
| 31.4 | 28.0 | 23 | 23 |
| 24.4 | 22.0 | 24 | 24 |

*Frequency (percent) of "Familiar" Scores*

*Note:* Both groups scored photos for familiarity after the hike, but group 1 also viewed the photos before the hike.

Paradigm: $P_1 - \boxed{P_2}$

$- P_1$

$- \boxed{P_2}$

The percentage scores were similar, and only two photos were somewhat discrepant in their ranked position (Table 6.5). The lack of influence of prior visual information suggests that the familiarity ratings were based on the on-site cognitive experience rather than on exposure to the prior photos.

The influence of prior visits on visual recall can be examined in terms of differences in familiarity scores for first-time visitors versus repeat visitors. Only one photograph showed any significant difference (chi-square test) in familiarity rating as the number of previous visits to the bog increased. Thus it appears that a single on-site experience was sufficient for developing a sense of familiarity.

It is important to keep in mind that in this study only visual recall of on-site scenes was measured as an indicator of familiarity. This does not mean that repeat visitors might not be more familiar with the environment if other indicators of familiarity were measured. Nevertheless, it is important to know the degree to which visual information enters memory as a result of on-site experiences, for this certainly can be important in the initial phases of cognitive model development.

It is also intriguing that visitors were so cognizant of the visual information they had processed while engaged in a recreational activity. The behavior of visitors while hiking the trail (or for that matter, participating in any other recreational activity) would lead one to believe that visitors "are just having a good time and the acquisition of information is the last thing taking place." Yet information-processing theory predicts that visitors necessarily have an efficient cognitive system for "knowing" the natural environment.

### The Familiarity and Visual-Preference Relationship

When the preference and familiarity scores were ranked and compared, a positive relationship was revealed (rho = .53). However, as Figure 6.7 indicates, the majority of the scenes show a stronger relationship than indicated by the rho value. Two scenes that were highly preferred but low in familiarity are feature-oriented but were not available for visitor viewing during the on-site hike. Visitors liked the

ships. Even though Group 1 viewed photographs (and rated them for preference) *before* the hike, they had no apparent advantage over Group 3 (which did not view photos before the hike) when both groups rated the photos for familiarity at the end of their hikes (rho = .97).

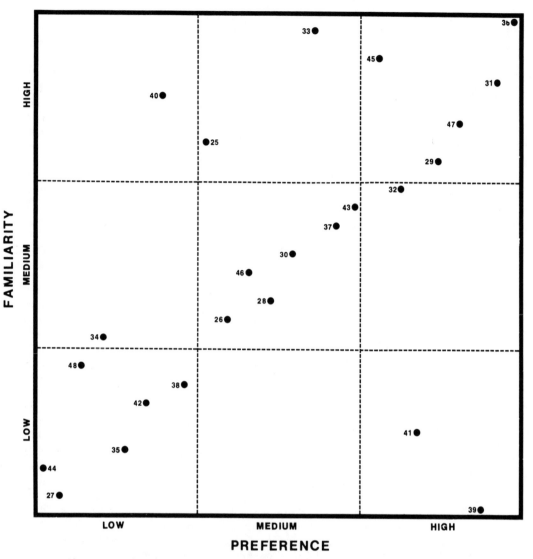

**Figure 6.7.** Relationship of preference to familiarity for photographs of a bog (n = 274, rho = .53).

scenes and, perhaps because they were distinctive, were quite sure they had not seen them onsite. Photo 40 (not reproduced here) represents the only instance of low preference but high familiarity. The scene was of an uprooted tree, a negative feature in the pattern of boardwalk events, which visitors did not appreciate but had no difficulty recalling.

How might the relationship between familiarity and preference be explained in terms of en-

vironmental cognition and the mental models that humans develop during on-site experiences? When an environmental setting is nondistinct, featureless, and offers little opportunity for individuals to become visually involved, they might be expected to pay less attention or to pass more rapidly through such areas. In preferred environmental settings they are likely to pay more attention and thus increase contact and familiarity. Also, operating along with greater attention for preferred scenes is the fact that one prefers scenes that are more distinctive, that help in orientation, and distinctiveness is easier to remember. Thus an environmental scene high in the cognitive domains of "distinctiveness" and "involvement" is more likely to be attended, and such prolonged contact should enhance familiarity. It is further proposed that the enhanced familiarity is a component of cognitive model development during on-site engagements.

Although preference appears to lead to familiarity, a cautionary note is in order. While high preference for a scene tends to be associated with a high degree of familiarity, one is reminded that the opposite situation—of high familiarity being associated with low preference—can also occur. Familiarity can lead to increased preference, but familiarity per se is an insufficient basis for appreciation. One can be very familiar with nonpreferred aspects of an environment.

## Summary and Implications

Preference ratings indicate that visitors rated most aspects of the bog environment fairly high, but that they also had definite preferences for certain aspects of the bog. The enclosed bog forest areas surrounding the open bog mat were given greater preference than the bog mat. These two types of habitats differ strikingly in terms of physical attributes as well as in the opportunity they afford for visual and cognitive involvement. The marked contrast in visitors' preference for the bog forest over the bog mat led to a cautionary note for resource managers: In one's eagerness to show the visitor the ecologically interesting bog mat habitat, do not ignore the visually interesting bog forest. Both aspects of the bog resource need to be considered.

Of particular interest to visitors were distinct, novel features and the inviting opportunity to explore for additional visual information within the environment. Bogscapes that contained an element of hidden but available information, which encouraged visitors to enter scenes to explore, were highly preferred. The bog forest rated high in this component, and the boardwalk trail offered easy access for its exploration. The open bog mat, on the other hand, offered far less visual information and opportunity for perceptual involvement.

Familiarity ratings indicated that visitors were quite cognizant of what scenes they had or had not viewed during the on-site bog experience. The ratings further indicated that people process visual information in bog environments efficiently, with only one exposure seemingly enough for much of the information to be incorporated into memory. First-time visitors were as accurate at recalling visual scenes as were repeat visitors. First-time "experiences" or "environmental encounters" can be significant in the development of cognitive structures. The initial experience is often the most important in building a cognitive structure of any environment, and it probably greatly influences much other information to be incorporated into it during additional experiences. Devlin (1976) found the initial cognitive maps of new residents to a town to be sketchy frameworks of key locations with additional experiences serving to fill in the gaps with details. Such cognitive structures form rapidly and are facilitated by on-site experience. Thus the resource planner or designer must carefully plan settings to enhance the informational properties of initial experiences.

Familiarity, in terms of prior information and experiences, was shown to affect preference. The viewing of photographs before the bog hike tended to "dampen" the post-hike responses of visitors. Visitor's lack of previous experience and thus of a cognitive structure of bog scenes was suggested as one reason for the "dampening effect". Preference was, however, shown to increase directly with number of previous trips to the bog. Preference continued to increase even after three or more prior visits.

The role of photographic images in the area of environmental perception for bogs differed depending on whether the photographs were viewed before or after an on-site experience. The pre-trip viewing of isolated, unrelated, and non-familiar photographs was of little value to visitors, except for those repeat visitors who had a well-structured cognitive model to which the images could relate. Yet, after the on-site experience, the photographs were very effective at evoking memories and were no longer isolated, unrelated, or non-familiar images for the visitors. Visual stimuli are most efficiently perceived when experienced as related, meaningful images in reference to past experiences and cognitive structure.

Preference and familiarity were shown to be closely related, provided visitors had the opportunity to view scenes during the on-site experience. A strong implication of this finding is the relationship among information processing, preference-appreciation, and familiarity-memory. A simplified sketch of this relationship might be as follows:

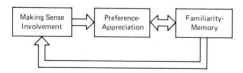

An environment whose informational components "make sense" and are legible to the viewer, and at the same time offer opportunity to become cognitively involved in terms of processing additional information, will be appreciated and preferred. The appreciated and preferred environment also appears to be more strongly coded into cognitive structure in terms of familiarity and memory. Yi-Fu Tuan (1977, pp. 4–5) refers to the memory-appreciation relationship: "Remembrance is an important component of appreciation. We tend to think of remembrance as warmed-over experience, forgetting that it can itself be an exquisite pleasure."

Knowing that humans are efficient at determining visual scenes they prefer, and at remembering what is viewed, leads to several implications for planning-designing the visual aspects of recreational opportunities. Trails can be designed to include preferred aspects of a bog environment or to expose visitors to those aspects of the visual resource that managers want visitors to become familiar with (Hammitt, 1980; Hammitt and Cherem, 1980). That preferred environmental scenes have been shown to aid familiarity also has implications in the area of environmental interpretation (Hammitt, 1978). More germane to the cognitive processes by which visitors acquire an appreciation for bog environments is the role that familiarity plays. It provides visitors with cognitive structures for incorporating future experiences. After all, it is the continuing sequence of experiences

that eventually shape a person's thinking and behavior.

While the reviewed technique and approach for measuring visual preference and familiarity of bog environments has greatest application in planning and designing preferred environmental experiences, there are various other visual resource and land management situations to which it can be adapted. The fact that the methodology is economical, requires little statistical software, and is an approach that involves on-site public involvement in the management of visual resources should encourage its future use.

## References

Appleton, J. 1975. *The experience of landscape.* New York: John Wiley & Sons.

Arnheim, R. 1969. *Visual thinking.* Berkeley: University of California Press.

Attneave, F. 1957. Transfer of experience with a class-schema to identification-learning of patterns and shapes. *Journal of Experimental Psychology* 54:81–88.

Bruner, J. S. 1957. On perceptual readiness. *Psychological Review* 64:123–52.

Daniel, T. C., and Boster, R. S. 1976. Measuring landscape esthetics: The scenic beauty estimation method. USDA Forest Service Res. Paper RM–167. Fort Collins, Colo.: Rocky Mountain Forest and Range Experiment Station. 66 pp.

Devlin, A. S. 1976. The "small town" cognitive map: Adjusting to a new environment. G. T. Moore and R. G. Golledge, eds. In *Environmental knowing.* Stroudsburg, Pa.: Dowden, Hutchinson and Ross. Pp. 58–66.

Gallagher, T. J. 1977. Visual perception for alternative natural landscapes. Ph.D. dissertation, University of Michigan, Ann Arbor.

Hammitt, W. E. 1978. A visual preference approach to measuring interpretive effectiveness. *Journal of Interpretation* 3(2):33–37.

———. 1980. Designing mystery into landscape-trail experiences. *Journal of Interpretation* 5(1):16–19.

———. 1981. The familiarity-preference component of on-site recreational experiences. *Leisure Sciences* 4(2):177–93.

Hammitt, W.E., and Cherem, G. J. 1980. Photographic perceptions as an on-site tool for trail design. *Southern Journal of Applied Forestry* 4(2):94–97.

Kaplan, R. 1975. Some methods and strategies in the prediction of preference. In E. H. Zube, R. O. Brush, and J. Gy. Fabos, eds. *Landscape assessment: Value, perceptions, and resources.* Stroudsburg, Pa.: Dowden, Hutchinson and Ross. Pp. 118–29.

_____. 1976. Way-finding in the natural environment. In G. T. Moore and R. G. Golledge, eds. *Environmental knowing.* Stroudsburg, Pa.: Dowden, Hutchinson, and Ross. Pp. 46–57.

Kaplan, S. 1973. Cognitive maps in perception and thought. In R. M. Downs and D. Stea, eds. *Image and environment.* Chicago: Aldine Press. Pp. 63–78.

_____. 1975. An informal model for the prediction of preference. In E. H. Zube, R. O. Brush, and J. Gy. Fabos, eds. *Landscape assessment: Value, perceptions, and resources.* Stroudsburg, Pa.: Dowden, Hutchinson and Ross. Pp. 92–101.

_____. 1978. On knowing the environment. In S. Kaplan and R. Kaplan, eds. *Humanscape: Environments for people.* North Scituate, Mass.: Duxbury Press. Pp. 54–58.

Kaplan, S., and Kaplan, R., eds. 1978. *Humanscape: Environments for people.* North Scituate, Mass.: Duxbury Press.

Kulik, J. A.; Revelle, W. R.; and Kulik, C. 1970. Scale construction by hierarchical cluster analysis. Unpublished paper, University of Michigan, Ann Arbor.

Levin, J. E. 1977. Riverscape preference: On-site and photographic reactions. Master's thesis. University of Michigan, Ann Arbor.

Lingoes, J. C. 1972. A general survey of the Guttman-Lingoes nonmetric program series. In R. N. Shepard, A. K. Romney, and S. B. Nerlove, eds. *Multidimensional scaling,* Vol. 1. New York: Seminar Press. Pp. 52–68.

Lynch, K. 1960. *The image of the city.* Cambridge, Mass.: MIT Press.

Shafer, E. L., Jr., and Richards, T. A. 1974. A comparison of viewer reactions to outdoor scenes and photographs of those scenes. USDA Forest Service Res. Paper NE–302. Upper Darby, Pa.: Northeastern Forest Experiment Station. 26 pp.

USDA, Forest Service, 1977. Personal communication, Cranberry Glades Visitor Information Services Staff, Monongahela National Forest, West Virginia.

Welsh, G. S. 1966. The perception of our urban environment. In R. E. Stipe, ed. *Perception and environment: Foundations of urban design.* Chapel Hill: Institute of Government, University of North Carolina. Pp. 1–10.

Tuan, Yi-Fu. 1977. Experience and appreciation. In Children, nature, and the urban environment. USDA Forest Service Gen. Tech. Rep. NE–30. Upper Darby, Pa.: Northeastern Forest Experiment Station. Pp. 1–5.

# PART III

# Field Classification of Wetland Attributes

# 7 Classifying Visual Attributes of Wetlands in the St. Lawrence– Eastern Ontario Region

MOLLY BURGESS MOONEY

## Introduction

The problem dealt with in this chapter is to produce a descriptive analysis based on visual values for wetlands that can be used by planning agencies in the land-use decision-making process. Richard Smardon's 1972 study dealing with visual assessment of wetlands developed an evaluative model to analyze the visual quality of inland wetlands in Massachusetts. His method, involving measuring many elements in the landscape and feeding this information into a data bank for processing, was adapted and modified using nonnumerical measures and applied to selected study areas using map interpretation and fieldwork. This study differs from Smardon's because it produces a descriptive analysis, based on classifying wetland types, instead of producing comparative aesthetic judgments of wetlands. It makes no attempt to compare the quality of one type with another by rating or ranking. Both kinds of methods, evaluative and descriptive, are commonly used in landscape assessment.

A classification of wetlands by visual character provides an understanding of the distribution, nature, and extent of different types of wetland landscapes in a given context, be it state, regional, or local. A descriptive system can be used by the St. Lawrence Eastern Ontario Commission to determine what different visual types of wetlands exist within the region. Coupled with an evaluation, this information could be used as a data base in the process of selecting wetlands for priority of protection. The wetland classification in this study draws upon the visual values Smardon identified for wetland assessment.

The physical attributes of wetlands found to be important to visual values are water bodies, landform, surrounding land use, and wetland vegetation (Smardon, 1972, p. 102). The key visual attributes identified are visual contrast and visual diversity of the wetland and its surroundings (ibid., p. 103).

Visual contrast and visual diversity are attributed to resource variables. Each of the variables is briefly defined below.

*Water-body size* is the existence and quantity of open water that borders, goes through, or is part of a wetland.

*Surrounding land-use contrast* is the difference in edges, or height contrast, of the surrounding land uses.

*Surrounding landform contrast* is the scale of the surrounding landform in relation to the size or scale of the wetland.

*Internal wetland contrast* is the differences in vegetation edges, or height and textural contrast, of the internal edges of the wetlands.

*Water-body diversity* is the types of associated water bodies adjacent to or part of a given wetland.

*Surrounding landform diversity* is the variety of landforms surrounding or adjacent to a wetland.

*Surrounding land-use diversity* is the number of different land-use types that border a given wetland.

*Wetland-type diversity* is the number of wetland types found within a wetland.

*Wetland-edge complexity* is the complexity of the physical boundary of the wetland where it meets a landform or vegetation edge.

## Study Objectives

The following objectives were established based on the previous assumptions:

1. To clearly and systematically identify and describe visual attributes important to wetlands and their surrounding landscape context
2. To adapt and test a method of visual description in selected areas within the St. Lawrence–Eastern Ontario region
3. To ensure that the descriptive classification has utility to planners and designers so that the visual attributes of wetlands can be protected.

## Study Procedure

The descriptive analysis began with a classification of land use and landform to develop *landscape units*. Wetland vegetation and water bodies were then classified to develop *wetland units*. The landscape units and wetland units were synthesized to form the final character

areas. Figure 7.1 shows the overall process that was used to classify the visual attributes of the wetlands and their surroundings.

The specific method employed is one used in environmental assessment and has specifically been used for generating land-suitability maps (McHarg, 1969). The method begins with the identification of *factors* to be examined. In this case the factors are land use and landform, and wetland vegetation and water bodies. The first step was to map the distribution of *types* for each factor. Hopkins (1977, p. 388) defines factors as "distinct dimensions along which variations among parcels of land can be described" and types as "nominal labels of particular characteristics along a particular dimension." Types are the particular characteristics of the factors. For example, the landform "factor" includes many "types" such as valleys, plains, and islands. All the steps of the method are illustrated in Figure 7.2, using land use and landform as examples of the factors. In the actual study many more types are included than those in Figure 7.2, but they have been eliminated from the illustration to avoid confusion.

The second step consists of overlaying the individual factors maps to produce a composite map showing the spatial pattern of the types (see Figure 7.2). The potential number of combinations is enormous when overlaying a set of factors each with a number of types. Hopkins (1977, p. 394) states that "most of the possible combinations will not occur on a real site due to spatial correlation among ecological factors." However, a final composite map should represent those areas or regions that actually exist in a study area in a manner that is valid and is not unwieldy to use in a planning context. For this reason *decision rules* must be made to combine factor types into homogeneous areas (Step 3 in Figure 7.2). Decision rules are expressed in terms of verbal logic, and their function is to assign the initial composite types into realistic and workable sets of combinations. They are based on design theories that the authorities (designers and planners) agree upon and are substantiated by literature reviews. The result of the application of decision rules is a final composite map showing the spatial pattern of landscape units (Step 4 in Figure 7.2). A verbal description of each final landscape unit accompanies the final composite map.

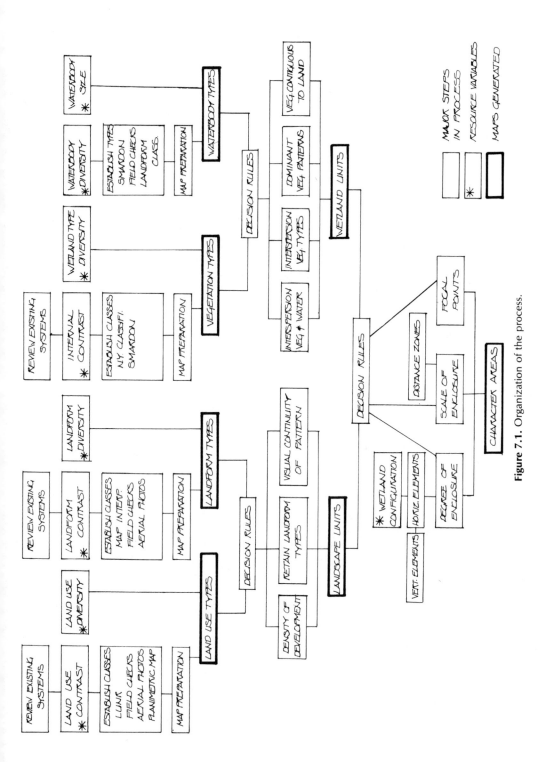

**Figure 7.1.** Organization of the process.

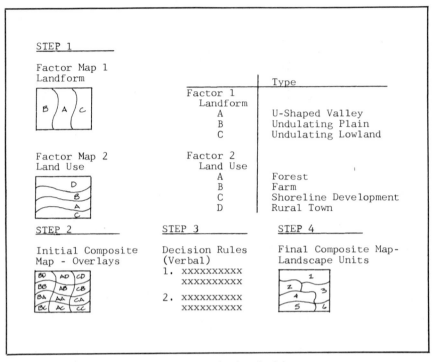

**Figure 7.2.** Example of methodology.

## The Study Areas

### Study-Area Selection

Three study areas were selected along the shoreline of Jefferson County, New York. The Jefferson County shoreline contains numerous wetlands of various size that have been influenced by conflicting pressures for shoreline use. More than 51 percent of the land along the shoreline had been converted to some form of agricultural or developed land use by 1972 (Geis and Kee, 1977, p. 5).

What follows is a discussion of the criteria established for selecting the study areas. The criteria are based on consideration of the users of wetlands, or those most likely to view wetlands and their surrounding landscapes. Three steps were involved in selecting the study areas:

1. Determining the number of study areas
2. Determining the size of the study areas
3. Determining which wetlands to study within each study area

1. The number of study areas was determined by the number of physiographic coastal provinces, or landform patterns that were delineated in a visual assessment study by Felleman (1975) in Jefferson County. It was decided that each of the three physiographic provinces in Jefferson County should be represented.

2. The size of the study area was determined by the limits of the most critical distance from which an observer would view a landscape. The middleground, or intermediately distant landscape, is the most critical because linkage between separate parts of the landscape can be seen (Litton, 1968, p. 4).

Since middleground usually does not exceed five miles, the size of the study areas was limited within a five-mile radius of the selected wetlands, but it was not less than three miles.

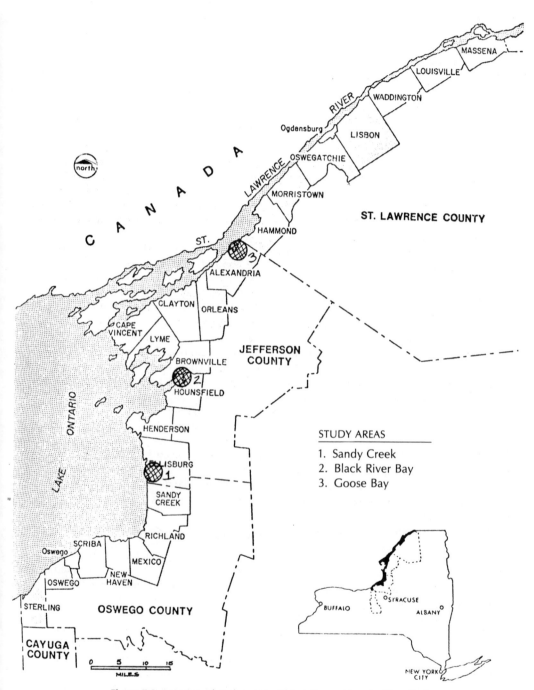

**Figure 7.3.** Location of study areas within Jefferson County, New York.

3. Determining the wetlands to be studied in each area had to satisfy the following criteria:

a. That wetlands with a great amount of physical access be represented

b. That wetlands with a variety of cover types be represented

c. That wetlands associated with rivers suggested for study as Wild, Scenic, and Recreational Rivers be represented

d. That each of the three typical wetland types identified in a study by Geis and Kee (1977) be represented

## Description of Study Areas

The following is a brief description of the study areas that were selected. Figure 7.3 shows the location of the areas.

### Sandy Creek

Sandy Creek is a large flood-pond complex occurring in a depressional area physically separated from the lake by a beach barrier. Two major streams drain through the complex. The wetlands here are associated with creeks that may eventually be designated as recreational rivers.

### Black River Bay

The Black River complex occurs on shallow sediments at the mouth of the Black River in Black River Bay. Wetlands occurring in the bay are associated with Black River, which may be designated a recreational river in the future.

### Goose Bay

Goose Bay is the largest bay along the St. Lawrence River. Islands and upland peninsulas constrict the mouth of the bay and protect it from the main body of the river.

## Landscape Units

Landform and land-use types were identified and then synthesized to form landscape units, which describe the visual character of the study areas. This process started with a review of existing pertinent classification systems (visual and nonvisual) and selection of data sources that

would be used. Two things were considered important when analyzing classification systems for their utility: (1) the classifications must be representative of landscape types found in the study areas, and (2) systems developed according to visual characteristics and for visual assessment should be reviewed.

### Land Use

The source selected to classify land-use types was the Land Use and Natural Resource Inventory of New York State (LUNR), a system that provides more than 130 land-use characteristics. Supplementary sources included aerial photographs, New York State Planimetric Maps, and field checks.

The two resource variables for land use, land-use contrast, and land-use diversity were applied. *Land-use contrast* was determined by delineating height classes and visual continuity. Height classes were determined by comparing land uses occurring in the LUNR system with the land uses in each height class identified in the classification used by Smardon (1972). From this, height classes assigned by Smardon could be applied to various land uses in New York State. Visual continuity was determined in the field by driving the roads in each study site and simply noting which elements were visually continuous because of their use, form, color, surface, and/or nearness of parts. Surrounding *land-use diversity* was determined by locating the different land-use types bordering the wetlands.

### Map Preparation for Land-Use Types

The process of mapping the data required making a map of each study site that showed all of the LUNR information, then overlaying this map on aerial photos and the planimetric maps to pick up the supplementary information and update obvious changes. The field checking required driving the roads in each study area and comparing the information on the map with firsthand observation in the field. Any discrepancies found between the mapped information and field observation were noted. The field observation was most useful for describing the general appearance and condition of the various land uses. Forty-one types of land use as defined by LUNR were found. These types were

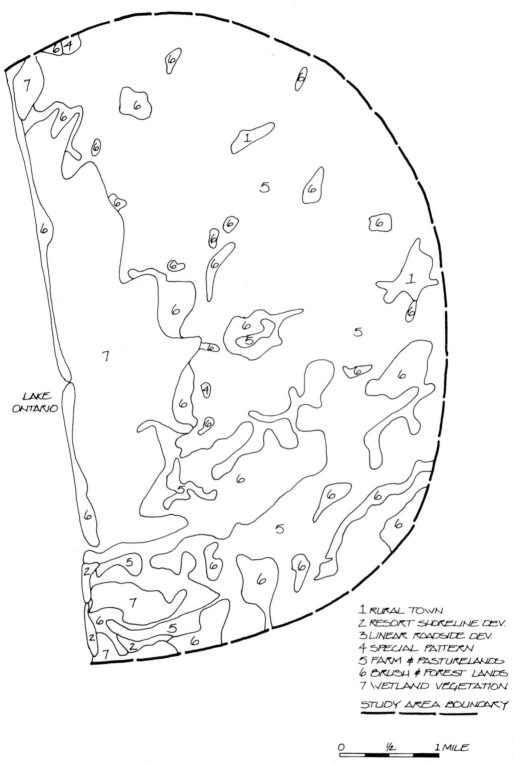

LAKE
ONTARIO

1 RURAL TOWN
2 RESORT SHORELINE DEV.
3 LINEAR ROADSIDE DEV.
4 SPECIAL PATTERN
5 FARM & PASTURELANDS
6 BRUSH & FOREST LANDS
7 WETLAND VEGETATION

STUDY AREA BOUNDARY

0    ½    1 MILE

N

**Figure 7.4.** Land-use types, Sandy Creek study area.

aggregated by drawing lines around and lumping together those uses defined as one "type" according to the height classes and continuity of use. The types were listed in order from most developed to least developed; the description was simply a listing of each of the LUNR uses. The aggregate land-use types determined were (1) rural town, (2) shoreline resort development, (3) linear roadside development, (4) special pattern, (5) farm and pasture lands, (6) brush and forest lands, and (7) wetland vegetation. Land-use types for the Sandy Creek study area are shown in Figure 7.4.

### Land Form

A landform classification system of the New York State coastal zone was developed for use in visual assessment by Felleman (1975) and was applied in this study. Felleman's method used topographic map interpretation to identify landform patterns and developed a list of shoreforms found within the coastal zone. Additional sources included aerial photographs and field checks. The two resource variables, landform contrast and landform diversity, were applied. *Landform contrast* usually refers to the variable of landform relief (Smardon, 1972, p. 126). The St. Lawrence–Eastern Ontario region is relatively flat (the greatest height difference is 200 feet), so, based upon height differences, very little contrast existed. However, definite landform patterns did stand out and were delineated based upon the principle of visual continuity defined and used for land-use types. This was done on topographic maps by drawing lines around areas that appeared continuous or to contain many of the same elements (i.e., a flat plain with a number of linear hills). Questionable areas were flagged and checked in the field by driving the roads and noting if the areas in question were visually continuous or not. *Landform diversity* refers to the different landforms on and around wetlands. The assumption is that wetland diversity increases as the number of landform types increase. The number of different types can be located on the landform maps.

### Map Preparation for Landform Types

The process of classifying landform patterns required overlaying a sheet of paper on the topographic maps and identifying patterns according to the list of shoreforms defined by Felleman (1975). The maps were then overlaid on aerial photographs and adjusted to show any recent changes in landform patterns. The field checking was done by driving the roads and viewing the study area from a variety of locations to confirm the topographic map interpretation. The landform types identified were (1) undulating plain, (2) undulating lowland, (3) U-shaped valley, (4) island/river, (5) wetland areas, (6) beach barrier/dunes, (7) open bay, (8) river, and (9) lake. Landform types for the Sandy Creek study area are shown in Figure 7.5.

### Landscape Units: Synthesis of Land Use and Landform

Because the relationship of landform and land use creates the visual character, they were synthesized to form units. When landform and land-use types are overlaid for a given site, many combinations or mixtures of land use and landform occur. An observer would not necessarily perceive so many individual and separate characters, nor is it workable for a designer or planner to use too many sets of combinations. Thus the landscape units were formed by aggregating areas based on decision rules.

*Decision Rule 1:* Different densities of development create different identifiable landscape characters. Density of development was the important factor used to identify locations within the landscape continuum, or to define differences among areas.

*Decision Rule 2:* All landform types should be represented in the final landscape units. Few landform patterns emerged within the study areas, and it was decided not to aggregate them further.

*Decision Rule 3:* The visual continuity of land-use and landform types determines a particular pattern.

### Map Preparation for Landscape Units

The decision rules were applied and the landscape units were delineated on a transparent overlay by identifying (1) the areas of most to least or no development, and (2) the landform types. Visual continuity of the landform and land-use combination was determined by driv-

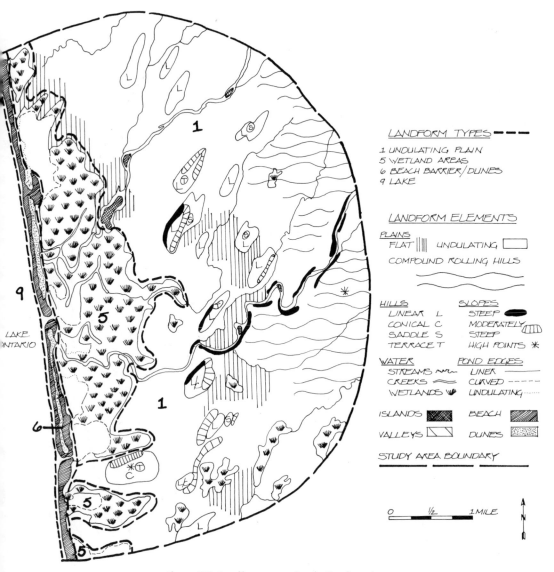

**Figure 7.5.** Landform types, Sandy Creek study area.

ing the roads in the study areas and noting where patterns changed on the map.

### Landscape Units

Ten basic visual units were formed. Each type has its own identifiable visual continuity and density of development. The units are (1) rural town, (2) shoreline resort strip, (3) farm and pasture lands, (4) U-shaped valleys with resort development, (5) U-shaped valleys with forest

and water features, (6) islands, (7) forested land, (8) undeveloped lowland, (9) sandy beach and dunes, and (10) flood-pond complex. Landscape units for the Sandy Creek study area are shown in Figure 7.6.

## Wetland Units

Pertinent wetland classification systems were reviewed for their use in a visual study. Wetland vegetation types and water-body types were

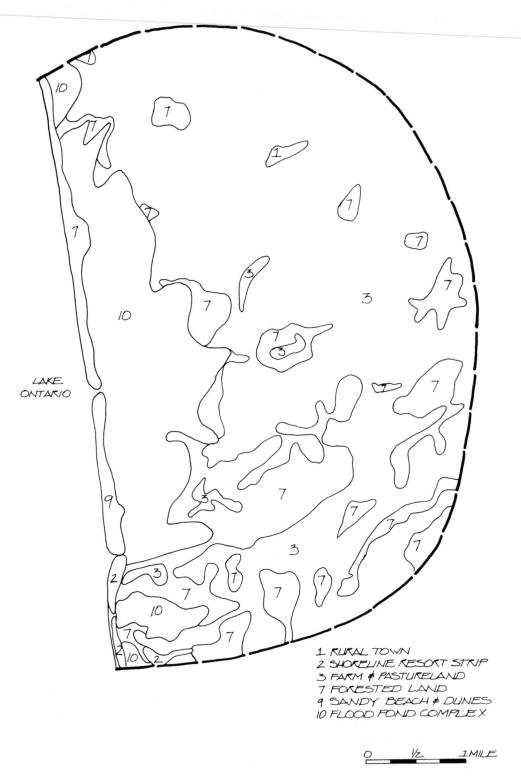

LAKE
ONTARIO

1 RURAL TOWN
2 SHORELINE RESORT STRIP
3 FARM & PASTURELAND
7 FORESTED LAND
9 SANDY BEACH & DUNES
10 FLOOD POND COMPLEX

0    ½    1 MILE

**Figure 7.6.** Landscape units, Sandy Creek study area.

then delineated. Previous wetland classification systems that were reviewed (Geis and Kee, 1977; Golet and Larson, 1974; New York State Fish and Wildlife Service, 1975; and Shaw and Fredine, 1956) used the criteria of vegetation, soils, and water level to differentiate wetland types. The New York State system was selected because it was similar to other existing systems, readily available to agencies in New York, and adaptable to a regional or local scale.

## Wetland Vegetation Types

*Internal wetland contrast* is provided by changes in vegetation (Smardon, 1972). Height and texture were the qualities used to delineate wetland vegetation in this study. Height classes for vegetation were provided by the New York State wetlands classification system (Fried and Gardner, 1977). Textural qualities were determined in the field by looking at each cover type and noting its general texture. The height and texture classes form the vegetation types used in this system. *Wetland-type diversity* is dependent upon the number of wetland types found within a wetland. The amount and location of diversity that would occur within the wetlands could be seen by referring to the mapped wetland vegetation types. Wetland vegetation types for the Sandy Creek study area are shown in Figure 7.7.

## Map Preparation for Wetland Vegetation Types

The mapping for wetland vegetation types was done by overlaying a transparent sheet on the New York State wetlands classification maps and delineating the dominant vegetative cover types, which were further delineated according to height classes and textural qualities. Cover types consisting of an area of one acre or less were not used because they were not visually significant at the scale of concern.

## Wetland Water-body Types

Two characteristics of water influence its distinction in the landscape: size and diversity (Smardon, 1972). *Waterbody-size* classes were not established because there were not enough to provide a range of sizes that would accommodate such a classification. *Water-body diversity* is simply the number of different water-body

types that border, go through, or are part of a wetland. Five types were identified in this study: (1) natural ponds, (2) tributary rivers and streams, (3) major river, (4) natural lake, and (5) bays. Water-body types were then described according to their clarity and general textural qualities.

## Map Preparation for Water-body Types

The mapping for water-body types was done by overlaying a transparent sheet on USGS topographic maps and delineating the types identified above. Water-body types for the Sandy Creek study area are shown in Figure 7.8.

## Wetland Units: Synthesis of Water Bodies and Vegetation

The patterns created by the relationship of wetland vegetation and water bodies were determined to form the wetland units. Two primary decision rules, based on size, were used to formulate units.

*Decision Rule 1:* The size of a wetland vegetation type in relation to a water-body type determines a particular pattern.

*Decision Rule 2:* The size of a wetland vegetation type in relation to other wetland vegetation types determines a particular pattern. To apply these decision rules an initial composite map was made by overlaying the wetland vegetation type map and the wetland water-body type map for each study area. The overlay showed each water-body and vegetation type that occurred. The first decision rule was then applied by drawing a line around one vegetation type and its contiguous water-body type. Each time a vegetative type or water-body type changed, a new unit was formed.

In applying Decision Rule 2, a line was drawn around vegetation types. Each time a vegetation type changed, a new unit was formed. At this point, dominant patterns characterizing the wetlands were seen. Because the final units should be realistic and workable sets of combinations, a third decision rule was established.

*Decision Rule 3:* Only dominant vegetative spatial patterns should be considered in forming units. This was applied by eliminating as separate units those areas where small amounts of vegetative interspersion occurred, except at the periphery of the wetlands. When vegetation

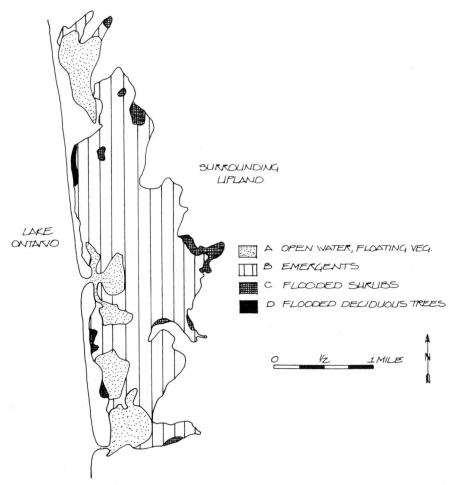

**Figure 7.7.** Wetland vegetation types, Sandy Creek study area.

types were interspersed in sizable amounts, and this interspersion did not occur at the periphery, one unit that included both vegetative types was formed.

In bay areas some wetland vegetation is connected or contiguous to land, and in some instances it is not. A fourth decision rule was made to delineate this difference.

*Decision Rule 4:* Wetland vegatation occurring contiguous to land forms a different spatial pattern than vegetation that does not occur contiguous to land. This was applied by delineating between vegetated areas that were or were not contiguous to land. Thirteen wetland units were identified by applying the decision rules: (1) stream-emergent, (2) pond-emergent, (3) shrub patches, (4) deciduous patches, (5) stream-shrub, (6) Lake Ontario, (7) bay-emergent fringe, (8) bay-scattered emergents, (9) bay-emergent and floating vegetation, (10) bay-floating vegetation fringe, (11) stream-floating vegetation, (12) stream-emergent border, and (13) bay/major river/stream-emergent. Wetland units for the Sandy Creek study area are shown in Figure 7.9.

### Character Areas: Synthesis of Landscape and Wetland Units

The information produced by the classifications was synthesized and developed into a framework that could be used by planners and designers. The synthesis required aggregation of the landscape and wetland units into character

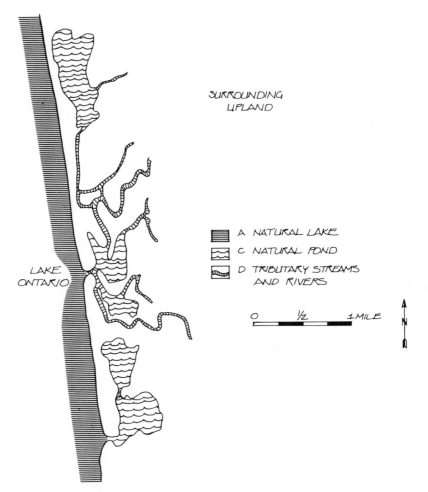

**Figure 7.8.** Water-body types, Sandy Creek study area.

areas. Spatial concepts were defined and applied to develop the character areas. The following decision rules were used based upon concepts of spatial definition.

*Decision Rule 1:* The configuration of a wetland's shoreline and the vertical space defining elements determine several identifiable degrees of spatial enclosure.

*Decision Rule 2:* The scale of enclosure or exposure can be identified on the basis of distance zones.

In applying the decision rules it was necessary to examine the edge configuration for the wetlands and identify areas where enclosure and exposure could occur, as well as areas in between. It was necessary to consider scale when determining if an area would be enclosed.

Distance zones of foreground, middleground, and background were established by estimating the distance and field testing. The distances for the scales of landscape zones were foreground (0–¼ mile), middleground (¼ to ½ mile), and background (more than 1 mile). Distance was used to establish enclosed and exposed areas.

### Enclosed Areas

If a recessed area was ¼ mile or less across at its mouth, it would be dominated by foreground distance and could be considered enclosed.

### Exposed Areas

Exposed areas are those that project outward from the shoreline (see Figure 7.10). Totally ex-

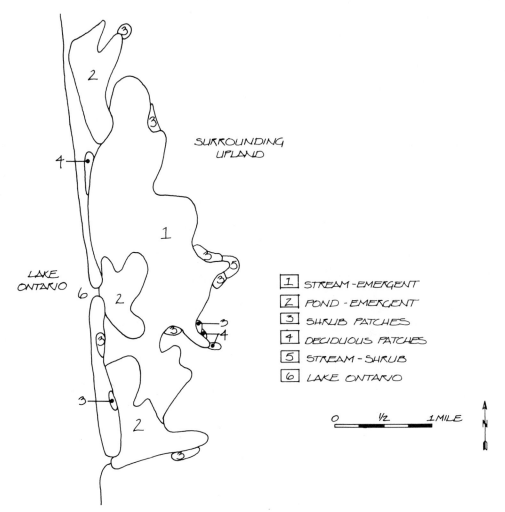

**Figure 7.9.** Wetland units, Sandy Creek study area.

posed areas were identified as those in which space-defining elements were absent within the foreground distance.

It was necessary to note the type of vertical space-defining elements of landform and vegetation within each designated area. An area was considered open if the bordering upland unit consisted of grassland vegetation and closed if woodland vegetation occurred. Litton's (1974) vegetative-edge types (butt, transitional, digitate, and diffuse) were used to determine the presence or absence of enclosure and contrast produced by vegetation.

A third decision rule was developed to identify areas dominated by focal points.

*Decision Rule 3:* A strong focal point can dominate an area. In this study the focal points used in the formation of character areas were natural focal points. They occur where tributary streams and rivers enter bays or where natural ponds connect to natural lakes. Visual movement is directed toward these areas where attention becomes concentrated.

## Micro and Macro Areas

Character areas were developed at two scales. Areas showing the general character of large segments of the wetland and surrounding upland were delineated and called macro areas.

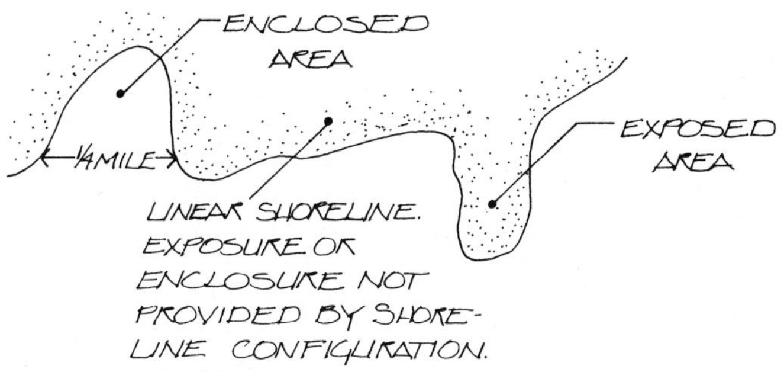

**Figure 7.10.** Spatial enclosure based on shoreline configuration.

Smaller segments within the macro areas showing individual characteristics were delineated and called micro areas.

### Micro Areas

The micro areas were delineated by analyzing the map overlays to determine the type of spatial definition present. The analysis required the identification of the presence and relative prominence of space-defining elements and the type of shoreline configuration. The application of these observations developed for spatial definition is shown in Table 7.1.

### Macro Areas

The macro areas were delineated by identifying major changes in (1) landform patterns and (2) scale. Areas where symmetrical and asymmetrical enclosure occurred adjacent to the wetlands were delineated and then used as a basis for delineating macro areas. Large areas where the middleground dominated were distinguished from those where the foreground dominated. The macro areas further serve to distinguish among the three broad categories in which wetlands are found: in the region-bays, flood-pond areas, and along tributaries.

### Map Preparation for Character Areas

The decision rules for the character areas were applied by the following mapping process.

*Micro Areas*

1. The landscape and wetland units maps were overlayed with a transparent sheet. Exposed and enclosed areas were identified by measuring the recessed areas to determine if the foreground was dominant (¼ mile or less at the mouth of the area) and located by drawing lines around each of the recessive, linear, and exposed areas of the shoreline configuration.

2. The different types of vegetative edges (butt, transitional, digitate, diffuse) were then delineated on the transparent sheet by using Litton's (1974) description of each edge. This identified the space-defining types of vegetation at the wetlands' edges (spatial definition from landform was minimal and was used to define macro areas).

3. Focal areas were identified by noting where streams and ponds entered larger bodies of water and then were labeled on the overlay.

4. Each area was observed to determine which description in Table 7.1 was appropriate and then was labeled accordingly.

*Macro Areas*

Macro areas were identified by separating micro areas dominated by foreground from those dominated by middleground and drawing lines on the overlay around each group of micro areas formed by the separation. In addition, elongated corridors of symmetrical and asymmetrical landforms were identified from the landscape units map, and lines were drawn around all the adjoining micro areas encompassed by the corridors, forming macro areas

**Table 7.1    Spatial-Definition Descriptions:   Micro Areas**

| Areas | Descriptions |
|---|---|
| 1. Extremely enclosed | Space-defining elements of vegetation and/or landform produce dominant enclosure approaching a canopy. Immediate foreground dominates. Shoreline configuration is recessed. |
| 2. Moderately enclosed | Space-defining elements of vegetation and/or landform, produce enclosure, no canopy present. Shoreline configuration recessed. Foreground dominates. |
| 3. Average enclosure | Space-defining elements are present and provide identifiable scale. Shoreline configuration is linear or undulating with occasional small inlets, but no strong recessed or projecting areas. Foreground and middleground awareness. |
| 4. Moderately open | Space-defining elements are present, but shoreline configuration projects outward and is exposed. Foreground and middle-ground awareness with emphasis on middleground. |
| 5. Extremely open | Space-defining elements are minimal. Middle ground dominates. Shoreline configuration may be linear, exposed, or recessed. |

based on landform definition. The character areas for the Sandy Creek study area are shown in Figure 7.11.

## Utilization of the Study

The following products were generated by this study: (1) descriptions and maps of landscape units of three study areas in the St. Lawrence–Eastern Ontario region, (2) descriptions and maps of wetland units found within the three study areas, (3) descriptions and maps of the character areas of the wetlands and surrounding uplands. It is important to understand the utility and limitations of this information. Uses of the study are outlined in this section.

The visual management of resources usually begins with a descriptive analysis of the resource. Laurie (1970) emphasized the distinction between character and descriptive studies (classificatory) and quality studies, which are essentially analytical (evaluative).The classification often precedes the evaluation, or rather it provides the information base for the evaluation in visual management systems. The descriptive classification can be generated for utility by itself in the planning and design process, or it can be generated for use as a data base for evaluation.

To determine visual quality using the character areas as a data base, it would be necessary to apply a procedure for rating and ranking the areas. A number of procedures could be used. It should be pointed out that the descriptive classification is one part of the visual management system, with evaluation another important part. If a ranking procedure were applied to the character areas, the comparison of areas could contribute more information for use in a visual management system. Specifically, ranking the wetlands regionwide would show which wetlands have a higher or lower visual value. This helps determine priority of wetland protection and suggests priority of purchase for open-space uses.

The information from visual assessment could be used by private firms and governmental agencies for environmental-impact statements that involve visual values of wetlands. The SLEO region is economically dependent upon tourist trade and is trying to increase that trade. Thus it is important that the region's attractions be preserved. An identification and description of the visual character of resources is one of the first steps in understanding how proposed programs may affect that character.

A 1972 shoreline study done for the SLEO Commission by the College of Environmental Science and Forestry introduced the idea of a "natural-history interpretation system," which would focus on the unique and important natural areas, mainly the wetlands (Webb et al., 1972). The system would afford an opportunity for people to learn about the natural history and ecology of the region and provide additional justification for protection, preservation, and management of the wetlands.

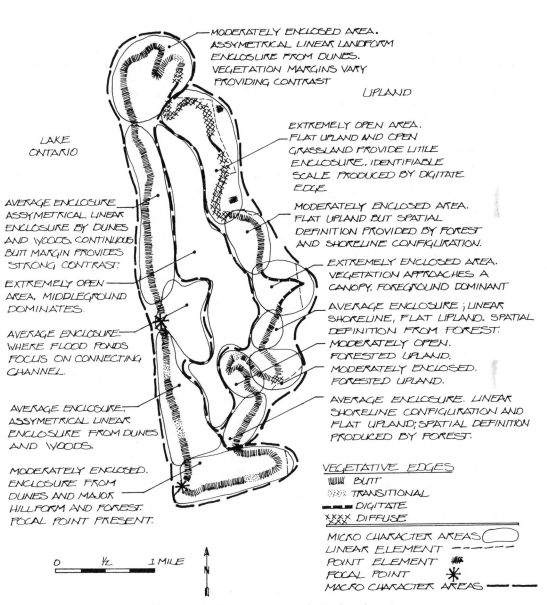

MODERATELY ENCLOSED AREA.
ASSYMETRICAL LINEAR LANDFORM
ENCLOSURE FROM DUNES.
VEGETATION MARGINS VARY
PROVIDING CONTRAST

UPLAND

LAKE
ONTARIO

EXTREMELY OPEN AREA.
FLAT UPLAND AND OPEN
GRASSLAND PROVIDE LITTLE
ENCLOSURE. IDENTIFIABLE
SCALE PRODUCED BY DIGITATE
EDGE

MODERATELY ENCLOSED AREA.
FLAT UPLAND BUT SPATIAL
DEFINITION PROVIDED BY FOREST
AND SHORELINE CONFIGURATION.

AVERAGE ENCLOSURE
ASSYMETRICAL LINEAR
ENCLOSURE BY DUNES
AND WOODS. CONTINUOUS
BUTT MARGIN PROVIDES
STRONG CONTRAST.

EXTREMELY OPEN
AREA. MIDDLEGROUND
DOMINATES.

AVERAGE ENCLOSURE
WHERE FLOOD PONDS
FOCUS ON CONNECTING
CHANNEL.

AVERAGE ENCLOSURE.
ASSYMETRICAL LINEAR
ENCLOSURE FROM DUNES
AND WOODS.

MODERATELY ENCLOSED.
ENCLOSURE FROM
DUNES AND MAJOR
HILLFORM AND FOREST.
FOCAL POINT PRESENT.

EXTREMELY ENCLOSED AREA.
VEGETATION APPROACHES A
CANOPY. FOREGROUND DOMINANT

AVERAGE ENCLOSURE ; LINEAR
SHORELINE, FLAT UPLAND. SPATIAL
DEFINITION FROM FOREST.

MODERATELY OPEN.
FORESTED UPLAND.

MODERATELY ENCLOSED.
FORESTED UPLAND.

AVERAGE ENCLOSURE. LINEAR
SHORELINE CONFIGURATION AND
FLAT UPLAND; SPATIAL DEFINITION
PRODUCED BY FOREST.

VEGETATIVE EDGES
〰️〰️ BUTT
░░░ TRANSITIONAL
▬▬▬ DIGITATE
XXXX DIFFUSE

MICRO CHARACTER AREAS ⬭
LINEAR ELEMENT — — — —
POINT ELEMENT ✳
FOCAL POINT ✳
MACRO CHARACTER AREAS — ▬ —

0    ½    1 MILE

N

**Figure 7.11.** Character areas, Sandy Creek study area.

The descriptive analysis of the wetlands could be used in planning interpretive facilities at different scales. The character areas provide a framework that could be used for planning various sequential experiences along a trail or canoe route. A planner or designer could provide a diversity of educational, recreational, and visual experiences and reduce visual fatigue by planning a route through several different types of character areas. It could also be used by the SLEO Commission as a basis for the establishment of a visual inventory system for the analysis of wetlands in the region.

Coupled with an evaluation, the system could be used to identify key areas and visually distinctive sections. Zones could be located relating to a variety of land uses based upon visual quality. For instance, observation or viewing points could be established in key visual zones reserved for protection, while areas of lower quality could be designated for recreational activity.

The descriptive analysis might also serve as an information base to proposed alteration of shoreline character. It may be beneficial to plant trees to produce enclosure in certain areas, direct or modify views, or open up areas of vegetation. In this study the analysis has the advantage of generating a mapped product that could be used directly by designers and planners in decisions involving the visual management of wetlands.

The analysis relies heavily upon the decision rules for its outcome or final product—the character areas. The decision rules themselves, although based on design theories considered important in visual assessment, cannot be considered the only important rules that could be used in such a process. The use of other concepts should be explored.

One advantage of the descriptive analysis is that it generates the landscape and wetland units as separate products and later synthesizes them, which means that either process could be applied and used alone for assessment purposes. For instance, the landscape units could be generated for assessment of areas where the intent is not necessarily to focus on wetlands, but on the landscape in general.

Probably more subjectivity is involved in the application of the variables in this study than in Smardon's 1972 study. The decision rules are largely abstract concepts or dimensions that in some cases can lend themselves to different interpretations by various assessors. Smardon's use of the variables involves more clearly defined measurement techniques, which would leave less room for variation in interpretation. Subjectivity may be reduced by involving others in the decision-making process in the selection and application of decision rules and variables.

# References

Felleman, John. 1975. *Coastal landforms and scenic analysis: A review of the literature, with a preliminary examination of New York's shoreline.* Syracuse: SUNY College of Environmental Science and Forestry, School of Landscape Architecture.

Fried, Eric. 1973. *Wetlands inventory: Methods and uses.* Albany: New York State Department of Environmental Conservation.

Fried, Eric, and Gardner, Charles B. 1977. *Freshwater wetlands overlay user information.* Albany: Bureau of Wildlife Division of Fish and Wildlife. New York State Department of Environmental Conservation.

Geis, James W., and Kee, Janet. 1977. *Coastal wetlands along Lake Ontario and St. Lawrence River in Jefferson County, New York.* Syracuse: SUNY, College of Environmental Science and Forestry, Institute of Environmental Program Affairs.

Golet, Francis C., and Larson, Joseph S. 1974. *Classification of freshwater wetlands in the glaciated Northeast.* Resource Publication 116. Washington, D.C.: U.S. Government Printing Office, Fish and Wildlife Service, U.S. Department of Interior.

Hopkins, Lewis D. 1977. Methods for generating land suitability maps: A comparative evaluation. *AIP Journal* (July):386–400.

Laurie, Ian C. 1970. Objectives of landscape evaluation. Landscape Research Group Conference II.

Litton, R. Burton, Jr. 1968. *Forest landscape description and inventories: A basis for land planning and design.* USDA Forest Research Paper PSW–49. Berkeley, Calif.: Pacific SW Forest and Range Experiment Station.

Litton, Burton R., Jr.; Tetlow, R. J.; Sorensen, J.; and Beatty, R. A. 1974. *Water and landscape.* Port Washington, N.Y.: Water Information Center.

McHarg, Ian L. 1969. *Design with nature.* New York: Doubleday/Natural History Press.

Office of Planning Services. 1974. *Land use and natural resource inventory of New York State.* Albany, N.Y.

Shaw, S. P., and Fredine, G. C. 1956. *Wetlands of the United States.* Circular No. 39, 67 pp. Washington, D.C.: U.S. Fish and Wildlife Service.

Smardon, Richard C. 1972. Assessing visual-cultural values of inland wetlands in Massachusetts. Master's thesis, Department of Landscape Architecture and Regional Planning, University of Massachusetts, Amherst.

_____. 1975. Assessing visual-cultural values of inland wetlands in Massachusetts. In E. H. Zube, R. O. Brush, and J. Gy. Fabos, eds., *Landscape assessment: Value, perceptions and resources.* pp. 289–391. Stroudsburg, Pa.: Dowden, Hutchinson and Ross.

Webb, William; Bart, Jonathan; and Komarek, Constance. 1972. Technical Report Wildlife Resources. In *St. Lawrence Eastern Ontario Shoreline Study.* Watertown, N.Y.: St. Lawrence Eastern Ontario Commission. April.

# 8 Evolutionary and Cyclical Change as Fundamental Attributes of the Estuary

## ROWAN A. ROWNTREE

## Introduction

The two decades of literature in landscape evaluation have focused more on the static than on the dynamic. While this preoccupation with current form was necessary to establish basic principles, a means must now be found for incorporating short- and long-term change into the philosophy and method of visual analysis. This chapter looks at the visual-cultural attributes of (1) the morphologic evolution and (2) the tidal cycles of estuaries. Both forms of landscape change are considered to be intrinsic characteristics of the resource, although emphasis is placed on evolution.

### The Philosophy of Change as Meaning

Meaning is the ultimate phenomenon we seek to grasp in landscape evaluation, whether we are landscape manager or casual viewer. Certain categories of meaning take higher priority in our minds than others. The concept of change and all that is means is commonly ap-

plied to what we sense. We are unlikely to ask consciously about landscape change as we move about our daily routine. Yet when we look at a wetland and consider it as a significant part of our environment, we are capable of inquiring about its past and future states.

If, as Suzanne Langer says, the landscape operates as a language to convey meaning, we can think of visual analysis as having advanced to the point of identifying the important elements of vocabulary and syntax. What remains is to find ways of employing these static elements in a dynamic grammar that communicates richer and more complete landscape meanings. We know that a snapshot of another person is an incomplete picture of that person. It is easy to think beyond that image and see the person as having evolved from youth, of having a future morphologic state, and of having the ability to move about in his or her current morphologic state. We have acquired the information necessary to envisage the total image of another person from our own experience and from learned concepts of human maturation and development. However, the important concepts of wetland dynamics and maturation are only recently being made available to us.

The "uninformed" viewer of wetlands will be content to look for a pleasing texture and assemblage of color and perhaps a similarity to known landscapes: a lake or a field of wheat. Others will seek meaning about the scene from an explanation that may have been suggested to them. Thus, our task is to organize visual information about wetlands to convey an understanding of change.

### Cyclical Change

Most landscapes undergo some form of cyclical change: That is, the viewer is aware of repetitive transformations in the set of visual attributes. If we think of the deciduous forest landscapes of the Adirondacks, the Rocky Mountains, or the Midwest, the sequence is predictable and cyclical. The estuary landscape is dominated by the tides. They undergo visual (and functional) change daily, monthly, and seasonally. These cyclical events are linked with the directional process of succession and evolution because tidal action determines how sediment erosion, transport, and deposition will combine with marsh invasion to transform the estuary slowly into a coastal meadow.

### Wetland Evolution

Wetlands have been called the ephemeral landscape. While there are certain wetland forms that are relatively stable, we must assume that change is a fundamental characteristic of most wetland types.

Until fifteen years ago wetlands were a neglected and unappreciated landscape, being neither sound land nor good water. Then, in a wave of concern over their imminent loss, the public began to appreciate the attributes of marshes, bogs, swamps, and estuaries.

Not only succession but also the rate at which estuaries were evolving inspired a concern for preservation. This concern stemmed at first from the evidence that humans had transformed, through dredge and fill, much of our national estuarine resource into sound land and good water. The subsequent realization that Nature was at work, too, led to the conclusion that — in contrast to forest succession where the end product is still forest — the terminal condition for estuarine evolution was extinction of the resource and creation of a new landscape, the coastal meadow.

It was argued that some estuaries were "in their last stages of maturity" and others were "suffering from senescence," soon to be lost to the next successional state. The political dimensions of this controversy often centered on the question of whether to preserve the natural process of succession or to manipulate the hydrology of an estuary to arrest succession and preserve the wetland landscape.

### Human Influence on Change

If we accept the premise that the human influence on nature and the visible changes it brings about is easily comprehended by most people, how in confronting the dynamics of an estuarine landscape can the visual analyst include in his or her interpretation an understanding of this dimension? Human influence of course is not to be thought of in only negative terms. A viewer of landscape often relates more easily to the human imprint, the artifacts of his species, than to the natural. Nature, to some, is alien. A touch of humanity provides a point of reference, especially if there are hints of antiquity and the raw edges of human action have been visibly worn by time. Insofar as we look to the landscape for meanings about our identity, relations among people, and, for some observers, relations between people and their dieties, we must assume that any landscape view is a medium for understanding the theater of life.*

We will consider human influence on the dynamics of the estuary primarily in terms of

---

*Glacken (1967) argues that human modification of the natural environment is one of the great themes of Western civilization. He bases his argument on an analysis of the literature, but others agree that, along with time and space, negotiations ("conquest" is too simple, and it often exaggerates the relationship) with nature is a fundamental dimension of human life and not just a preoccupation of the literati.

succession. While tidal dynamics constitute an important visual consideration, human influences on cyclical change are of secondary importance. The types of human influence on successional change to be discussed are those activities that increase or decrease (1) the deposition rate and/or (2) the rate of plant invasion and development in the estuary.

The following section elaborates on the concept of estuarine evolution and describes the principal morphologic units of an estuary with an eye to how they typically change over time. The third section explains how to document estuarine evolution. The fourth section discusses how the visual characteristics of an estuary change during the tidal cycle. The fifth and sixth sections deal with the geographic and political contexts for interpreting cyclical and evolutionary change.

## The Morphologic Evolution of Estuaries

The life cycle of an estuary begins when a coastal valley is flooded by coastal subsidence or rising sea levels. Its ontogeny is complete when under stable sea-level conditions the embayment is completely filled with sediment and invasion of terrestrial (nonwetland) vegetation creates a coastal meadow. Sea levels began their rise at the end of the last glaciation some ten to fifteen thousand years ago. Until about two to three thousand years ago, when sea levels began to stabilize, deposition rates in coastal embayments were seldom greater than the rate of sea-level rise. Only during the more recent period when sea levels became relatively stable did estuaries become "wetland landscapes" with elements of marsh, mudflat, and channel.

During the period of human habitation of the watersheds and littoral zones of the world's estuaries, sedimentation rates have increased, partly because of land use. In general, with sea levels remaining roughly what they are today, many estuaries and lagoons will enter the last phases of their lives within the next fifty to one hundred years. In some cases the speed with which they grow old will be influenced by humans: in some cases increased, in others decreased.

During the life cycle the most visible changes will be the creation of extensive mudflats, the constriction of channels, and the expansion of marsh, finally spilling into the channels to clog this circulatory system with vegetation. The direct visual consequences of morphologic change will be the changes in the relative extent of the three morphologic units: marsh, mudflat, and channels. Indirect consequences will follow. Changes in speciation and frequency of visible biota, primarily birdlife, will result from changes in the lower strata of their food chain (i.e., speciation and frequency of organisms inhabiting each morphologic unit).

### Approaches to Describing Estuarine Evolution

The terms used in this chapter need some refinement. The classical notion of "succession" implies changes in plant and animal communities: changes in the presence and dominance of species and changes in production at various trophic levels. For some, succession implies an end state or "climax" that involves stabilization of the species mix and system equilibrium. Succession has been applied to generalized modes of wetland evolution in introductory texts in physical geography and ecology. The common example shown in Figure 8.1 employs morphologic units of vegetation and describes evolution using a sequence of profiles with some attention to the stratification of peat soils. Beyond this, there is no discussion of trophic changes or shifts in diversity and speciation at various stages in the successional sequence. It would seem obvious that wetland succession does not stabilize at a terminal climax but continues through the transition into a terrestrial sequence of succession. At the beginning of the terrestrial sequence, the wetland as a landscape entity becomes extinct.

More appropriate to the topic is Redfield's (1972) portrayal of the development of Barnstable Marsh in Massachusetts. For the period 1300 B.C. to A.D. 1950 Redfield employs a sequence of maps that shows changes in four morphologic units: upland, sand dunes, intertidal marsh, and high marsh (Figure 8.2). If the visual analyst and land manager are to characterize the evolution of an estuary, the selection of morphologic units must be based only on intrinsic wetland attributes. Thus the method presented in this chapter varies from Redfield's ap-

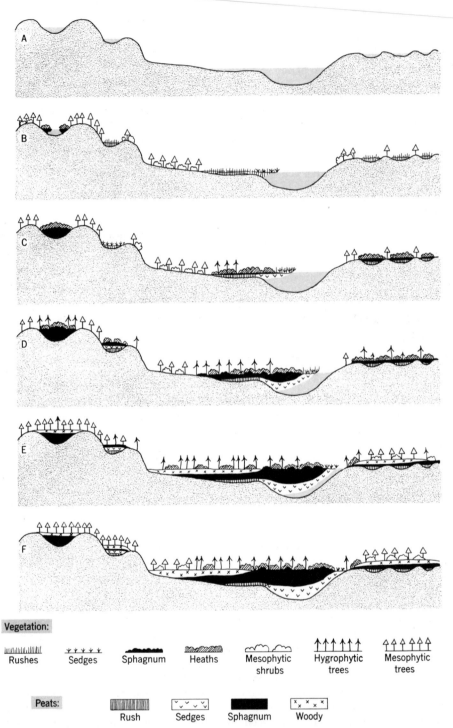

**Vegetation:**

| Rushes | Sedges | Sphagnum | Heaths | Mesophytic shrubs | Hygrophytic trees | Mesophytic trees |

**Peats:**

| Rush | Sedges | Sphagnum | Woody |

**Figure 8.1.** A typical model of wetland succession. Vertical profiles of autogenic bog succession from A. N. Strahler, *Physical Geography*, 3rd ed. (New York: John Wiley & Sons, 1969), p. 336. After Dansereau and Segadas-Vianna, 1952, *Canadian Journal of Botany* 30. Reprinted by permission.

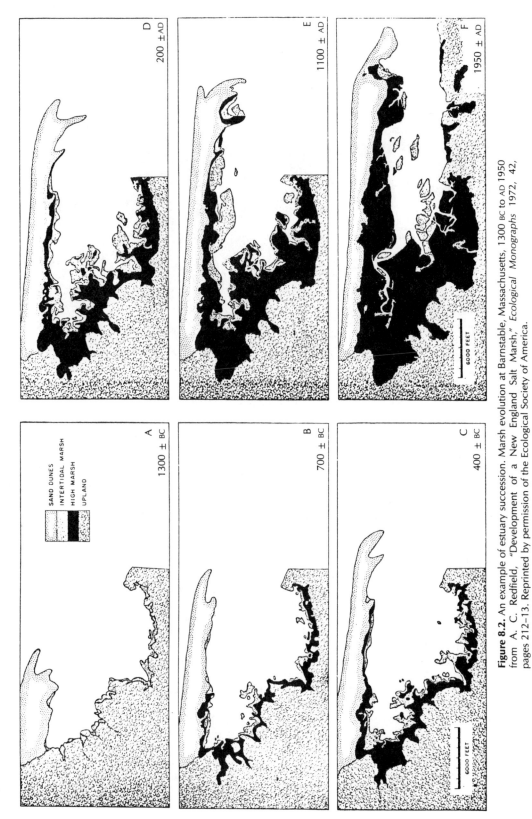

**Figure 8.2.** An example of estuary succession. Marsh evolution at Barnstable, Massachusetts, 1300 BC to AD 1950 from A. C. Redfield, "Development of a New England Salt Marsh," *Ecological Monographs* 1972, 42, pages 212–13. Reprinted by permission of the Ecological Society of America.

123

**Figure 8.3.** Morphologic units of an estuary as principal visual components. (1) Intertidal marsh, extending from right margin of photograph; (2) mudflats, a rich substrate for feeding shore birds; and (3) channels full of water, even at low tide.

proach by eliminating upland and sand dunes because they are elements of the terrestrial landscape and generally lie above the traditional boundaries of the estuary, mean high water. Furthermore, no distinction is made between high marsh and intertidal marsh. In California, where I did my field studies, the high-marsh community of *Distichlis spicata* (saltgrass) was more often than not of relatively minor areal extent, in contrast to the large fields of saltgrass contiguous to eastern estuaries. Also, historical references rarely distinguished between high and intertidal marshes, making it difficult or impossible to reconstruct the evolution of an estuary employing that boundary. Finally, two additional morphologic units have been added — mudflats and channels — to those used by Redfield to allow for a more comprehensive treatment of estuarine evolution.

### The Principal Morphologic Units of an Estuary

I have divided the estuary into three morphologic units: (1) the intertidal marsh, (2) the mudflat, and (3) the channel (Figure 8.3). These compose the gross visual structure under either static or dynamic conditions and are valid units for both visual analysis and ecological function. Thus in this classification are the principal components that compose the food chain and act together to engineer estuarine succession. This congruence of apparent visual attributes with ecologic attributes qualifies the estuary as a landscape potent for interpretation and meaning.

*The Intertidal Marsh:* From the line of mean high water (MHW: on the Pacific Coast, mean higher of high water, or MHHW) down to the lower edge of the intertidal vegetation, several plant communities exist in zones determined mostly by elevation and tidal submergence. The upper boundary between intertidal marsh and the adjacent terrestrial vegetation is not well delineated: often it shows a "diffuse" edge. (The visual terminology is from Litton et al., 1974). Within the marsh the boundaries between communities are either "digitate" or "butt." These fairly clear lines of demarcation result from differences in the physiology of the dominant species, especially with respect to salt tolerance and the ability to withstand submergence.

One of the most important visual considerations in the marsh component of estuaries is the distinction between those estuaries with a predominantly *Salicornia* marsh as opposed to those with a *Spartina* marsh. In many of the world's estuaries the marsh is dominated by the low-growing pickleweed, *Salicornia*, which forms a bunchy cover. In a *Spartina* marsh fields of tall cordgrass undulate in the shore breeze in an entirely different visual display (Figure 8.4).

*The Mudflats:* The unvegetated zone lying between the marsh and the channel is the mudflat or tidal flat. At first encounter, this zone seems visually barren. Yet much of the estuary action takes place here. Loaded with benthic organisms, the mudflat is an important feeding ground for shorebirds. They take worms and ghost shrimp from the mud as the tide goes out and cull young fish from the first incoming waters of the flood tide. In addition, this is the zone of active marsh invasion, where fingers of vegetation reach out to claim the rich substrate.

*The Channels:* The remaining portion of the estuary below the mean low water line (MLW: on the Pacific Coast, mean lower of low water, or MLLW) can be termed "channel." Even at low tide these winding incisions in the estuary bottom are full of water. A complex of tributary channels, lying technically above the MLW elevation, together with the main channels, constitutes the estuary's circulatory system. The complete network forms a sinuous branching pattern that is one of the estuary's more predominant visual characteristics. While some of the channels may shift their location from year to year, the pattern is essentially permanent, given repeated visual emphasis by the *galleria* of shorebirds waiting along the channel banks at each incoming tide.

Ulrich (1976) asserts that observers prefer those landscapes that display "ordered or patterned complexity" and show low preference for those that exhibit unordered or random complexity. The incised, branched network of estuarine channels is a familiar pattern in the environment of *Homo sapiens,* and it conforms to Ulrich's definition of ordered complexity. The tides flow through, visually unifying the principal components of the estuary.

# A Method of Documenting Morphologic Evolution

The purpose of describing morphologic evolution for visual assessment is to provide a picture of the areal extent of each of the three morphologic units — marsh, mudflat, and channel — at intervals during which there are adequate data. Most often these intervals are restricted to the tenure of human habitation or exploration. A picture of the historical evolution of an estuary provides a basis for making estimates of how the morphology will change, and at what rate, under different future conditions. The first step is to characterize the estuary's present morphologic status.

### Delineating Current Morphologic Status

The work cannot proceed easily without a set of aerial photographs taken at the scale and resolution determined by the analyst to be appropriate to the morphologic complexity of the estuary. The choice of black and white or color in any of the spectral classes is often determined by how well the photography allows one to separate (1) upper marsh from terrestrial vegetation, (2) lower marsh from mudflat, and (3) mudflat from water in the channels. Black-and-white infrared or color infrared provides good delineation in most estuaries. The investigator should be aware of the problem of algae deposition on the mudflats, which will give a reflectance somewhat similar to that given by lower marsh at small scales and low resolution.

The air photography should be taken at a time of year when vegetation reflectance signatures provide clear distinctions and at a time of the day when the tide is at MLW, the elevation at which channel units are distinguishable from mudflat. The best conditions, both in terms of plant color differences and atmospheric clarity, are often found in fall and spring along all three coasts of the United States.

If possible, an elevation and distance survey should be conducted to allow accurate calculations of areal extent of marsh, mudflat, and channel units. (Most estuaries are near survey benchmarks.) This is the only means of determining the line of MHW (MHHW) that serves as the boundary of the estuary. This boundary

**Figure 8.4.** Comparison of *Spartina* and *Salicornia* form. (*Left*) Wheatlike *Spartina* (cordgrass) occurs as tall, undulating fields (specimens of *Spartina foliosa* shown here are shorter than the aggressive *Spartina alterniflora* of the Atlantic and Pacific coasts), compared with (*center*) low, bunchy *Salicornia* (pickleweed) that produces dense mat. (*Right*) Field of *Spartina foliosa* (California), colonizing the mudflat abutting the channel, is one of the principal visual features of many estuaries.

sometimes coincides with a vegetational transition that can be seen on the air photographs, making the delineation fairly simple. In many estuaries the transition from high marsh to terrestrial vegetation occurs at an elevation above MHW.

The upper and lower elevations of each morphologic unit can be very useful to ecologic interpretations, which will add meaning to any understanding of cyclical or directional change. For example, elevations of the lowest marsh plants indicate the rate and form of mudflat conversion to marsh and how fast channel patterns are being stabilized by marsh vegetation. Elevations of this kind can be compared to those for other estuaries to suggest relative rates of marsh invasion and consequently to determine whether the estuary is changing morphologically more slowly or faster than others in the same geographic region.

As part of the survey, the general distribution of dominant marsh species should be noted. This will assist in estimating the rate and form of marsh invasion of mudflat units. For example, in many California estuaries *Spartina foliosa* (cordgrass) is a more active invader of the mudflat than *Salicornia* (pickleweed), the other common marsh plant. Each has its own pattern of invasion. However, *Spartina* is not present in all California estuaries, and it is absent from most estuaries in Oregon and Washington. Consequently, those estuaries with *Spartina* dominating the lower marsh will exhibit a different pattern and rate of morphologic evolution than those estuaries where *Salicornia,* exclusively, composes the marsh. Because both occur in nearly pure stands, noting their presence and location also helps in describing the static visual characteristics of the estuary. During tidal transformations estuaries dominated by either *Spartina* or *Salicornia* will look quite different from one another.

### Interpreting Historical Patterns of Change

One can work backwards in time, seeking first the most recent historical map of the estuary, then uncovering earlier documentation. However, there is no reason why the investigator should not go directly to the first coastal survey. It is critical to remember that the information contained on any particular map will be related to the purpose of the map and mission of those doing the mapping and cartography. The following examples taken from Bolinas Lagoon in Marin County, California, will emphasize this point.

The first map (1897) constructed by the U.S. Geological Survey of Bolinas Lagoon and vicinity occurs as part of the Tamalpais Quadrangle (Figure 8.5). It would appear that the lagoon was in a "youthful" stage of its morphologic evolution, exhibiting no marsh and mudflat components. The picture conveyed by this map is one of a simple embayment with a bar and inlet. However, the mission of the USGS was to map terrestrial features, not wetland environments. The map is of no use for documenting morphologic change within the estuary. The first map of Bolinas Lagoon done by a legitimate agency capable of accurately documenting estuarine geography was constructed by the U.S. Surveyor General in 1858 to confirm the boundaries of the Baulinas Rancho land grant (Figure 8.6). In 1858 the government wanted to survey only lands above the approximate line of mean higher of high water and to delineate ground solid enough for grazing, agriculture, and the construction of rancho homes. There was no intention of including tidal land unsuitable for these purposes, and therefore it is not surprising that the map omits marshes, mudflats, deltas, and islands or a full rendering of the bar across the embayment.

In contrast to and predating these two maps, the first U.S. Coast Survey map of Bolinas Lagoon dated 1854 is an excellent base for reconstructing the estuary's morphology (Figure 8.7). To prepare a morphologic picture from this map, one must use Aaron Shalowitz's "Shore and sea boundaries, with special reference to the interpretation and use of Coast and Geodetic Survey data" (1964). The following sections should be noted: "Symbolization of Topographic Surveys" (pp. 188–92); "The Line of Mean High Water" (pp. 172–76); and "The Low Water Line" (pp. 183–89). The heavy solid line on the map represents the line of mean higher of high water, which is assumed for purposes of morphologic analysis to be the boundary of the estuary. Where marshes exist, the seaward edge of the marsh represents only the edge of the vegetation, as noted by the surveyor, and does not conform to a particular tidal plane. The in-

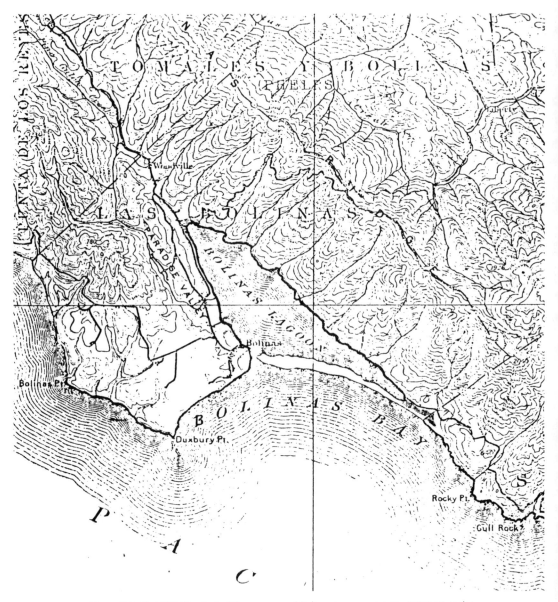

**Figure 8.5.** First U.S. Geological Survey map of Bolinas Lagoon vicinity, 1897. Note the absence of morphologic detail within the estuary.

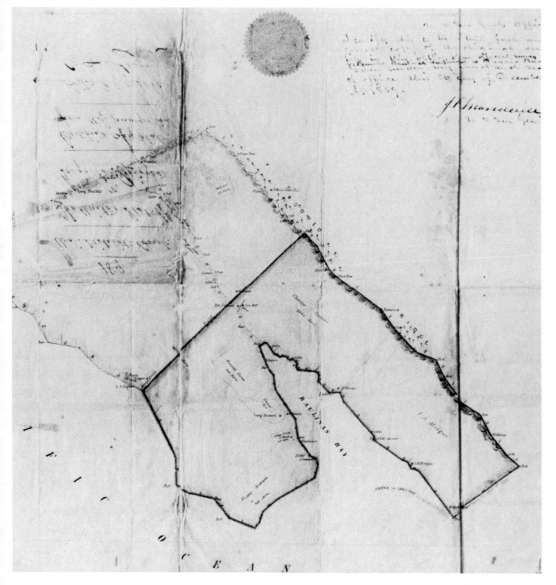

**Figure 8.6.** First U.S. government map of Bolinas Lagoon vicinity, done by Surveyor General, 1858. Note the absence of morphologic detail in the estuary and token (erroneous) representation of the sandspit across the mouth of the lagoon.

**Figure 8.7.** First accurate survey of estuary conducted by U.S. Coast Survey, 1854. (Representation of marsh, mudflats, and channels provides a good picture of the lagoon's morphology.)

ner edge of the marsh, shown on the map, for the most part corresponds to the line of mean higher of high water. Where it was difficult for the surveyor to discern the MHHW line of the marsh, the inner edge will not conform precisely to that elevation.

The U.S. Coast Survey (later the U.S. Coast and Geodetic Survey) completed two sets of maps for most areas. They are denoted as either "topographic" or "hydrographic" maps. The topographic maps show marshes and lines of MHW (MHHW), MLW (MLLW), with some upland vegetation and selected roads or buildings. The hydrographic maps note the depths of navigable water at spot locations using the topographic map as a base. The hydrographic map for Bolinas Lagoon (1854), a companion to the topographic map in Figure 8.7, indicates water depths in the bay outside the lagoon entrance and in the entrance itself. No depths are given within the lagoon proper. Hydrographic maps of other estuaries that I have seen provide similar information. When they are available, the U.S. Coast Survey topographic and hydrographic maps can be used together to construct a morphologic picture of an estuary for that time. Those who are fortunate will find several sets spanning a century, which together can provide a fine sequence of morphologic evolution.

### Sedimentation Rates as Supplemental Indexes of Change

The process of sedimentation is the fundamental mechanism that creates morphologic change. Many people are concerned about increases in sedimentation rates—as an index of rapid evolution of the estuary—that result from land uses such as logging and residential development on the estuary's watershed. Analysts should know the possibilities and pitfalls of using sedimentation as another measure of evolutionary rate. They can then respond more effectively to public interest about how fast an estuary is changing under natural conditions, compared to how fast it would change if different types of human activities were allowed in any of the three sedimentation locales: the estuary itself, the watershed, or the littoral zone.

Sedimentation is a process of erosion, transport, and deposition. All material eroded from

the watershed or adjacent littoral bluffs and beaches may not be transported to the estuary, and what is transported may not remain there. Some of it is removed by the tides. Thus, simply calculating erosion rates from the watershed under natural versus cultural conditions will not provide an accurate estimate of deposition rates in the estuary.

The interpretation of evolutionary change eventually focuses on the following questions: How fast did the estuary change in precultural times (essentially, before European man)? How fast has it been changing in recent years (under "current land-use conditions")? How fast will it change in the near future (given increases or decreases in human activity)? And how long before the estuary is extinct as a wetland landscape? An understanding of deposition rates in the estuary helps to answer some of these questions, but good data are hard to come by. This is one of the reasons why characterizing morphological change is perhaps more practical as well as inherently more suitable for visual-cultural assessment.

Human influences on how fast a natural feature like an estuary will evolve into maturity, senescence, and extinction are often best described using estimated sedimentation rates only as comparative measures for different intensities of human activity. Conventional wisdom assumes that aboriginal man increased erosion rates over those rates existing before human habitation and that "modern man" has sped up the rate of erosion even more. Table 8.1 illustrates this using hypothetical data from a small estuary. Documenting the history of deposition in relation to land use is difficult. The best method is to analyze sediment cores from the estuary. In the absence of cores, deposition rates may be estimated. This involves a series of speculative extrapolations from partial data on streamflow, tidal volume, and the like to rates of sediment transport into the estuary and then to rates of actual deposition. The procedure becomes more speculative when one attempts to reconstruct historical patterns.

The person who assesses visual-cultural values of estuaries will probably operate within the context of controversy over how fast the estuary is evolving toward extinction and what human activities in the vicinity of the estuary are doing to speed or slow the process. The partici-

**Table 8.1** **The Role of Human Influence on Estuary Evolution, Using Estimated Deposition Rates for Five Historical Periods**

| Historical Period | Rate (1,000 meters³/year) |
|---|---|
| 1. Preaboriginal: Estuary evolving at a rate representative of truly natural conditions. | 20 |
| 2. Aboriginal: Hunter-gatherer tribes; no agriculture but occasional fires that could produce episodes of increased sedimentation. | 21 |
| 3. European: Farming and logging by settlers; occasional fires. | 25 |
| 4. Contemporary: Limited suburban and second home development; limited logging, grazing, and farming. | 30 |
| 5. Future: | |
| Growth: Continued suburban and second-home development, logging, and road building; diminished grazing and farming; no removal of sediment from estuary. | 35 |
| Management: Restrictions on rate and locale of building, logging, and roads to minimize sedimentation; removal of sediment from estuary. | 28 |

Time to Extinction

(assumption: tidal prism to MHW is $1,400 \times 10^3$ meters³)

Tidal prism divided by future "management" rate = 50 years.
Tidal prism divided by future "growth" rate = 40 years.

pants in the controversy may speak in terms of deposition rates, for they are a convenient means for describing the rate of evolution and the relative influence of man and nature. However, without an accurate technique for measuring contemporary deposition rates, and in the absence of sediment cores for historical analysis, the primary effort of characterizing the evolution of an estuary should be restricted to the depiction of morphological change using historical maps and air photography.

### The Portrayal of Morphologic Evolution

Morphologic evolution can be depicted in both tabular and cartographic form. Figure 8.8 portrays morphologic evolution of Bolinas Lagoon over the 170-year period from about 1850 to 1970. This sequence was constructed from interpretations of historical maps, descriptive records, and recent air photographs. Table 8.2 provides areal data for morphologic units at four dates during the period.

It would be a simple matter to extend this portrayal back in time to the point where sea levels stabilized and the estuary began its evolution. The first map, dated perhaps two or three thousand years ago, would show a thin fringe of marsh with an incipient delta at the mouth of the major stream. The estuary would be quite open to the sea, with segments of a spit beginning to develop. This could be said to represent preaboriginal conditions, although at that date there may have been small bands of coastal Indians in the vicinity of the lagoon. A second map, dated about a thousand years ago, would show the stream delta somewhat enlarged, with two small islands emerging inside the lagoon. In the interim between the two maps, there would have been significant growth of the spit or bay mouth bar. A third map could be added for the period around A.D. 1500 to suggest how Bolinas Lagoon would have looked to the first European explorers, perhaps even to Sir Francis Drake himself, who is reported to have come ashore not far from this estuary. The main fluvial delta and the tidal delta (the two islands inside the mouth of the estuary) would have grown. The spit across the seaward face of the lagoon would now be more fully developed, but it still might be segmented, being breached by high tides and storm waves at regular intervals.

A sequence of morphological maps as described here is an effective means of communicating the history and future of evolutionary change. Used as a medium for public interpretation, the morphologic stages can be characterized along a time line beginning with stabilization of sea level (two to three thousand years ago) and ending with conversion to a coastal meadow. The information in Table 8.1

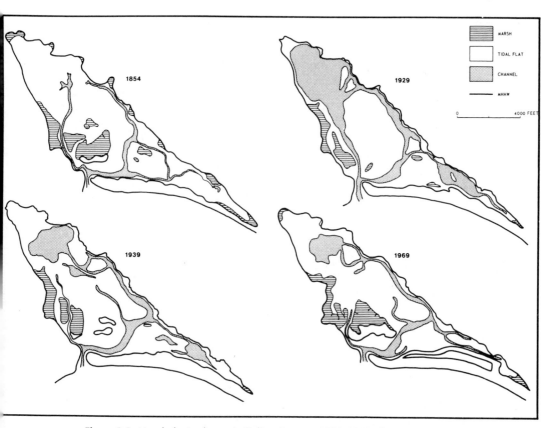

**Figure 8.8.** Morphologic change in Bolinas Lagoon, 1854–1969. (Sources: 1854–U.S. Coast Survey; 1929–U.S. Coast and Geodetic Survey; 1939–U.S. Army Corps of Engineers survey; 1969–air photographs.)

and Figure 8.8 has been combined in Figure 8.9, to illustrate how alternate future patterns and time to extinction can be incorporated in one presentation.

### Marsh Invasion and Rate of Evolution

The primary colonizers invading the bare mudflat help to determine the visual character of the estuary in both static and dynamic terms. In both respects the major distinction is between two common invaders, *Salicornia* (pickleweed) and *Spartina* (cordgrass). On the west coast of England, *Salicornia* is the dominant colonizer. Along the English Channel, *Spartina* (the aggressive hybrid, *S. townsendii*) has within several decades changed the visual character of a large number of estuaries. *Spartina foliosa*, a cousin of the European species,

actively expands onto the lower elevations of selected California estuaries. *Spartina alterniflora* covers the marsh in estuaries along the Atlantic, and to a lesser degree on the Gulf Coast of the United States (this species is also prevalent on the east coast of South America and in the English Channel). *Spartina* is generally absent from the estuaries of Oregon and Washington.

There is a marked visual difference between marshes boasting the tall (three to five feet), wheatlike *Spartina* and those having a low (six to ten inches) mat of *Salicornia* (Figure 8.4). The thick, shiny-leafed cordgrass undulates in the shore breeze, presenting a clear edge to adjoining communities and to the bare mudflat. It browns in winter, whereas the pickleweed remains a grayish-green. Circular groves of cordgrass are commonly seen standing amid an ex-

**Table 8.2   Morphologic Elements of Bolinas Lagoon Expressed as Acres and as Percentage of Total Estuary Areas, 1850–1970**

| Year | Area of Lagoon | Marsh Acres : % | Mudflats Acres : % | Channel Acres : % |
|------|-----|-----|-----|-----|
| 1850 | 1216 | 157 :13 | 909 :75 | 150 :12 |
| 1930 | 1130 | 72 : 6 | 653 :58 | 402 :36 |
| 1940 | 1096 | 88 : 8 | 742 :68 | 266 :24 |
| 1970 | 938 | 118 :13 | 654 :70 | 166 :17 |

tensive pickleweed mat or along the lower edge of the mat in a distinct band ten to twenty yards wide. These are the static attributes of *Spartina* and *Salicornia* communities, but what are the dynamic aspects?

*Spartina* is thought to be the more aggressive colonizer. Once it is introduced to an estuary, rates of morphologic change are likely to increase there. The cordgrass is able to withstand longer periods of tidal submergence; consequently it extends itself farther down on the mudflats than the pickleweed. Like other pioneer vegetation, cordgrass seems to thrive on disturbance. It is common for *Spartina* to invade tidal channels, and these aggressive plants are often torn out by the rushing water of a heavy rainstorm occurring at low tide. If they are not removed this way, the cordgrass-clogged channels may be dredged to restore the flushing action of the estuarine circulatory system. In either case the broken but viable *Spartina* rhizomes float off to sprout new colonies elsewhere. Many estuaries in central and northern California have previously had only moderate amounts of cordgrass, but these colonies are expanding and in the near future will probably dominate these landscapes.

# The Tides: Visual Attributes of Cyclical Change

To this point, the discussion has focused on morphologic evolution, with the implicit understanding that tidal cycles work in conjunction with morphology to produce an estuary's set of visual attributes. Each morphologic change produces a different stage on which the tides produce different visual scenes.

When a viewer comes to an estuary, he or she may hold the image of a placid body of water. Confronting the estuary in reality may be disappointing because at low tide it looks like a drained reservoir. To characterize the estuary visually as a body of water is simply a technical error. As shown by the tide curve in Figure 8.10, the estuary is full only 20 percent of the time and empty 20 percent of the time. During flooding or ebbing ("midstage" in Figure 8.10), the mudflats are teeming with birdlife. Thus to overlook the visual attributes of a half-filled estuary is to neglect the most common as well as the richest stage of its tidal cycle.

## The Tides as a Unifying Medium

In the tidal cycle we can find a solution to the old conflict between visual complexity and visual unity. Litton et al. (1974) identified three critical aesthetic criteria for the evaluation of environmental stimuli: unity, vividness, and variety. "Unity is that concern or expression whereby parts are joined together to a coherent and single harmonious unit" (p. 105). But, he goes on to say, "Variety does have a potential conflict with unity" (p. 107) unless there can be found some cohesion in diversity. (The terms *variety, diversity,* and *complexity* are used synonymously to denote the array of elements in a landscape display.) To see unity in a *static* landscape, the observer must infer some degree of structural cohesion or coherence among the parts. To see unity in the *dynamic* landscape of the estuary, the observer witnesses the repeated linking of morphologic units by tidal action. These units are the visible components of the estuarine system. Tidal flow is the dynamic medium that unifies them by immersion. This unifying process is given visual elaboration by the action of shorebirds at each tidal stage. As the incoming tide begins to join channel with mudflat, mudflat with marsh, the diggers move about poking in the mud for worms and small crustaceans, while the egrets and herons stand in deeper water and wait for fingerlings. Birds fly back and forth between channel, marsh, and mudflat, and the observer can see with ease the estuary as an intergrated whole composed of distinct parts.

# Historical Sequence of Morphological Change

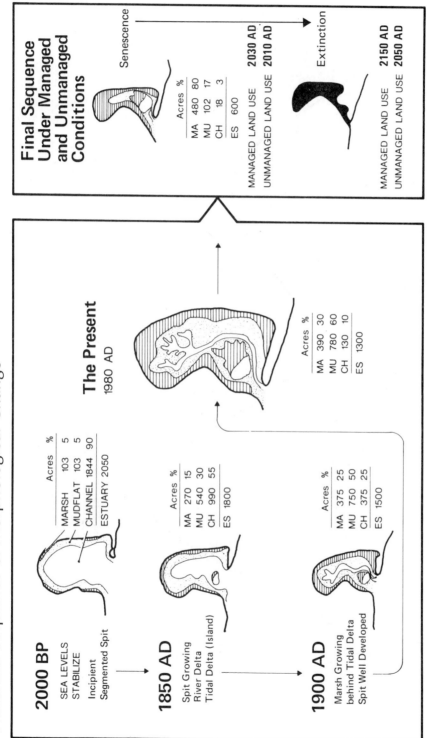

**Figure 8.9.** Estuarine evolution can be portrayed so that the time to "senescence" and, finally, "extinction" is seen as resulting from the decision to manage, or not manage, land use in and around the estuary. This idealized picture is created from existing knowledge and presents the question in terms of a choice to extend the life of the estuary. Dates and time periods will vary greatly among estuaries having different geographic properties.

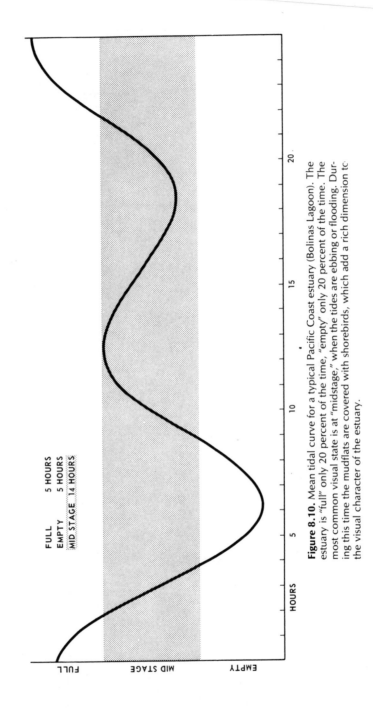

**Figure 8.10.** Mean tidal curve for a typical Pacific Coast estuary (Bolinas Lagoon). The estuary is "full" only 20 percent of the time, "empty" only 20 percent of the time. The most common visual state is at "midstage," when the tides are ebbing or flooding. During this time the mudflats are covered with shorebirds, which add a rich dimension to the visual character of the estuary.

## Evolutionary Changes in Visual Attributes of the Tidal Cycle

As an estuary ages, the visual attributes of the tidal cycle change. The direct changes are by now obvious and have been touched on above. A youthful estuary, when full of water, looks like a lake; when empty, it looks like a muddy, drained reservoir. A water-filled, mature estuary with extensive marsh appears as a grassland; but when flooded to three-fourths the height of the *Spartina*, it looks like a true "marsh." A mature estuary lacking *Spartina* may be flooded above the height of the *Salicornia* or *Distichlis*, giving more the impression of a lake than a marsh. A senescent estuary with deeply incised channels among raised marsh beds may never give the visual impression of being a wetland if the flood-tide water is contained in the channels.

The morphologic evolution of a given estuary continuously reapportions a finite number of acres among the three morphologic units. For example, the more marsh, the less mudflat. Consequently, the kinds and abundance of birds that appear at different times in the tidal cycle will change with each stage of morphologic evolution. The mudflat supplies the food for the medium-sized and smaller shorebirds (Figure 8.11, bottom). Primarily diggers, the swarms of sandpipers, aggressive willets, dowitchers, dunlins, and oystercatchers are squeezed out as the ratio of marsh to mudflat increases. The mudflat stage offers prime visibility, a dance floor on which the trophic ballet is repeated with each tidal cycle. In the last stages of evolution, when the marsh abuts the channels, those smaller birds that still use the estuary will be hidden from view. The large birds—herons, egrets, and cranes—remain with an estuary after the mudflat unit has disappeared (Figure 8.11, top). They can stand knee-deep in the channels and feed, although they, too, will often be hidden from view as the channels become narrow and constricted.

*Tidal Range and Visual Character:* Tidal ranges (the vertical distance from MHW to MLW) vary from place to place. The variation is several feet in southern California and four times that in northern Maine. An average annual tidal curve similar to the one in Figure 8.10 could be used as the basis for calculating the area and duration of tidal filling. The vertical axis would represent the elevational scale, and once the estuary was surveyed, the area covered by—and the duration of—any stage of the tide could be calculated and graphically documented. A variation of this method would be necessary if no survey could be done. Using standard tide tables that note the time of day of high and low tides, an estimate could be made as to when a given stage would occur. Photographs could then be taken of the estuary landscape at, for example, low water plus one foot, low water plus two feet, midtide, low water plus three feet, and high tide. The photographs would be correlated with the duration (taken from the tidal curve) at each stage to document the visual attributes for different percentages of time for the daily cycle.

The tidal range of an estuary determines the range of visual conditions that will be produced. At low tide, estuaries with large tidal ranges, such as those in Maine, exhibit a great expanse of mudflat. Under these conditions the mudflat component of the estuary may visually overwhelm the presence of marsh and any remaining water in the channels. The relationship between tidal range and the rate and form of morphologic evolution is unclear. Some hypothesize that those estuaries with small tidal ranges evolve more rapidly than those with ranges of six feet or more.

# The Geographic Context for Interpretation

In the Introduction it was suggested that the visual attributes of landscape—those inventoried in conventional assessments—were analogous to the static elements of a language, and the challenge was to find a way of using these elements in some dynamic grammar to convey meaning. Yet, pursuing the analogy further, a well-constructed sentence taken out of context may not be able to convey meaning adequately or accurately.

For any single estuary the meaning of morphologic change and rate of evolution emerges best when the case at hand is compared to other estuaries, measured against a theoretical norm, or set among the range of evolutionary conditions found within a geographic region. A good point of departure is the question of abundance and form of estuaries taken at the national scale.

**Figure 8.11.** Long-legged egrets, herons, and cranes (*top*) fish in the channels and rest in the marsh, employing the mudflat only minimally. Short-legged diggers (*bottom*) dine on mudflats and leave the estuary in its senescent state. (Photographs by Clerin Zumwalt. Courtesy of Audubon Canyon Ranch, Stimson Beach, CA.)

The American estuarine landscape varies dramatically from east to west. An equivalent length of Atlantic coast boasts neary forty-two times more acres of tidal marshes and mudflats than California. Estuaries on the West Coast appear as small discrete entities compared to those along the Atlantic and Gulf coasts, where the estuarine landscape often seems ubiquitous.

Thus, in a geomorphic region where estuaries are comparatively few, a given potential increase in deposition rates from increased urbanization (Table 8.1) will be viewed differently than in a region where they are more abundant. Beyond this, the evolutionary status of other estuaries within the same geomorphic or geographic region will serve to judge more or less critically a given rate of change of the estuary in question. In a region where a good number of estuaries are thought to be on the verge of extinction, for example, there may be a desire to do whatever is necessary to slow morphologic change. (The political implications of this are discussed in the section "The Cultural and Political Context.")

### The Present Evolutionary Status of Estuaries

Placing estuaries into evolutionary categories, while useful for comparative purposes, involves some difficult taxonomic problems. Is a "youthful" estuary one with a high percentage (of total area) in channel and a low percentage colonized by marsh? Conversely, would a "mature" estuary have a high amount of marsh and relatively little channel? A successional model would certainly point to these as normative cases.

To test this approach, California estuaries are divided in Table 8.3 into three categories—Youth, Maturity, and Senescence—using percentage of channel as the single criterion. If this procedure is followed, the analyst must understand that the visual attributes may vary somewhat within each category, depending on the ratio among the three landscape elements—Channel, Mudflat, and Marsh.

The "youthful" estuaries have a high percentage of water and a low percentage of marsh, but the percentage of mudflat varies in this example from 3 to 13 percent. An observer would see "youthful" estuaries primarily as water bodies, but at low tide San Francisco Bay would appear much more "mature" than, say, Klamath River because of the significantly higher percentage of mudflat in the former.

At the other end of the spectrum, a truly "senescent" estuary like Elkhorn Slough (97 percent marsh) appears from the perimeter road as a flat plain of low gray Salicornia. Bolinas Lagoon could be said to be in "early senescence" with more than half of its acreage in mudflat. The ratio of mudflat to marsh (which can be used as a second criterion for more refined divisions) helps to distinguish "mature" cases from "senescent" ones. As an estuary moves from "maturity" to "senescence," the ratio will diminish as mudflats are colonized by the expanding marsh. However, the divisions between these three categories in Table 8.3 are arbitrary in that no dictum states rigidly where they must be made. The analyst should be aware that labels such as these have powerful implications in the cultural and political context.

### Variations in the Morphologic-Evolution Model Resulting from Geologic Events

If things have meaning only in relation to other like phenomena, then stark exceptions to the norm require some consideration here. This is not to say that the power of meaning increases (proportionately) to the magnitude of deviation, for those estuaries that conform nicely to the general model of evolution will have great interpretive value. The error of any general model or theory is to assume that all things behave in much the same way. In estuarine evolution the factors discussed that bear on the process and rate of change are (1) sea levels, (2) sedimentation, (3) marsh invasion. Human influences on sedimentation will be discussed again. An important determinant of morphologic change that has been omitted to this point is the large-scale uniform or eposodic geologic event.

Subsidence or emergence of the coastal shelf are geologic events of long-term, uniform dimensions that affect the rate and form of morphologic change. Subsidence produces a flooding of the estuarine basin. Emergence lifts the basin and allows the descent of the marsh down the mudflat gradient to occur more rapidly than under stable geologic conditions. Because the effects of emergence or subsidence

Table 8.3    Evolutionary Status of Selected California Estuaries

| Location | Channel | | Mudflat | | Marsh | |
|---|---|---|---|---|---|---|
| | Acres | % | Acres | % | Acres | % |
| **Youth (66 percent water)** | | | | | | |
| Bodega Bay | 840 | 90 | 45 | 5 | 50 | 5 |
| Klamath River | 4,250 | 80 | 165 | 3 | 870 | 17 |
| San Francisco Bay | 258,000 | 78 | 41,600 | 13 | 32,000 | 19 |
| Smith River | 3,825 | 76 | 230 | 5 | 920 | 19 |
| **Maturity (33 percent to 66 percent water)** | | | | | | |
| Tomales Bay | 5,950 | 64 | 2,900 | 31 | 440 | 4 |
| Drakes Estero | 1,290 | 62 | 580 | 28 | 200 | 10 |
| Eel River | 2,300 | 59 | 500 | 13 | 1,050 | 27 |
| Big River | 120 | 47 | 90 | 35 | 45 | 18 |
| Humboldt Bay | 4,500 | 45 | 5,000 | 50 | 500 | 5 |
| **Senescence (33 percent water)** | | | | | | |
| Bolinas Lagoon | 370 | 30 | 720 | 58 | 150 | 12 |
| Ten-Mile River | 40 | 24 | 100 | 58 | 30 | 18 |
| Morro Bay | 600 | 23 | 1,400 | 55 | 575 | 22 |
| Elkhorn Slogh | 97 | 3 | 0 | 0 | 2,840 | 97 |

*Source:* Unpublished data, California Department of Fish and Game, 1968. Acreage estimates were made from air photos. Tidal stages on the air photos were roughly the same for all estuaries inventoried. The evolutionary divisions are the author's.

are often difficult to measure, assessors of estuary visual attributes are cautioned not to let this factor weigh too heavily on their methodology.

The effects of earthquakes—an episodic geologic event—are, on the other hand, more easily seen in morphologic analysis and should be part of the context of any assessment, particularly in California, where active faulting is associated with a number of estuaries. Bolinas Lagoon is a case in point. Referring back to Figure 8.8 and Table 8.3, one can note that the morphologic sequence does not conform to the general picture of estuarine evolution. Between 1849 and 1929, instead of the area of marsh and mudflat expanding at the expense of channels, just the reverse occurred. The marsh decreased by 54 percent, the mudflats shrunk by 28 percent, and the channel expanded by 168 percent of the 1850 area.

Bolinas Lagoon lies astride the San Andreas Fault. During the 1906 earthquake in central California, the sediments in Bolinas Lagoon were probably compacted, thus lowering the surfaces of the mudflat and marsh units. In evolutionary terms the lagoon was "rejuvenated" and set back in its sequence, consequently extending its lifetime. Another earthquake of approximately the same magnitude as the 1906 event—expected by many to occur within the next ten to twenty years—may have a similar effect. One might conclude from the sequence of maps that the lagoon was set back in its evolution by approximately one hundred years. It is true that in 1970 the relative distribution of total estuary area among the three morphologic units was much as it was in 1850: Marsh, 13 percent and 13 percent; Mudflats, 75 percent and 70 percent; Channel, 12 percent and 17 percent (see Table 8.3). However, the total area of estuary is shrinking despite seismic rejuvenation—23 percent from 1850 to 1970. So, while Bolinas Lagoon exhibits a variation of the theme, its long-term pattern conforms to the general model of evolution.

Bolinas Lagoon = 12,344 meters$^3$/year/mile$^2$

Tomales Bay = 5,120 meters$^3$/year/mile$^2$

### Geographic Factors Affecting Deposition Rates: A Summary

Deposition is the primary factor causing morphologic evolution. It is possible to generalize roughly as to what causes more or less deposition in an estuary:

1. *Climate:* The higher the annual rainfall – all other things being equal – the more water available to carry sediment from the watershed into the estuary.
2. *Orientation and exposure:* Estuaries exposed to ocean storms will receive more littoral sediment than those protected by headlands and well-developed spits.
3. *Areal ratio – watershed to estuary:* The amount of sediment transported to the estuary increases with the size of the watershed. Small estuaries with large watersheds should evolve at higher rates than large estuaries with proportionately smaller watersheds.
4. *Geologic factors:* These include uniform and episodic events covered above, plus erodibility of the watershed and the proximate sources of littoral sediments.
5. *Tidal factors:* The unclear set of relationships between deposition rate and the mix of tidal factors includes tidal prism (volume of estuary) and tidal form (semidaily, diurnal mixed, equatorial, tropic). Thus, while tidal factors are recognized here, no general relationship is stated.
6. *Land use:* Human influences on the process of sediment erosion, transport, and deposition have been touched on above and relate principally to land uses that either increase or decrease (dams) sediment transport to the estuary or remove sediment (e.g., dredging).

The unique combination of these factors operating on a specific estuary makes that estuary very different from even its next-door neighbors. This is said to alert the visual analyst to potentially great variations in morphologic process within the same geographic region. For example, two estuaries only ten miles apart with similar geology, soils, climate, and tidal form experience vastly different deposition rates. Annually, deposition occurs, per square mile, in Bolinas Lagoon at nearly three times the rate as in Tomales Bay to the north.

A look at the geographic factors affecting deposition in these two estuaries suggests just the opposite case: higher deposition rates in Tomales Bay. The areal ratio of watershed to estuary is much greater for Tomales Bay (14:1) than for Bolinas Lagoon (9:1). Land use on the Tomales Bay watershed includes potato farming, dairying, and grazing, compared to less erosive land uses at Bolinas Lagoon. A closer look, however, leads to at least a partial explanation of the anomaly. Dams and lakes on the lower tributaries of Tomales Bay have captured much of the sediment. Bolinas Lagoon, on the other hand, lies near a formation of highly erodible sea cliffs that produce large amounts of sediment that enter the lagoon on each flood tide.

The lesson is clear: The documentation of estuary evolution as part of visual-cultural assessment should be place-specific, relying on as much local information as possible. Each estuary has its own story, and each can differ enough from its neighbor to yield fascinating, if perplexing, comparisons.

## The Cultural and Political Context

On the geologic time scale, estuaries are an ephemeral landscape. Our view of estuaries has changed only within the last two decades. Historically, we have cherished only one morphologic unit – the channel. When mudflat or marsh encroached, we fought them back. Dredge and fill became a convenient means for keeping the estuary open and providing solid ground for buildings and roads. Much of the destruction of marsh and mudflat came just before our attitudes changed and indeed may have been the catalyst for the tidelands preservation movement. Between 1950 and 1964, New York State lost nearly 30 percent of its tidelands. Between 1940 and 1970, 90 percent of the salt marshes along the San Diego County coast in California were destroyed. By 1970, San Francisco Bay had lost about 60 percent of its marshlands.

Most estuaries, in terms of morphologic evolution, are several thousand years old, if we count from the time sea levels stabilized. The marshes

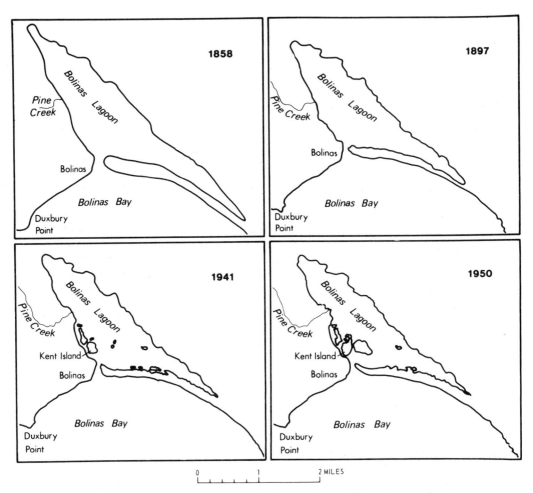

**Figure 8.12.** Erroneous sequence of morphologic evolution of Bolinas Lagoon, showing the estuary as transformed from a deep-water embayment to a "senescent" lagoon in less than 100 years. (Source: U.S. Geological Survey, 1969, p. 9.)

and mudflats destroyed by dredge and fill were created in part by natural processes of sedimentation, but often they were significantly enhanced by erosive human activities on the watershed. Hydraulic mining in the Sierra foothills during the California Gold Rush provided a large amount of sediment to nourish San Francisco Bay's tidelands. Humans have been a part of both the creation and destruction of the estuarine landscape. Consequently, the history of an estuary may be interpreted in one way or in another by various individuals or groups having a vested interest in its future.

An earlier study (Rowntree, 1975) docu-mented how cultural context heavily influenced the interpretation of an estuary's evolutionary history. Cultural context is the fabric of extant myths, folklore, and conventional wisdom held by individuals and groups about the manner in which an estuary evolves, how fast it evolves, and what role humans have played in that evolution. Political context is the manifestation of these beliefs in a more formalized decision-making environment. Normally, scientific interpretation of landscape process is free of influence by cultural-political beliefs. In this case, however, the folk interpretation of estuary evolution seemed to the scientists conducting the investigation to be in conformance with general textbook models of estuarine process. Their "official" interpretation of morphologic change took this model for granted and overlooked important facts that would have produced a true picture of that estuary's evolution. The example is worthy of a brief summary.

Bolinas Lagoon was a lively shipbuilding and lumbering port in the latter half of the nineteenth century. As a result of a number of controversies over land planning, the lagoon had become in the late 1960s something of an icon for environmentalists and remained as part of a strong sense of place shared by the established citizens of two small communities on either side of the estuary. Part of this sense of place was a deep feeling for the history of the lagoon, its evolution, and the role people had played in that evolution. Folklore said that the lagoon was morphologically youthful prior to lumbering and shipbuilding in the mid-1880s. It could be used as a port, and there were few mudflats and marshes. Siltation from redwood cutting (to build San Francisco) transformed the embayment into the senescent, marshy lagoon. It was thought to be on the verge of extinction as a wetland ecosystem and useless as a port of refuge for pleasure boats.

A federal agency was called in to document the form and rate of evolution and to propose a set of recommendations for the estuary. The authors of this report were provided with maps by local residents that seemed to document morphologic transformation in the lagoon as a result of siltation from logging. The agency scientists apparently did not examine these maps closely, thinking that they were appropriate evidence for a "normal" sequence of estuary evolution. Consequently, the government report institutionalized an erroneous picture of morphologic change (Figure 8.12) that served as a foundation for public policy recommendations.

What can be learned from this? In the previous section it was shown that unique combinations of geographic and geologic factors produce significant variations in evolutionary pattern, even within the same region or locale, a fact that renders most evolutionary models useful only as a point of departure for interpretation. This requires that the visual analyst pay close attention to the specifics of the estuary in

question without being unduly influenced by the local folk wisdom about morphologic change. Local sources of information are rich and in most cases invaluable if sifted and judged with a discerning eye. Beyond this, the reservoir of local belief about the past, present, and future of a wetland is in fact a powerful resource that can energize whatever interpretation the analyst feels is valid and appropriate.

Obviously, the myths and folklore about estuary evolution are not in themselves irrational or conspiratorial. Indeed, in the minds of those who believe in them, they are rational hypotheses about how things came to be. Depending on the outcome of his or her investigations, the analyst or interpreter may find himself working in concert with these beliefs or in opposition to them. Whichever is the case, he *will* have the advantage of the investment these people have made in their beliefs to power an interesting, yet accurate, interpretation of estuarine change.

## Summary

A dynamic interpretation of wetlands provides a richer and indeed more valid picture of the landscape than visual analysis of static qualities. Estuaries are excellent candidates for this approach to assessment because they are visually dynamic at two temporal scales: the short-term cyclical and the long-term evolutionary scales.

The "morphologic evolution" of estuaries is susceptible to visual interpretation because it can be described graphically using changes in the three major units of the estuary: marsh, mudflat, and channel. What makes this approach more powerful is that these units are valid on both ecological and visual grounds. Thus visualized changes in morphology can explain fundamental changes in ecological structure and function.

The principal method for documenting morphologic change employs historical maps and air photos supplemented by data on rates of sedimentation. The method is straightforward, but it has many pitfalls.

The tides are a visually unifying medium for the diverse and complex estuarine landscape. The precise visual attributes of the tidal cycle change with the morphologic evolution of the estuary. A common set of six geographic factors determine evolutionary rate and form. These factors operate uniquely on individual estuaries to produce greatly differing rates for even neighboring cases.

The visual analyst must be aware of folklore about the dynamics and evolution of cherished landscapes. These myths and beliefs have the same inherent weaknesses as generalized scientific models, even though they can facilitate acceptance and appreciation of truly valid interpretations of cyclical and evolutionary dynamics.

### Postscript: Central Premise for Documenting Wetland Change

With the help of trained interpreters, landscape observers can grasp and benefit from a picture of wetland dynamics. All viewers of landscape seek meaning in one form or another and their search for meaning will follow certain lines of inquiry previously learned, particularly when these lines of inquiry pertain specifically to the type of landscape before them. Simply, viewers are taught to understand landscape dynamics, having been provided with the right conceptual and emotional tools.

To accept this premise, there has to be proof that ample concepts of both a general and specific nature are available to a majority of viewers that will enable them to comprehend cyclical and evolutionary change. General concepts of cyclical change derive from common experience with cyclical time—days and years—and the general concept of evolution derives from the experience of human physiological maturation and development. It would be difficult to argue that these common dimensions of the human experience did not provide at least a framework for the comprehension of cyclical and evolutionary change. Yet, what about the availability of more specific concepts—that can provide them with real points of reference to the idea of a functionally evolving estuary?

There is a prevalence of ecological ideas of an evolutionary nature in the popular literature. The concept of succession, for example, began as a scientific theory, but now it enjoys popular usage in nonscientific and quasi-scientific discussions of the world about us. (We know, too, that it was popular in sociology about fifty years ago.) More particularly, in the literature of wetlands, there is always some mention—even a theme—about evolution and change. Unquestionably, however, the challenge is great for the visual analyst and interpreter of wetland landscapes to create a valid and comprehensible notion of dynamic change as a fundamental attribute of the resource.

Visual-cultural assessment is commonly done under the auspices of a search for visual quality. Indeed, the field of visual analysis was mandated by the need to know more about the landscapes around us and to have a defensible method for justifying what we save and what we throw away. People want some objective measure of how the viewscape will change if certain processes, both human and natural, are allowed to exist. Thus it would seem that visual analysis would logically incorporate a concern for change. To speak to this concern, a land manager or planner ideally should try to comprehend how the landscape got to be the way it is, how fast it is likely to change as a result of natural processes, and how human influences on those natural processes can modify the rate and form of evolutionary change.

Certainly, this will not always be possible, and the approach should be employed only when dealing with a class of landscapes that are thought to be changing relatively rapidly. Estuaries—in fact, most wetlands—fall into this class. Thus incorporating short-term and long-term change into visual-cultural assessment is not just a matter of *enriching* interpretation. It is a case of documenting *fundamental* attributes of this type of landscape.

## References

Glacken, C. J. 1967. *Traces on the Rhodian shore: Nature and culture in western thought from ancient times to the end of the eighteenth century.* Berkeley: University of California Press.

Litton, R. B., et al., 1974. *Water and landscape: An aesthetic overview of the role of water in the landscape.* Port Washington, N.Y.: Water Information Center.

Redfield, A. C. 1972. Development of a New England salt marsh. *Ecological Monographs* 42(2): 201–37.

Rowntree, R. A. 1975. Morphological aging in a California estuary: Myth and institutions in coastal resource policy. In H. J. Walker, ed. *Geoscience and man,* Vol. 12, pp. 31–42. Baton Rouge: Louisiana State University Press.

Shalowitz, A. L. 1964. *Shore and sea boundaries, with special reference to the interpretation and use of Coast and Geodetic Survey data,* Vol. 2. U.S. Coast and Geodetic Survey Publication 10–1. Washington, D.C.: Government Printing Office.

Strahler, A. N. 1969. *Physical geography.* 3rd ed. New York: John Wiley and Sons.

Thomas, W. L., Jr., et al., eds. 1956. *Man's role in changing the face of the earth.* Chicago: University of Chicago Press.

Ulrich, R. S. 1976. Some factors in environmental preference. In D. B. Harper and J. D. Warbach, eds. *Visual quality and the coastal zone.* Syracuse: SUNY College of Environmental Science and Forestry. Pp. 40–41.

U.S. Geological Survey. 1969. *Preliminary studies of sedimentation and hydrology in Bolinas Lagoon.* U.S. Geological Survey Open File Report. USGS, Menlo Park, Calif.

I am indebted to R. Burton Litton, Jr., George Hopkins-Rowntree, Lester B. Rowntree, and Richard C. Smardon for their careful and constructive review of an earlier manuscript of this chapter.

# PART IV

# Wetland Visual-Cultural Valuation and Evaluation

# 9 A Model for Assessing Visual-Cultural Values of Wetlands: A Massachusetts Case Study

## RICHARD C. SMARDON and
## JULIUS GY. FABOS

## Introduction

This chapter addresses itself to the problem that land-use decisions affecting inland wetlands are being made without consideration of visual-cultural values because allegedly these values, which preempt their place in the decision-making process, cannot be "quantified." Chapter 9 summarizes the first known attempt to develop a fairly rigorous model for assessing visual-cultural values of wetlands.

### Landscape Resources and Models

To deal with the values of wetlands in connection with land-use decisions, the Commonwealth of Massachusetts pioneered wetland legislation with the Hatch Act (1966) and the Inland Wetlands Protection Act (1968). Both acts and a few others are included in the umbrellalike Wetlands Protection Act (Commonwealth of Massachusetts, 1971). Many other states have drafted wetland protection legisla-

tion since 1966, the date of the initial Massachusetts Hatch Act.

A multidisciplinary inland-wetlands research project started at the University of Massachusetts soon after the Inland Wetlands Act became law. The objective of the project's organizer, Joseph S. Larson, was to create a tool that would help decision-makers reach better land-use decisions concerning inland wetlands. Larson assembled a team to formulate the decision-making tool and to investigate the many different types of inland-wetland resource values. This interdisciplinary study included a wildlife biology subproject, which assessed the wildlife values; an aerial photogrammetry subproject, which provided the wetland resource data; a hydrogeology subproject, which assessed the water supply and quality; a resource economics subproject, which assessed the economic value of each major wetland resource; and a landscape planning subproject.

The landscape planning subproject specifically addresses the issues of how to develop conceptually an overall model and how to incorporate the visual-cultural resource values of wetlands into the decision-making process. This has not yet been done comprehensively in any state under any legislation.

This chapter details how the landscape planning subproject of the inland-wetlands research team articulated the visual-cultural values of inland wetlands and designed a multistage assessment model to measure these values.

### Study Objectives

The major study objectives were:

1. To identify, analyze, and classify inland wetland types and surrounding landscape types that are important for discerning and identifying different types of visual-cultural values.
2. To identify the major visual-cultural values that can be attributed to inland wetlands in Massachusetts and design an assessment model to estimate those values.
3. To design the inland wetlands assessment model for visual-cultural values as a module submodel in a larger inland-wetlands assessment model that inludes other inland wetland values.
4. To ensure that the inland-wetlands assessment model for visual-cultural values has utility at all decision-making levels and scales.

### Definition of Critical Terms

Certain terms that are used throughout the chapter should be defined.

*Resources:* "Resources are entities which are useful and finite. They are like money held in the bank; they are available for human use, but scarcity dictates that some mechanism be established defining the objectives of use and the allocation of resources according to those objectives. Planning processes are one type of response to defining objectives and allocating resources" (Fabos, 1973, p. 1).

*Visual-cultural:* Refers to the visual landscape portion of the physical environment. "It consists of natural entities such as soil, trees, landform, water and various cultural entities or artifacts such as farms, recreational developments and housing. These entities or artifacts have various perceptual attributes and characteristics" (ibid, p. 2).

*Wetlands:* In this chapter, freshwater wetlands. Freshwater inland wetlands include marshes, swamps, meadows, and bogs by themselves, adjacent to, or part of streams, rivers, lakes, ponds, and reservoirs. They can be generally characterized as having a year-round surface or above-surface water level with submergent, surface, and emergent aquatic vegetation or herbaceae and woody vegetation resistant to frequent flooding.

*Visual-cultural wetland resources:* The finite natural resources available for human use that are perceived, found within, or associated with wetland areas. Examples of human use that treat wetlands as a visual-cultural resource are outdoor classroom use for natural history, canoeing, or hiking.

*Visual-cultural wetland values:* "Values are defined by human individuals and groups. The reason for segregating visual-cultural resource values for separate study is that they have received relatively little attention by the American decision-making process. A basic premise of this paper is articulation and definition of visual-cultural [wetland] values, even if through primitive quantitative techniques, will increase societies' favoring more explicit consideration of these values in individual and group decision-making processess" (ibid., p. 2).

*Landscape resource variables:* "Landscape resource variables represent a given quantity and quality of a resource [for example, visual contrast or wildlife productivity] that may have a number of different values" (ibid., p. 2). For instance, landform contrast may vary from high, owing to a 1,000-foot-high mountain situated adjacent to a wetland, to low, owing to no perceptual height difference of any landforms adjacent to a wetland. "The quantity (height difference) and quality all represent different values. They vary and yet they are still quantifiable within the metric; hence the term landscape resource variable" (ibid.).

*Landscape dimension:* The metric unit or measurement process used to rate a given landscape resource variable. In the case of landform contrast, the two landscape dimensions are relative relief measured in feet and ratio of relative relief to wetland width, a pure number.

*Measurement:* "A process which estimates the

magnitude of a visual-cultural wetland value at a given point in time. The measurement of the value of the landscape resource variable or the measurement of several attributes (parameters) of a landscape resource variable is directed toward defining physical units useful in considering collective human values" (ibid., p. 3).

*Rating:* "The process which orders [visual-cultural] values of a landscape resource variable in a hierarchy [from high value to low value] in respect to a larger geographic area" (ibid., p. 3).

*Assessment:* "The process which combines the measurements and ratings of all landscape variables" (ibid., p. 3).

## Inland-Wetland Assessment Model

The visual-cultural assessment submodel developed as an integral part of the overall inland-wetland assessment model (Figure 9.1). This was done to ensure that all the different subproject efforts would culminate in an effective interdisciplinary tool for assessing wetland resource values.

The inland-wetland assessment model has three major parts: classification, natural cultural resource evaluation, and economic valuation. The classification part of the assessment model necessitated a separate classification for each of the three subprojects: wildlife, visual-cultural, and hydrogeologic. The second part, the natural-cultural resource evaluation section, has three different levels, which constitute an eliminative system in that a wetland is "eliminated" from further deliberation or analysis if the wetland has a high value or scores high within any given level of evaluation. A wetland receiving a high value early in the evaluation process may require top priority for preservation or protection and is accordingly eliminated from further evaluation.

Level 1 evaluates a given wetland for a possible single outstanding natural or cultural value (for example, is it a major flyway and feeding area for large numbers of migratory waterfowl?). If a single outstanding value is not found, the wetland area is assessed at Level 2, which evaluates a wetland for several possible values simultaneously (for example, water-supply quantity and quality; wildlife-habitat quality and quantity; visual diversity and contrast) by rating the natural attributes and characteristics of the

wetland area. If the combined value of the natural attributes is not substantial, the wetlands cultural attributes (for example, accessibility or proximity to urban areas) are then evaluated at Level 3. In each evaluation level the wetlands can be ranked from most to least valuable for wildlife and for visual-cultural and water-resource values.

The third major part of the assessment model deals with the economic evaluation of the combined values of each of the three subprojects: wildlife, visual-cultural, and hydrogeologic. In addition, it assesses the flood storage value of the wetlands. This assessment model can be used with or without the economic evaluation by the decision-maker, who has the option of using any combination of levels and resource factors, depending on the types of wetland values with which he or she is concerned.

## Framework of the Visual-Cultural Submodel

The visual-cultural submodel (Figure 9.2), as part of the wetland assessment model, has two basic parts: the wetland and landscape context classification system; and the visual-cultural resource evaluation as a three-level eliminative process, described in detail by Smardon (1972).

Level 1 evaluates a given wetland for a possible single outstanding value (for example, an outstanding natural area for nature education). If outstanding values are not present, the wetland is further evaluated at Level 2. At this level, visual, recreational, and educational values (landform contrast, land-use diversity, associated water body size, and so forth) are rated by the attributes and characteristics of wetland and its surroundings. If the combined value is not substantial, the wetlands cultural variables (educational proximity, physical accessibility, and ambient quality) may be evaluated at Level 3 and rated from the most to the least valuable.

## Visual-Cultural Classification Systems

A two-part inland-wetland classification system (see Figure 9.2) was developed as part of the visual-cultural assessment submodel. One classification system served to differentiate the interior landscapes of inland wetlands them-

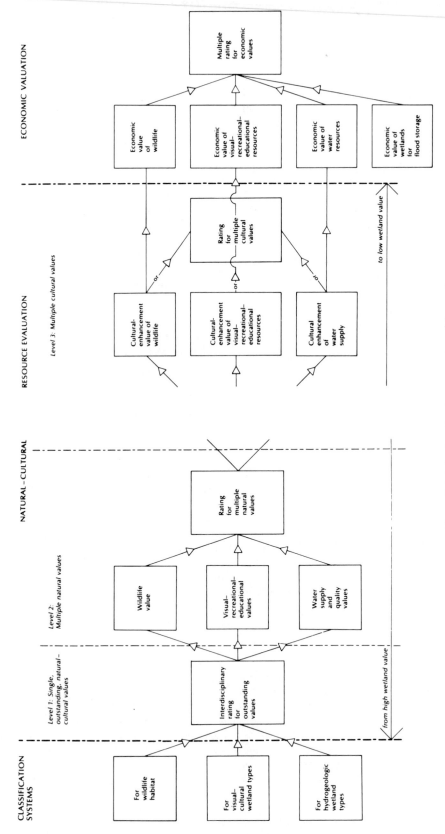

**Figure 9.1.** Inland-wetland assessment model.

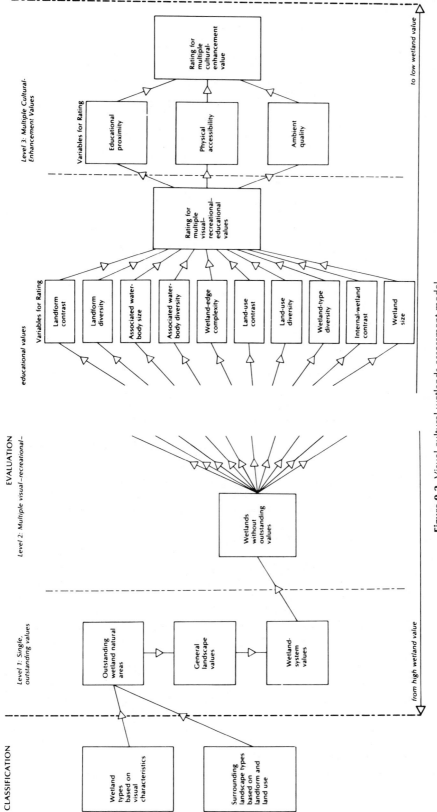

**Figure 9.2.** Visual-cultural wetlands assessment model.

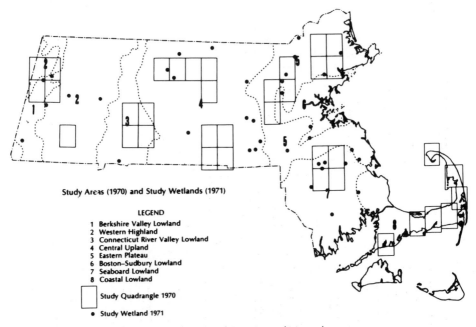

Study Areas (1970) and Study Wetlands (1971)

LEGEND

1 Berkshire Valley Lowland
2 Western Highland
3 Connecticut River Valley Lowland
4 Central Upland
5 Eastern Plateau
6 Boston–Sudbury Lowland
7 Seaboard Lowland
8 Coastal Lowland

☐ Study Quadrangle 1970

• Study Wetland 1971

**Figure 9.3.** Physiographic regions of Massachusetts.

selves. The second system was needed to identify and differentiate the many different land scape contexts in which wetlands are found.

### Identifying and Classifying Inland Wetland Types

Previous wetland classification systems (Lacate, 1969; Shaw and Fredline, 1956; USDI, Fish and Wildlife Service, 1954a) used the criteria of water level, vegetation, and soils to differentiate wetland types.

MacConnell and Garvin's wetland classification system was used to identify and map inland wetlands in Massachusetts in 1952. This system (1956) was slightly revised by MacConnell and is presently being used to identify and map wetlands in Massachusetts, using 1971–72 photos (MacConnell, 1971). The utility of this system (composed of mapped data from 1951–52 and 1971–72) and its similarity with the Shaw and Fredline and U.S. Fish and Wildlife Service systems made it acceptable for adaptation to the visual-cultural wetland submodel.

This inland-wetland classification system then was tested in the field. The types tested included open freshwater, deep fresh marsh,

shallow fresh marsh, shrub swamp, wooded swamp, and bog (see Figures 9.3–9.10).

### Identifying and Classifying Surrounding Landscape Contexts

Wetlands cannot be separated from their surrounding physical landscape. To evaluate the visual-cultural values of inland wetlands that were dependent on the immediately surrounding landscape, it was important to be able to identify and classify that landscape accurately. There are two components or parts of the surrounding landscape context: (1) the land use, and (2) the landforms underlying the land use.

*Land Use:* The continuum of cultural or man-affected land use can be classified from center city to forest wilderness. A number of descriptive systems were reviewed that classified the cultural characteristics of the landscape (Lewis et al., 1969; Olin et al., 1971; Zube et al., 1970). MacConnell's land-use and vegetative types were used to identify and classify the surrounding vegetation. Land use of the one to five U.S. Geological Survey quadrangle map areas were picked out within the physiographic region to best represent all wetland types occurring

**Figure 9.4.** Typical cross-section and examples of open freshwater.

Definition: water less than 10 feet deep bordered by emergent vegetation: pondweed, naiads, wild celery, water lilies. (Photos by R.C. Smardon; cross-section by C.H. Greene.)

within the region. Each study area included all the wetland types as well as large complexes of wetlands and small isolated wetlands (see Figure 9.3).

The actual study procedure consisted of documenting individual wetland attributes and characteristics using field sheets and photography (see Smardon, 1972). Study-area results indicated that MacConnell's aerial photogrammetric land-use and vegetative-cover maps, as well as the wetland types and surrounding land-use types, were accurate and usable for the general assessment of visual-cultural values. A more refined classification system for wetlands was desirable at the time the study was done (Golet, 1973). No suitable set of detailed landform types existed in mapped form for the purpose of visual-cultural evaluation.

*Landforms:* Little work has been done in Massachusetts to identify and describe distinct landform types in the same detail as has been done for land use. Physiographic regions for Massachusetts, however, have been suggested (Beaumont, 1956; Fenneman, 1938; U.S. Fish and Wildlife Service, 1954). Each of these studies uses a gross continuous pattern of similar landforms. The landforms of the surrounding

landscapes were identified using similar criteria suggested by these studies. The visual-cultural subproject, together with the wildlife and geology subproject, used criteria such as topography, surficial geology, bedrock geology, and drainage patterns to define physiographic regions for Massachusetts. Through the application of this process, eight distinct physiographic regions were identified (see Figure 9.3).

## Visual-Cultural Valuation

The results of the classification indicated that different kinds of visual-cultural values could be related to wetlands or to wetlands and their landscape contexts. Three potential visual-cultural values were identified:

1. That inland wetlands themselves have educational and scientific values as outstanding natural areas.
2. That inland wetlands and their landscape contexts have visual, recreational, and educational value at a given site because of the attributes of the wetland, surrounding landform, water bodies, and surrounding vegetation and land use.

**Figure 9.5.** Typical cross-section and examples of deep fresh marsh. Definition: soil covered with 6 inches to 3 feet of water. Cattails, reeds, bulrushes, spike rushes, wild rice. (Photos by R.C. Smardon and F.C. Golet; cross-section by C.H. Greene.)

3. That large inland wetland complexes have visual-cultural values not found in small individual wetland sites.

The following evaluation section of the submodel defines the visual-cultural values indicated and includes methodologies for the measurement of these values. The process used here is the same as discussed earlier under the inland-wetland assessment model; that is, a three-level eliminative model.

### Level 1: Individual Outstanding Values

Certain wetlands may have a single natural visual or cultural value that merits top priority for preservation or protection. These single outstanding attributes in most cases were jointly identified and defined by all the subprojects within an interdisciplinary framework.

It was concluded that certain unique wetland resources should not be assessed quantitatively. It was also concluded and widely accepted by the interdisciplinary team that there could be no monetary value attached to outstanding wetland resources, and that their greatest value to society is their present natural state. It was therefore proposed to use social norms to preserve outstanding wetlands similar to those used to create national parks, wildlife refuges, and wilderness areas. Thus the purpose of level 1 is to flag those wetland areas that are outstanding either by virtue of a single attribute or a number of attributes. Three types of values are examined in Level 1:

**Figure 9.6.** Typical cross-section and examples of shallow fresh marsh. Definition: soil waterlogged during growing season, often covered with 6 or more inches of water. Grasses, bulrushes, spike rushes, cattails, arrowhead, smartweed, pickerelweed. (Photos by R.C. Smardon and F.C. Golet; cross-section by C.H. Greene.)

1. Outstanding wetland natural area, such as an endangered-species habitat
2. General landscape values, such as a scarce wetland type within a region
3. Wetland system value, such as several significant wetlands interconnected with rivers and lakes

The first and third values cannot readily be separated into subproject areas because they draw on all subproject research areas. The second value represents primarily a visual-cultural value.

*Outstanding wetland natural areas:* This submodel defines wetland areas with high or outstanding visual, educational, or scientific value. Previous attempts to deal with this type of value in assessment literature have resulted in the concept of "uniqueness" (Leopold, 1969) or "being unique" (USDI, National Park Service, 1954). The similar concept of "outstanding areas" corresponds closely with the concept of nationally significant natural areas used by the National Park Service (1954b). The only difference is that wetland natural areas can be "outstanding" in a statewide or regional context. "Natural areas" as defined in the literature are "areas where at present natural processes predominate and are not significantly influenced by either deliberate manipulation or interference by man" (Maryland State Planning Department, 1968, p. 1).

Criteria for the identification of outstanding natural wetland areas were derived from professional judgment and other existing criteria (USDI, National Park Service, 1954b; Natural

**Figure 9.7.** Typical cross-section and examples of fresh meadow. Definition: without standing water during growing season; waterlogged to within a few inches of surface. Grasses, sedges, rushes, broadleaf plants. (Photos by R.C. Smardon and F.C. Golet; cross-section by C.H. Greene.)

Areas Criteria Committee, 1972) for identifying outstanding natural areas.

*General landscape values:* There are two kinds. One is the value of a wetland type that is relatively scarce within a specific geographic or physiographic region. Scanning of the aerial photogrammetric land-use and vegetative-cover maps of the state produced several relatively scarce wetland types within physiographic regions (Table 9.1).

The second general landscape value is that of visual contrast. Visual contrast is produced by a wetland providing openness in a predominantly forested landscape with little physical relief, or providing both forest and openness in a predominantly urban landscape. Visual contrast is provided in the landscape by keeping or in-troducing landscape types that contrast in height or texture with the general surrounding landscape. Table 9.2 summarizes the outstanding wetland types that provide visual contrast to the various geographic or physiographic regions.

*Wetland system value:* Wetland systems are combinations of wetlands, rivers, streams, lakes, and ponds. Because of their size and interconnectedness, large wetland systems have many conservation and open-space values. From the visual-cultural point of view, an important role is structuring urban development by providing open-space linkages; giving visible form to towns to improve their perceptual identity; serving as buffers or wedges between incompatible land uses or different areas of development; and

**Figure 9.8.** Typical cross-section of examples of shrub swamp. Definition: soil waterlogged, often covered with 1 or more feet of water. (Photos by F.C. Golet; cross-sections by C.H. Greene.)

by defining and separating towns, cities, and metropolitan areas (Central Massachusetts Regional Planning District, 1967; Lynch, 1960; USDA, Economic Research Service, 1968).

Because of the open-space values that a large system has, all wetlands within the system should be protected if the wetland system values are to be kept. The criteria developed for identifying large wetland systems within a New England landscape context are:

1. The wetland should be connected to another wetland by a large river or stream of at least fifteen miles navigable length; or
2. A wetland must be connected to another

wetland by a lake, pond, or reservoir of more than 200 acres in area; or
3. The wetland should constitute a continuous 1,000 acres in size.

If a wetland does not meet any of the criteria for individual outstanding values in Level 1, it is then further evaluated at Level 2.

### Level 2: Multiple Visual, Recreational, and Educational Values of Inland Wetlands

The purpose of Level 2 is to evaluate the large bulk of wetland areas that may not have a single outstanding visual, recreational, or educational

**Figure 9.9.** Typical cross-section and examples of wooded swamp. Definition: soil waterlogged, often covered with 1 foot of water. Along sluggish streams, shallow lake basins, and flat uplands. (Photos by F.C. Golet; cross-sections by C.H. Greene.)

**Figure 9.10.** Typical examples of bogs. Definition: soil waterlogged, spongy covering of mosses. Heath shrubs, sphagnum, sedges. (Photos by F.C. Golet.)

characteristic. However, several attributes together may result in a wetland with a high value in each characteristic. Level 2 is more quantitative and more complex than Level 1.

This part of the model is developed on the premise that values of the wetland benefit both recreational and educational uses. Primary recreational uses are fishing, hunting, bird watching, and nature study. Other recreational uses include hiking, photography, canoeing, boating, and ice skating. Recreational uses of areas adjoining the wetland could include camping and picnicking; recreational activities involving movement include using trails and roads adjacent to wetlands for walking, cycling, horseback riding, cross-country skiing, and pleasure driving. Educational uses of wetlands include outdoor educational and scientific laboratories.

Obviously, there is a great overlap among the visual-recreational-educational attributes of a wetland. For example, a wetland has recreational value for canoeing, visual value for the scenery experienced while canoeing, and educational value for the species of fauna and flora that can be seen and identified while canoeing.

Key attributes were used to derive *variables,* which indicate differences in the visual, recreational, and educational quality of inland wetland sites. The two significant visual variables selected and substantiated were *visual contrast,* which can be attributed to the variables of landform contrast, water-body size or length, surrounding land-use contrast, and internal wetland contrast, and *visual diversity,* which can be attributed to the variables of landform diversity, wetland-edge complexity, and wetland-type diversity.

The *recreational carrying capacity* of wetlands was also estimated. It, too, can be attributed to the variables of landform diversity and wetland-edge *complexity;* but water-body size or length are equally important. Opportunity for *recreational diversity* and *educational diversity* of wetlands can be attributed to the variables of landform diversity, water-body diversity, surrounding land-use diversity, wetland-edge complexity, and wetland-type diversity. As a result of this rationale, the following resource variables were identified and measured.

**Table 9.1  Scarce Wetlands within Specific Geographic Regions of Massachusetts**

| Physiographic Region | Scarce Wetland Type |
|---|---|
| Western highlands | Seasonally flooded flats |
| | Deep fresh marsh |
| | Shallow fresh marsh |
| | Fresh meadow |
| Berkshire valley lowland | Seasonally flooded flats |
| | Bogs |
| Connecticut valley lowland | Seasonally flooded flats |
| | Bogs |
| Central upland | Seasonally flooded flats |
| Eastern plateau | Seasonally flooded flats |
| | Bogs |
| Boston–Sudbury basin | Bogs |
| Seaboard lowland | Seasonally flooded flats |
| Coastal plain | Seasonally flooded flats |
| | Wooded swamp |

**Table 9.2  Wetlands with Outstanding Visual Contrast within Specific Geographic Regions of Massachusetts**

| Physiographic Region | Wetland Types |
|---|---|
| Western highlands | Deep fresh marsh |
| | Shallow fresh marsh |
| | Seasonally flooded flats |
| | Fresh meadow |
| | Bogs |
| Berkshire valley lowland | All types |
| Connecticut valley lowland | All types |
| Central upland | Deep fresh marsh |
| | Shallow fresh marsh |
| | Seasonally flooded flats |
| | Fresh meadow |
| | Bogs |
| Boston–Sudbury basin | All types |
| Seaboard lowland | Deep fresh marsh |
| | Shallow fresh marsh |
| | Seasonally flooded flats |
| | Fresh meadow |
| | Bogs |
| Coastal plain | All types |

1. *Landform contrast* is the amount of visual edge manifested in the form of object dominance or spatial enclosure of the wetland in reference to a given landform.
2. *Landform diversity* is the variety of shape and/or mode or origin of landforms surrounding, adjacent to, or part of a wetland.
3. *Wetland-edge complexity* is the degree of irregularity of the physical boundary of the wetland where it meets a landform or vegetated edge.
4. *Associated water-body size* is the area of any lake, pond, or reservoir, or the length of a river or stream that borders, goes through, or is part of a wetland.
5. *Diversity of associated water bodies* is the number of different types of water features surrounding or comprising the given wetland.
6. *Surrounding land-use contrast* is the amount of contrast generated by the difference in vegetative and structural height and texture between the wetland and the adjacent land use or uses.
7. *Surrounding land-use diversity* is the amount of contrast generated by the different vegetative and compatible land uses bordering a wetland.
8. *Wetland-type diversity* is the number of variety of different wetland types or micro-landscapes within the wetland itself.
9. *Internal wetland contrast* is the amount of contrast generated within a wetland by differences in vegetative and water height and in texture.
10. *Wetland size* is the gross area of the continuous wetland area.

A measuring and rating procedure was developed on a scale from 1 to 5, with 5 the highest and 1 the lowest. The procedure was substantiated from research results of behavioral scientists. (For a full discussion of the development of and sources for the rating system, see Smardon, 1972 and 1975.) Table 9.3 displays the measuring and rating for the resource variables.

*Weighting the Visual-Resource Variables:* After each variable is rated, the score is adjusted by using significance coefficients based on two criteria, immutability and multiple value. Immutability is the degree of permanence. The landscape attributes that are more permanent are more valuable for visual-cultural values because they are less likely to be changed naturally or by man's actions. Immutability in the landscape attribute means long-term benefits without extra efforts, such as maintenance, to sustain visual, recreational, and educational quality (Fabos, 1971). Immutability was rated on a scale from 1 to 3, with 1 representing high mutability (vegetation) and 3 representing immutability (landform) (see Table 9.4).

The other criterion, multiple value, compensates for some variables having multiple-use values (visual, recreational, and educational), whereas other variables are significant for only one use value. The significance coefficients for visual resource variables are calculated by multiplying the number of use values (visual, recreational, and educational) that the given variable pertains to by the immutability number (see Table 9.4).

The overall visual resource is computed with the algebraic formula:

$$m = 1...11$$

$$\sum_{t=1} (RVm)SCm = X$$

where
$RV$ = visual-resource variable
$SC$ = significance coefficient
$m$ = number of visual-resource variables
$X$ = visual resource value

Higher scores indicate greater visual, recreational, and educational value. Thus evaluation Level 2, the visual-resource evaluation system, can be used to rate inland wetlands from the highest to the lowest values. If a wetland did not receive a high enough score to be eliminated from further analysis, the evaluation process continues to Level 3.

### Level 3: Multiple Cultural-Enhancement Values of Inland Wetlands

The purpose of Level 3 is to acknowledge the man-made or cultural attributes, both positive and negative, of wetlands. A cultural attribute may increase the visual-cultural value to society (for example, greater accessibility). At the same time, pollution may decrease the visual-cultural values of a wetland.

*Cultural-Enhancement Variables and Corresponding Landscape Dimensions:* Cultural variables are what Lewis et al. (1969) term "extrinsic," which can be defined as "man-made changes, adaptations, and additions to the natural resources" (p. 23). Thus cultural variables are concerned with the existence or nonexistence of man-made effects, which can both add to and detract from the natural resource value. The cultural-enhancement variables are briefly defined:

1. *Educational proximity* is the measure of elementary schools, high schools, and colleges to a wetland area.
2. *Physical accessibility* is the degree of accessibility to a wetland by trail or road, and accessibility within the wetland by boat, trail, or road.
3. *Ambient quality* is the physical condition of the wetland as indicated by the lack of water pollution, air pollution, high noise level, and visual misfits or noncompatible land uses.

Table 9.5 summarizes the measurement and rating processes of the cultural-enhancement variables. The rating scales are the same as Level 2 (see Figure 9.2).

*Weighting the Cultural-Enhancement Variables:* The cultural variables are weighted by using significance coefficients or multipliers. The criterion used was the relative importance of the variable to visual, recreational, and educational quality. A summary of the significance coefficients, the maximum points possible per variable, and the total number of points possible from the Level 3 evaluation are shown in Table 9.6.

A wetland's rank in relation to other wetlands may change from the rank received in Level 2 owing to the ratings given in Level 3. Its rank may increase or decrease.

A wetland's score after a Level 3 evaluation is the cultural-enhancement value of the wetland site for visual, recreational, and educational quality. This can be expressed algebraically as:

$$n = 1...3$$

$$\sum_{t=1} (CV_n)SC_n = Y$$

where
$$
\begin{aligned}
CV &= \text{cultural enhancement} \\
&\quad \text{variable} \\
SC &= \text{significance coefficient} \\
n &= \text{number of cultural variables} \\
Y &= \text{cultural-enhancement value}
\end{aligned}
$$

When a wetland is ranked with other wetlands after the Level 3 evaluation, it can be ranked on its cultural-enhancement value (y) alone, or with both scores from the visual, recreational, educational resource value and the cultural-enhancement value (x + y) to yield the total visual-cultural resource value (z). Furthermore, the visual-cultural resource values can be expressed in dollars if an economic valuation is conducted as developed by members of our economics subproject.

## Economic Valuation

The inland-wetland assessment model described earlier (see Figure 9.1) shows the evaluation of three separate resource values of wetlands: wildlife-habitat, visual-cultural, and water-resource values. Each separate study developed a submodel to assess the qualities of all wetlands in Massachusetts. The submodels did not valuate, however, the economic value to society of any of these resources. The landscape planner may rank a highly rated wetland for visual-cultural value as number 10 among 130 wetlands. But what can a decision-maker who needs to translate ratings into monetary values be told? He or she may use the economic valuation submodel developed by our resource economists.

The economics subproject of the wetland study developed techniques to estimate visual-cultural, wildlife-habitat, · and water-supply values of wetlands. In addition, benefits to society resulting from flood control by preserving wetlands were included (Gupta, 1973). We describe here only the technique used to obtain values for the visual-cultural wetland resources (Gupta and Foster, 1973).

The basis for the economic valuation of visual-cultural values was provided by data on land purchases made by conservation commissions in Massachusetts during the fiscal year 1972. The open-space value was assumed to correlate visual, recreational, and educational values in Level 2. Particular attention was paid to open-

**Table 9.3 Measuring and Rating Procedures for Visual-Resource Variables**

| Visual-Resource Variables | Landscape Dimensions | Measurement Process | Rating Procedure | |
|---|---|---|---|---|
| 1 Landform contrast | Relative relief | Calculate difference between wetland elevation and adjacent landform height. | Assign rating. | Adjacent landform height (ft) / Rating<br>800–1000  5<br>600–800  4<br>400–600  3<br>200–400  2<br>0–200  1 |
| | Ratio of relative relief to wetland width | Divide relative relief of adjacent landform by average width of wetland. | Multiply ratio by 3. | Average two ratings |
| 2 Landform diversity | Number of landform types | Count number of different landform types on and surrounding wetland. | Assign rating. | Number of landform types / Rating<br>6  5<br>5  4<br>4  3<br>3  2<br>2  1 |
| 3 Wetland-edge complexity | Wetland-edge configuration | Measure outer edge, length of wetland (S). | Plug into formula<br><br>$$\dfrac{S}{2\sqrt{\pi A}}$$ | Wetland-edge configuration / Rating<br>5.0  5<br>4–5  4<br>3–4  3<br>2–3  2<br>1–2  1 |
| | | Measure total area of wetland (A) | Assign rating | |
| 4 Associated water-body size | Navigable length of stream by canoe (100 CFS discharge) or acreage of pond or lake | Measure navigable length (mi.) or acreage. | Assign rating. | Miles / Rating  Acres / Rating<br>12–15  5   101+  5<br>9–12  4   51–100  4<br>6–9  3   21–50  3<br>3–6  2   9–20  2<br>3  1   8  1 |

| # | Factor | Description | Method | | Rating criteria |
|---|--------|-------------|--------|---|-----------------|
| 5 | Associated water-body diversity | Number of water bodies are in or adjacent to wetland | Count number of water bodies in or adjacent to wetlands. | Assign rating. | **Number of water bodies** — **Rating**<br>5+ — 5<br>4 — 4<br>3 — 3<br>2 — 2<br>1 — 1 |
| 6 | Surrounding land-use contrast | Difference between average height of wetland vegetation and average height of surrounding land use | Determine height class of wetland vegetation and height class of surrounding land use. | **Average heights** — **Height class**<br>0' — 1<br>0–2' — 2<br>2–4' — 3<br>4–15' — 4<br>15'+ — 5<br><br>Assign rating | **Height class combinations** — **Rating**<br>1/5 — 5<br>2/5, 1/4 — 4<br>1/3, 2/4, 3/5 — 3<br>1/2, 2/3, 3/4, 4/5 — 2<br>same heights — 1 |
| 7 | Surrounding land-use diversity | Number of height classes and wildlife habitat classes bordering wetland | Count number of height classes and wildlife habitat classes bordering on wetland and average both figures. | **Wildlife habitat classes**<br>woods<br>brush<br>grass<br>cultivation<br>water<br><br>Assign rating | **Average** — **Rating**<br>5 — 5<br>4 — 4<br>3 — 3<br>2 — 2<br>1 — 1 |
| 8 | Wetland-type diversity | Number of wetland types | Count number of different wetland types within a given wetland. | **Wetland types**<br>Bog<br>Deep fresh marsh<br>Shallow fresh marsh<br>Seasonally flooded flats<br>Fresh meadow<br>Shrub swamp<br>Wooded Swamp<br><br>Assign rating | **Number of wetland types** — **Rating**<br>5 — 5<br>4 — 4<br>3 — 3<br>2 — 2<br>1 — 1 |
| 9 | Internal wetland contrast | Internal wetland-edge contrast | Measure length of edges between different heights and measure total length of interior wetland edges, exclusive of perimeter. Determine percent of total edge occupied by each height-class combination (see 6 above). Multiply edge percentage by height-class combination rating (see 6 above) and add for rating. | Assign rating | **Rating**<br>5<br>4<br>3<br>2<br>1 |
| 10 | Wetland size | Size of wetland in acres | Measure wetland acreage. | Assign rating | **Acres** — **Rating**<br>501–1000 — 5<br>251–500 — 4<br>101–250 — 3<br>51–100 — 2<br>10–50 — 1 |

Table 9.4   Weighting the Visual-Resource Variables

| Natural Resource Variable | Landform (3) | Water Body (2) | Vegetation (1) | Visual (1) | Recreation (1) | Education (1) | Significance Coefficient | Highest Possible Rating | Highest Possible Total Score |
|---|---|---|---|---|---|---|---|---|---|
| Landform contrast | × | | | × | | | 3 | 5 | 15 |
| Landform diversity | × | | | | × | × | 6 | 5 | 30 |
| Associated water-body size | | × | | × | | | 2 | 5 | 10 |
| Associated water-body diversity | | × | | × | × | × | 6 | 5 | 30 |
| Wetland-edge complexity | × | | | × | × | × | 9 | 5 | 45 |
| Land-use contrast | | | × | × | | | 1 | 5 | 5 |
| Land-use diversity | | | × | × | × | | 2 | 5 | 10 |
| Wetland-type diversity | | | × | × | × | × | 3 | 5 | 15 |
| Internal wetland contrast | | | × | × | | | 1 | 5 | 5 |
| Wetland size | | | × | | × | | 1 | 5 | 5 |
| | | | | | | | | Total | 170 |

space lands for nonactive recreation, the purchase of which was made with the aid of a subsidy of 50 percent of the price through the "Self-Help" program using state funds.

Data were collected from twenty-nine municipalities that received "Self-Help" assistance from the Division of Conservation Services, Massachusetts Department of Natural Resources, to acquire forty-two parcels of open-space lands totaling 1,516 acres. The average price was $1,608 per acre.

The range of the five highest prices of land purchased was from $3,684 to $5,769 per acre. Based on these results, the resource economists estimated what they considered to be a fair maximum price that society had agreed to pay for high-quality open-space land, which was $5,000 per acre. If 5.375 percent is used as the capitalization rate of interest, the public cost of acquiring visual-cultural benefits on such lands was calculated to be approximately $270 per acre per year. If 7 percent is used, the figure would be $350 per acre per year. Based on the

assumption of maximum willingness, $270 was accepted as an economic-value measure of the annual productivity per acre of visual-cultural values of high-quality wetlands as assessed by the visual-cultural evaluation. This economic figure was correlated with the high-quality visual-cultural values assessed by our submodel.

Similar values for wildlife-habitat, water-supply, and flood-control benefits were also derived by the economics subproject. Table 9.7 summarizes the results in terms of high, medium, and low values of benefits per acre of wetlands per year.

These benefits were then translated through computer analysis into capitalized values for different types of wetlands. They were capitalized over a number of years using two different rates of interest. A summary of the results is presented in Table 9.8.

The figures in the two right-hand columns imply that, given a rate of interest, society is supposedly better off purchasing and preserving a wetland for its accrued benefits so long as its price is less than or equal to the respective figures in the table.

## Potential Utility of the Visual-Cultural Submodel

In this section we discuss the third study objective, which is to ensure that the visual-cultural wetlands assessment submodel has utility at all decision-making levels and scales. Illustrating the utility of the submodel can be done by showing who can use it, how they can use it, and what tasks it can be used for.

At the site scale, an inland wetland could be rated by a wetland owner—whether a private individual, conservation commission, state agency, or federal agency—to see if the individual wetland achieves a high, middle, or low score for visual-cultural values. The score may indicate the desirability of preserving or protecting the wetland, developing it for multiple or single use, or trading it for another use. Ideally, the wetland score for visual-cultural values as well as other values, such as water supply and wildlife habitat, could serve as a preliminary assessment for the wetland owner of the degree of difficulty the owner might expect from an agency in obtaining a permit to alter the wetland.

At the town scale, the ideal user would be

**Table 9.5 Measuring and Rating Procedures for Cultural-Enhancement Variables**

| Cultural-Enhancement Variables | Landscape Dimensions | Measuring Process | Rating Procedure |
|---|---|---|---|
| **1** Educational proximity | Proximity of elementary and high schools | Measure distance to closest school along existing roads. Measure distance to closest college along existing roads. | Distance zone (mi.) adjacent — Rating: 0–1 → 5; 1–5 → 4; 5–10 → 3; 10–15 → 2; 15+ → 1. Distance zone (mi.) adjacent — Rating: 0–10 → 5; 10–20 → 4; 20–30 → 3; 30–50 → 2; 50+ → 1. Average two ratings |
| **2** Physical accessibility | Number of access types | Check wetland and surroundings for different types of access to and on the wetland. Access types: Trail access, Boat access, Road access, Trail access | Access types — Rating: 5 → 5; 4 → 4; 3 → 3; 2 → 2; 1 → 1 |
| **3** Ambient quality | Number of ambient-quality problems | Check for number of ambient problems on or near wetland. Ambient problems: Water quality, Air quality, Noise level, Visual quality, Misfits | Number of problems — Rating: 0 → 5; 1 → 4; 2 → 3; 3 → 2; 4 → 1 |

**Table 9.6   Weighting the Cultural-Enhancement Variables**

| Cultural Resource Variable | Visual (1) | Recreational (1) | Educational (1) | Significance Coefficient | Highest Possible Rating | Highest Possible Total Score |
|---|---|---|---|---|---|---|
| Educational proximity | | | × | 1 | 5 | 5 |
| Physical accessibility | × | × | × | 3 | 5 | 15 |
| Ambient quality | × | × | × | 3 | 5 | 15 |
| | | | | | | — |
| | | | | | | 35 |

town or city conservation commissions, town selectmen, planning boards, and city-town planners. Conservation commissions in Massachusetts and their parallels in other states could use the visual-cultural submodel to rate various wetlands within their own towns or cities. The rated wetlands could then be ranked to help determine which wetlands should be acquired first, using money from the state's "Self-Help" program or the equivalent and/or federal outdoor-recreation programs. The visual-cultural resource value could be translated into the economic worth of the wetland by using the economic valuation. This would help to indicate whether the land is worth preserving

**Table 9.7   Monetary Equivalents of High, Medium, and Low Values of Annual Benefits of Wetland Preservation**

| Type and Nature of Benefits | Dollar Values of Benefits per Acre of Wetlands | | |
|---|---|---|---|
| | High | Medium | Low[a] |
| Wildlife | 70 | 35 | 10 |
| Visual-cultural | 270 | 135 | 30 |
| Water supply | 2,800 | 1,400 | 400 |
| Flood control | 80 | 40 | 10 |

[a] The dollar figures of low benefits bear no proportionate relationship to the high figures.

*Source:* Gupta, 1973, p. 153.

solely for its visual-cultural values for a certain acquisition price. A combined economic valuation, including water-supply, wildlife-habitat, and flood-control values, might indicate to the conservation commission that the purchase price is more than worth the combined values of the wetland.

At the regional scale, planning agencies or comparable agencies in other states would be ideal users. In Massachusetts, planning agencies could use the visual-cultural submodel to rate and rank wetlands on a regional basis to indicate priorities for preservation of wetlands, especially regional wetland systems.

At the state scale, planning agencies could use the visual-cultural submodel or the larger inland-wetlands assessment model to rate inland wetlands statewide. This could indicate preservation priorities for wetlands with visual-cultural values of statewide significance, water-supply values, wildlife-habitat values, wetlands with single "outstanding" values for educational and scientific use, and even wetlands for flood-control purposes as outlined in the economic valuation. The economic valuation would indicate whether the wetlands should be purchased with state funds.

Interstate users would be primarily federal wetland regulatory agencies, such as the Environmental Protection Agency and the Corps of Engineers under Section 404 of the Water Pollution Control Act, which pertains to dredge and fill permits in water bodies. Other potential federal users are land-management agencies, such as the Forest Service, the National Park Service, the Bureau of Land Management, the Bureau of Reclamation, Fish and Wildlife Service, and the Department of Defense. In addition, certain federal agencies offer specific programs and advice to local agencies. Wetland evaluation could become part of programs administered by the Soil Conservation Service, the Extension and Education Administration, and the National Park Service.

With some alteration the submodels could probably be used on a national scale for rating wetlands. The assessment systems could be used to indicate wetland areas of extremely high natural value or "outstanding" wetlands that would merit national status for preservation. River basins commissions and the Corps of Engineers could use the visual-cultural, wildlife-

Table 9.8  Summary of the Computer Analysis Showing the Nature of Benefits from Preserved Wetlands and Their Capitalized Values per Acre, Massachusetts, 1972

| | Nature of Benefits | | | Capitalized Value of Wetland Benefits per Acre at (percentage) | |
|---|---|---|---|---|---|
| Wildlife | Visual-cultural | Water supply | Flood control | 5.375 ($) | 7 ($) |
| High | High | High | High | 59,000 | 64,000 |
| High | High | Medium | High | 33,800 | 26,000 |
| High | High | Low | High | 15,200 | 11,700 |
| High | High | None | High | 7,800 | 6,000 |
| Medium | Medium | None | Medium | 3,900 | 3,000 |
| Low | Low | None | None | 700 | 500 |
| High | Low | None | None | 1,800 | 1,400 |
| Low | High | None | Low | 5,300 | 4,100 |
| Low | Low | None | High | 2,200 | 1,700 |
| Low | Low | High | Low | 53,000 | 40,700 |
| Low | Low | Low | Low | 8,300 | 6,400 |

*Note:*  Figures in the two right-hand columns have been rounded to the nearest $100.

*Source:*  Gupta, 1973, p. 175.

habitat, and water-supply submodels, and especially the economic valuation of flood-control benefits of wetlands, to rate wetland systems on an interstate river-basin scale.

This partial listing of possible users and the possible uses of the visual-cultural submodel or the overall inland-wetlands assessment model merely indicates the value of a comprehensive wetland assessment system. There are many more probable uses of the system at many different scales.

The visual-cultural submodel is an assessment system for measuring the visual-cultural values of inland wetlands. As an integral part of the overall inland-wetlands assessment model, it could help to facilitate better wetland-use decision making. It is needed now. Land-use allocation questions concerning wetlands are in the news every day and confront many decision-making bodies on many political levels and geographic scales.

It should be realized, however, that the system as a whole has not been thoroughly tested through actual use. Evaluation Level 2 has been extensively pretested in the field to deter-

mine if there is a good point spread between rating scores and to see if the variables account for reasonable differences in visual-cultural value. Level 2 sample ratings were also compared with expert panel ratings of the same wetlands. Evaluation Levels 1 and 3 have not been developed to the same degree.

To improve the model, research is proposed in three areas. First, the design of the model should be modified in such a way that the average conservation commission member could use it. Then, through the use of the model, additional necessary changes and modifications should be made to improve the submodel.

Second, the validity of the submodel should be improved through behavioral studies and by testing each variable and criterion, as well as the overall structure of the submodel. Perhaps new, additional variables should be developed to improve the value-rating procedure.

Third, assessment systems for evaluating the visual-cultural values of the large surrounding landscapes of wetland environment might be developed. Many of the variables and assessment principles used in this study are central to visual-cultural values for many other types of environments.

In short, much more research is needed in assessment systems to enable better environmental-resource decision-making.

# References

Beaumont, A. B. 1956. *Classification of soils in Massachusetts*. Washington, D.C.: U.S. Government Printing Office.

Central Massachusetts Regional Planning District. 1967. The nature of open space. In Chap. 2, *Open space and recreation*, pp. 7–8. Worcester, Mass.

Commonwealth of Massachusetts. 1966. *An act relating to the protection of flood plans*. Chap. 131, Section 40, General Laws, Dec. 20. Boston.

———. 1971. *An act permanently protecting the coastal marshes and inland wetlands of the Commonwealth*. Senate Bill 1439, May, Boston.

Fabos, J. Gy. 1973. *Model for landscape resource assessment: Part I of the Metropolitan Landscape Planning Model (METLAND)*. College of Food and Natural Resources Research Bulletin 602. Amherst: University of Massachusetts.

Fenneman, N. M. 1938. *Physiography of eastern United States*. New York: McGraw-Hill.

Golet, F. C. 1972. *Classification and evaluation system of freshwater wetlands as wildlife habitat in the glaciated Northeast*. Ph.D. dissertation, University of Massachusetts, Amherst.

Gupta, T. R. 1973. Economic criteria for decisions on preservation and alteration of natural resources with special reference to freshwater wetlands in Massachusetts. Ph.D. dissertation, University of Massachusetts, Amherst.

Gupta, T. R., and Foster, J. H. 1973. Valuation of visual-cultural benefits from freshwater wetlands in Massachusetts. *Journal of the Northeastern Agricultural Economics Council* 2(1):262–73.

Lacate, D. S. 1969. Guidelines for bio-physical land classification. In *Canada Land Inventory*. Ottawa: Department of Regional Economic Expansion.

Leopold, L. B. 1969. *Quantitative comparison of some aesthetic factors among rivers*. Geological Survey Circular 620, Washington, D.C.

Lewis, P. H., Jr., and Associates. 1969. *Upper Mississippi River comprehensive basin study. Appendix B: aesthetic and cultural values*. Madison, Wis.

Lynch, K. 1960. *The image of a city:* Cambridge: Harvard University and MIT Press.

MacConnell, W. P. 1971. *Remote sensing twenty years of change in the human environment in Massachusetts*. College of Agriculture Cooperative Extension Service, University of Massachusetts, Amherst.

MacConnell, W. P., and Garvin, L. E. 1956. Cover mapping a state from aerial photographs. *Photogrammetric Engineering* 22 (September): 702–7.

Maryland State Planning Department. 1968. *Catalog of natural areas in Maryland*. Publication 148. Baltimore: State of Maryland.

Natural Areas Criteria Committee of the New England Botanical Club, Inc. 1972. Guidelines and criteria for the evaluation of natural areas. A report prepared for the New England Natural Resources Center, Amherst, Mass., mimeo.

Olin, P., et al. 1971. Vermont scenery classification and analysis. Prepared for Planning Department, State of Vermont. Amherst, Mass.: Research Planning & Design Associates, Inc. Unpublished.

Shaw, S. P., and Fredline, C. G. 1956. *Wetlands of the United States*. Circular 39, USDI, Fish and Wildlife Service. Washington, D.C.: U.S. Government Printing Office.

Smardon, R. C. 1972. Assessing visual-cultural values of inland wetlands in Massachusetts. Master's thesis: University of Massachusetts, Amherst.

———. 1975. Assessing visual-cultural values of wetlands in Massachusetts. In E. H. Zube, R. O. Brush, and J. Gy. Fabos, eds. *Landscape assessment: Value, perceptions, and resources*. Stroudsburg, Pa.: Dowden, Hutchinson and Ross.

USDA, Economic Research Service. 1968. *Open space: Its use and preservation*. USDA Miscellaneous Publication 1121. Washington, D.C.: U.S. Government Printing Office.

USDI, Fish and Wildlife Service. 1954. *Wetlands inventory of Massachusetts*. Boston: Fish and Wildlife Service, Office of River Basin Studies, Region V.

USDI, National Park Service. 1954. *Parks for America*. Washington, D.C.: U.S. Government Printing Office.

Zube, E. H. et al. 1970. *North Atlantic regional water resources study. Appendix N: Visual and cultural environment*. Amherst, Mass.: Research Planning and Design Associates, Inc.

Portions of this chapter previously appeared as "Assessment of Visual-Cultural Values of Inland Wetlands in Massachusetts" in Ervin H. Zube et al., *Landscape assessment: Value, Perception and Resources* (Stroudsburg, Pa.: Dowden, Hutchinson & Ross, 1975). Reprinted by permission of the publisher.

# 10 Procedures and Methods for Wetland and Coastal Area Visual Impact Assessment (VIA)

## RICHARD C. SMARDON, with MICHAEL HUNTER

## Introduction

The purpose of Visual Impact Assessment (VIA) of any landscape is to determine the significance and/or severity of visual resource quality change from anticipated activities or land uses that are to take place on or adjacent to that landscape. Since the appreciation of visual resource landscape quality takes place through interaction of the landscape and the viewer, visual impacts are not restricted to the two dimensional geographic boundaries of the landscape itself. The landscape appreciated includes the total three-dimensional envelope of the area, its background, and atmosphere as perceived by the viewer. Examples of visual impacts are physical changes to the landscape, including, but not limited to, adding structures, changing or modifying landforms, water bodies, or vegetation, and obstructing views.

Consideration of visual impacts as a legally mandated procedure is clearly delineated by the National Environmental Policy Act[1] for federal actions. This legal mandate is also expressed by EPA's guideline regulations under Section 404[2] procedures as described in Chapter 2 and the President's executive order,[3] which neatly ties 404 procedures to the National Environmental Policy Act and specifies a broad range of federal activities to be included. Many state agency activities in the United States are potentially involved with environmental impact assessment procedures and more specifically visual or aesthetic impacts under mini-NEPAs. Specific consideration of VIA procedures depends on the language of these acts and the guiding regulations. Use of VIA for wetland landscapes in both inland and coastal contexts, in summary, depends on formal determination of a federal action under NEPA or

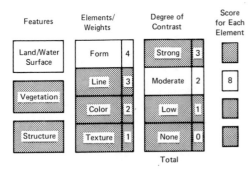

Figure 10.1. BLM's contrast rating system.

Section 404, a state action under mini-NEPA or state wetlands act (see Chapter 2 for specific acts), or in some instance where the visual impact of a proposed change to a wetland area is deemed to be a locally significant issue.

Previously, as with visual-cultural assessment in general, VIA was thought to be strictly a subjective assessment that cannot be methodologically defended or replicated. However, advances have been made in VIA methodology through research efforts. Of course there are still some problems with standards of practice and methodology, but they are equivalent to those experienced by other scientists working to develop accepted productivity assessment procedures for wetlands.

## Literature Review

An extensive amount of literature addresses visual resource management in general (see Smardon et al., 1982). The purpose in this chapter is to review VIA studies that pertain to (1) wetlands and coastal areas and (2) to current VIA methodology research. Some of the findings from this literature will then be incorporated in the VIA methodological framework to be developed later in the chapter.

VIA methods according to Palmer (1981) have involved three methodological approaches of: professional appraisal, predictive models, and public evaluation. In actuality, most of the VIA methods in the literature use a combination of these approaches, or they use research regarding predictive models and public appraisals to yield a field-effective professional appraisal method. VIA methods also differ in their focus of intended application. Some methods are meant to be used for all types of land-use changes, while some were developed for specific land-use changes.

### Agencywide VIA Methods

Probably the broadest methodology is the contrast-rating VIA system developed by the USDI Bureau of Land Management (1980a). The procedure as used by BLM operates in the following manner:

1. The landscape character as expressed by land features or water bodies, vegetation, and structures is described in terms of form, line, color, and texture.
2. The proposed activity for that particular locale is described in terms of form, line, color, and texture introduced or modified.
3. A contrast rating is then made by multiplying preestablished numerical values of form, line, color, and texture *for* land/water bodies, vegetation, and structures multiplied *by* the estimated degree of contrast (strong −3, moderate −2, weak −1, none −0) to yield subtotals of contrast ratings for land/water texture, vegetation, and structures (see Figure 10.1).
4. If the contrast ratings exceed "allowable" levels set according to the BLM Manual, then the project/feature element of greatest contrast is to be redesigned, the basic presumption being in most cases that too much contrast is "bad" or "not desirable."
5. The process is then repeated after the redesign.

This process is useful in that it provides a record of the landscape as it is and as it will be in the proposed project. It can be used to document which physical portion of the project needs to be reworked or redesigned (e.g., landfill cuts reduced, less vegetation disturbed, structures reduced in size). It can provide the legal documentation for taking action to ensure that mitigating actions are implemented, so from an administrative procedural point of view, the process provides many advantages.

The U.S. Forest Service uses a Visual Absorption Capability (VAC) analysis, primarily for assessing forest-harvesting-induced visual impacts.

VAC determines how much can be done to a

**VISUAL ABSORPTION CAPABILITY**

| Factors | | Variables | Rating | V1 | V2 | V3 |
|---|---|---|---|---|---|---|
| OBSERVER POSITION | Superior | +300' - +500' | 1 | | | |
| | | +100' - +300' | 2 | 2 | 2 | |
| | Normal | ±100' | 3 | | | |
| | | -100' - -300' | 4 | | | |
| | Inferior | -300' - -500' | 5 | | | |
| OBSERVER DISTANCE | Foreground | 0 - ¼ mi. | 1 | | | |
| | | ¼ - ½ mi. | 2 | | | |
| | Middle-ground | ½ - 1 mi. | 3 | 3 | 3 | |
| | | 1 - 2 mi. | 4 | | | 4 |
| | Background | 2+ | | | | |
| VIEW DURATION | Long | 30+ sec. | 1 | | 1 | |
| | | 10 - 30 sec. | 1 | | 1 | |
| | Short | 5 - 10 sec. | 3 | | | 3 |
| | | 3 - 5 sec. | 4 | 4 | | |
| | Glimpse | 0 - 3 sec. | 5 | | | |
| LANDSCAPE DESCRIPTION | | Feature | 1 | | | |
| | | Focal | 2 | | | 2 |
| | | Enclosed | 3 | 3 | 3 | |
| | | Panoramic | 4 | | | |
| | | Other | 5 | | | |
| SLOPE | Very Steep | 45+% | 1 | | | |
| | Steep | 30 - 45% | 2 | | | |
| | Moderate | 20 - 30% | 3 | | | |
| | Gentle | 10 - 20% | 4 | | | |
| | Very Gentle | 0 - 10% | 5 | 5 | 5 | 5 |
| Lowest rating is the Key Viewpoint | | | | 17 | 14 | 18 |

Summary

VISUAL ABSORPTION CAPABILITY

5 - 13 Low
14 - 16 Intermediate
17 - 23 High

**Figure 10.2.** Sample rating system showing visual-absorption capability.

landscape site before its visual absorption capability is exceeded. Contrast rating as used by BLM, on the other hand, determines whether a proposed change to the landscape would cause an acceptable or unacceptable level of contrast with that specific site.

VAC combines physical factors of the existing landscape, highly changeable perceptual factors, existing visual quality factors (form, line, color, texture), and proposed-activities factors (scale, configuration, duration, frequency) to determine the VAC score for that particular landscape (see Figure 10.2). A low VAC score is restrictive, and a high score means much more activity can be allowed. The VAC score range is then compared to the existing visual mangement objective(s) already determined for that area (see Figure 10.3).

These are the two existing federal-agency-related VIA methods. They are professional ap-

| LANDSCAPE MANAGEMENT GUIDE MATRIX | | | | |
|---|---|---|---|---|
| I-Most Restrictive ↓ V-Least Restrictive | VISUAL QUALITY OBJECTIVE | | | |
| | Retention | Partial Retention | Modification | Maximum Modification |
| Visual Absorption Capability — Low | I | II | III | V |
| Inter-mediate | I | III | IV | V |
| High | II | III | IV | V |

**Figure 10.3.** Matrix for identification of appropriate landscape management guides.

praisal methods in that they are meant to be used by professional VRM practitioners in the field. They are also meant to be predictive; the assumption is made that the key variables that explain most of the visual impact do, indeed, predict visual impact.

### Individual Practitioner/Academic VIA Methods and Research

Probably one of the earliest documented methods of VIA was developed by R. Burton Litton (1973). Litton explains how to study landscape visual impacts by setting up "landscape control points" (LCPs), a network of permanently established observation sites. The visible landscape can be plotted by direct field observations, by laying out a series of sections as rays from a single LCP, or by a computerized mapping technique. Photographs and sketches can be used to document landscape characteristics as they are and then with the modifications in place. A case study applied this VIA analysis to the Teton National Forest in Wyoming. This approach was strictly a professional appraisal, but it delineated some important principles of visual documentation and simulation.

Another early study, partially based on previous studies at Harvard University (Jacobs and Way, 1968), was done for the Corps of Engineers by Steinitz and Way (1970). The Urbanizing Watershed study dealt with the relationship of visual impact to land-use change "like/dislike," perceived "naturalness" of the landscape context, the vegetative opacity of the landscape, the area ratio of impacting land use to existing landscape, and the color spectral difference (or tonal difference) between land use and landscape. A photographic matrix containing different landscape/land-use combinations was used to elicit responses from study participants. Conclusions were that visual impact of land use can be predicted by (1) vegetative opacity of the landscape or the area ratio between land use and landscape and (2) their tonal contrast. These objective variables are screened, according to the authors, by a subjective evaluation (like/dislike) of the form (or land use) introduced to the landscape. The authors found that no significant differences existed between the visually trained and untrained subsamples. It should be noted that most landscapes used for this study were distinctly northeastern, which limits the relevancy of the vegetative opacity variable for many western landscapes. A later study (Hendrix and Fabos, 1975) done with a similar set of landscapes and land uses concluded that visual land-use compatibility, as judged by a cross section of respondents, played a significant role in explaining visual resource quality. Again, this study dealt with northeastern urbanizing landscapes. Note that the variable *compatibility* is well supported by the previous two studies.

The following literature deals with siting issues involved with large or dominant man-made alterations of the natural landscape. This is in contrast to the previous work, which dealt with less dominating activities in more urbanizing landscapes.

A substantial amount of work has been done through the firm of Jones and Jones in Seattle. This work was initiated through a joint project with Battelle Pacific Northwest Laboratories to develop a methodology to evaluate predictively changes in visual quality of a landscape as a result of siting a nuclear facility (Jones et al., 1975). This methodology uses the variables of *intactness, vividness,* and *unity* to account for change in visual quality. The basic method, combined with procedures to select representative viewpoints, amount of facility visibility, viewing distance, observer position, determination of viewing populations, and visual simulation, has been used to assess visual impacts from other activities, including dams, roads, and power lines. (Ady et al., 1979).

In recent work by Jackson, Hudman, and England addressing the issue of visual impact of high-voltage transmission lines, the factors that accounted for the largest percentage of variance include (1) dominance or harmoniousness of the introduced structure and (2) whether the poles are highly salient or close to the viewer:

Transmission lines become important in environmental assessment only when they are highly visible in environments which otherwise have little evidence of man's impact. The degree of negative impact in such settings increases as power lines become more visually *dominant.* In urban areas or other settings which are not regarded as 'natural', power transmission lines do not significantly distract from the aesthetic quality of the scene. (Jackson et al., 1978, p. 165)

This study involved 1,500 participants, who were shown eighteen sets of 35-millimeter transparencies of four scenes. Rankings were compared for each transparency through the use of preference proportions, Luce Scaling, and Thurstone Scaling. Analysis of scale scores revealed that environmental preference was highly uniform regardless of socioeconomic or other variables.

Daniel and Boster (1979) conducted visual assessments of forest stands using *scenic beauty* as the variable. They now have sufficient data to begin to develop a computer-aided management tool that will predict scenic beauty based on proposed management practices for specific forest types (Daniel and Schroeder, 1979). The scenic beauty estimation method has also been used to compare black-and-white sketches, color sketches, and color slides for simulating landscape modifications (Schomaker, 1978).

Finally, Wohlwill has done extensive research testing the variables *ambiguity, complexity, congruity,* and *novelty* in relationship to man-made structures introduced to the landscape (Wohlwill, 1978, pp. 3–5, 23; Wohlwill and Harris, 1980). This work involved two studies, using students as the predominant sample. The first involved visual simulation (photographs of scale models) of different land uses placed in three types of California coastal-zone environments. The second used slides of a mix of man-made structures in eastern park environments. Results from the coastal study showed that color and size contrast correlated highly with judgments of visual impact. However, judgments of appropriateness of land use with the environmental context was not straightforward (i.e., a lumber mill was judged appropriate to a "scenic" wooded coastal setting typical of northern California).

The second study showed a high level of agreement concerning the role of *congruity* or fittingness in evaluative judgments of different park scenes with varying amounts of man-made features (i.e., buildings, roads, bridges, signs and special purpose facilities for eating, entertainment, and recreation). In both studies the primary landscape alteration/modification was the addition or variance of the man-made structures. As will be noted later, there is a significant difference in the ease with which respondents react to structures introduced to the landscape as opposed to landform, water-body, and vegetational changes.

The development and use of VIA methods has proceeded rapidly in the last decade. Arising largely from a confluence of legal mandates, governmental administrative policies (Smardon, 1979), and the progressive accumulation of research on landscape perception (Craik and Feimer, 1979; Elsner and Smardon, 1979; Zube, 1976), these methods are generally intended to provide land-use managers with objective information concerning the impact of land-use activities on the aesthetic quality of the landscape. This information can be incorporated in the decision-making process, with aesthetic factors taking their place alongside the other important environmental, economic, and social factors concerning land-use options.

An important assumption underlying the inclusion of aesthetic factors through VIA systems in the decision-making process is that they will foster more effective, judicious decisions. That goal can be attained only if the information provided by VIA methods is accurate and systematic. Obviously, the greater the inaccuracy of a given measurement system, the greater is the likelihood and possible magnitude of an error in the decision. This issue is of critical significance where land-use management is concerned, since decisions involving land use often have long-term consequences. Thus the underestimation of the visual impact of a land use might result in unnecessary degradation of the visual quality of the landscape, while an overestimation might result in modification, curtailment, or disallowance of the activity, which in turn could cause considerable social and economic disruption. To avoid these pitfalls, VIA methods of sufficient technical quality should be employed (for a discussion of technical standards in VIA, see Craik and Feimer, 1979). Minimally, the technical-performance features of VIA systems must be evaluated so that decision-makers will know the margin of error.

Closely related issues to margin of error of any given VIA methodology are the legal issues of (1) adequacy of visual analysis given the context of existing laws and policy and (2) soundness of the basic methodology. Many federal and some state statutes call for explicit consideration and treatment of aesthetic or visual resources for certain federal/state actions or within certain land areas administered by federal/state agencies (Smardon, 1978).

Visual resource methodologies are being more closely scrutinized in courtrooms and administrative hearings, for basic adequacy and soundness. The ability of any VIA methodology to stand up to such legal tests is strongly related to the methodological properties of reliability, validity, and generalizability.

## Issues of Reliability, Validity, and Generalizability

The quality and utility of a measurement method is largely a function of three properties: reliability, validity, and generalizability. Reliability refers to the consistency and precision of measurement; it reflects the degree to which the obtained measures are replicable in the same or similar circumstances, as well as the attainable level of discrimination among the objects of interest. In the context of VIA, reliability represents the degree to which a measure accurately reflects variation among landscape and land-use conditions. Validity refers to the degree to which a measure represents the construct or variable of interest. Reliability has important implications for validity in that the reliability of a measure delimits its attainable validity. Validity provides an estimate of the degree to which a method is able to capture meaningful variations in the aesthetic quality of the landscape and to depict the impact of land-use activities upon it. Finally, generalizability refers to a specification of the conditions for which the attained levels of a reliability and validity are representative. Factors that could constrain the generalizability of reliability and validity coefficients might include physiographic landscape and land-use conditions, background characteristics of observers used in the VIA procedure, media of presentation of landscape and land-use conditions, and the extent of pertinent landscape and land-use information available to VIA users confronted with specific problems.

The research reported here is directed at an evaluation of the reliability, validity, and some aspects of the generalizability of selected observer-based VIA methods. The emphasis has been on VIA methods with a potentially wide application to a broad array of landscape and land-use contexts. Related findings on the reliability of VIA methods were reported by Feimer, Craik, Smardon, and Sheppard (1979). The following research and findings summarize three years of work done in two increments. The first research increment, which involved the author, Professor Nicholas Feimer of Virginia Polytechnic Institute, and Dr. Kenneth Craik of the University of California, also appears in an article by Feimer, Smardon, and Craik (1981).

## The First Increment: VIA Research

Nineteen pairs of landscape scenes were employed to assure the effectiveness of the VIA rating procedures. One member of each pair depicted the landscape before the imposition of a given land-use activity and the other after the imposition of that activity. Since preimpact and postimpact versions of scenes controlled for observer position, lighting, time of day, season, and other variables that are likely to affect ratings were not available, either the preimpact or postimpact version of each pair had to be simulated. Simulation entailed either removing or imposing the land-use activity by means of retouching and painting techniques. (USDI, Bureau of Land Management, 1980b). All stimuli were presented to subjects as 35-millimeter projected slides.

The landscape scenes and land-use activities selected include a broad range of conditions common to the western half of the United States. Landscapes ranged from densely forested mountains to sparsely vegetated desert, and land uses included agricultural, water management, mining, energy, and road development activities (see Smardon, 1979).

Research participants were drawn from three populations: (1) graduate and undergraduate students (n = 54) from the Berkeley and Davis campuses of the University of California; (2) federal agency administrative personnel (n = 87); and (3) landscape architects (n = 41) from the U.S. Department of Agriculture's Forest Service.

Ratings were obtained through three quasi-experimental treatment conditions. In one (Prepost) condition, participants were presented with the preimpact version of each scene; they completed direct ratings for all of the landscape dimensions except *importance* and *severity* (which implicitly apply to impacts) immediately after viewing each scene. Next, they were presented with the postimpact version of the scene and completed contrast ratings as well as the importance and severity ratings. Subsequently, the Visual Contrast Rating method (USDI, Bureau of Land Management, 1980a) was also completed. Thirty-nine members of the student subsample were in this condition.

In a second treatment (Post condition), participants were merely presented with the postimpact version of each scene and subsequently completed direct ratings on all landscape dimensions except importance and severity. Fifteen members of the student subsample were in this condition.

A two-hour training period preceded both the Prepost and Post conditions to familiarize raters

with the rating procedures, and with the contrast-rating method in particular. In addition, a subsample of the Post condition (students at the University of California, Davis; n = 27) was given feedback on its reliability levels periodically during the data collection period. However, no differential effects were found in conjunction with feedback and, hence, the subsamples were collapsed into one group for subsequent data analysis.

In the third treatment (Global condition), participants were presented with both the preimpact and postimpact version of each scene, with the order of presentation counterbalanced for subgroups within the condition. Immediately after viewing each version of the scene, the participants completed the scenic beauty ratings. After viewing both versions of each scene, severity (of visual impact) ratings were completed. After all ratings were completed, participants in this condition were asked to reflect on and then rank-order the criteria they employed for judgments of both scenic beauty and severity (of visual impact). The entire federal agency and BLM/Forest Service samples were in this condition. Because of time constraints, they completed only fourteen of the nineteen pairs of scenes.

The two different testing conditions were employed to provide contrast ratings and independent preimpact and postimpact direct ratings. The third testing conditions served primarily to provide an independent set of criterion data on evaluations of aesthetic quality to assess the generalizability of the direct and contrast ratings to observer groups from the first two conditions. Subjects were either untrained in VIA (federal agency sample) or trained but with differential training and experience (BLM/Forest Service sample).

### Reliability

Intraclass correlation (Ebel, 1951), the average reliability of a single rater was employed to assess the reliability of ratings. It is derived from a one-way analysis of variance, where scenes (n = 19) are a random variable that constitute the main effect; residual variance is the error term. Because of missing observations for some research participants on various scenes and rating dimensions, it was also necessary to use

**Table 10.1**   **Average Single-Rater Reliabilities for Direct and Contrast Ratings**

| | Rating procedure | | |
|---|---|---|---|
| | Preimpact | Postimpact | Contrast |
| Dimension | (n = 29)[a] | (n = 17) | (n = 29)[a] |
| Ambiguity | .19 | .07 | .04 |
| Color | .13 | .25 | .34 |
| Compatibility | .07 | .28 | .03 |
| Complexity | .49 | .13 | .15 |
| Congruity | .17 | .25 | .03 |
| Form | .45 | .14 | .15 |
| Importance | — | .27 | .13 |
| Intactness | .34 | .31 | .04 |
| Line | .19 | .05 | .22 |
| Novelty | .31 | .22 | .07 |
| Scenic beauty | .18 | .20 | .03 |
| Severity | — | .21 | .25 |
| Texture | .41 | .24 | .24 |
| Unity | .21 | .25 | .01 |
| Vividness | .26 | .24 | .10 |
| Mean | .26 | .21 | .12 |

[a] n is the average number of raters used in computation of reliabilities and follows Snedecor (1946).

an average value for the number of raters when calculating the reliability estimates. The appropriate value ($\bar{n}$) was obtained by an application of Snedecor's (1946) formula. The results of these analyses are given in Table 10.1. It is apparent that the reliability coefficients vary substantially within each rating condition. However, both preimpact and postimpact direct ratings tend to manifest higher levels of reliability than do contrast ratings. The average reliabilities for preimpact direct, postimpact direct, and contrast ratings are 0.26, 0.21, and 0.12, respectively. The lower reliability of contrast ratings is most likely a function of the cognitive complexity of the rating task. Rather than merely evaluating some aspect of the landscape and expressing it in terms of scale value, the contrast rating requires a quantitative appraisal of the difference between two variations of the same stimulus, with all the associated mental transformations. Nonetheless, even for direct ratings, the obtained coefficients are clearly below acceptable standards (generally coefficients of 0.70

and higher are desirable). However, these coefficients represent reliabilities for a single rater, and while single raters are often used in applied settings, higher reliability is generally obtained when composite ratings from panels of independent judges are employed (Craik and Feimer, 1979; Feimer et al., 1979; Zube, 1976). In the current context, for example, applying the Spearman-Brown prophecy formula (Guilford, 1954) to the average reliabilities of the respective rating procedures reveals that a panel of ten independent judges would increase the average reliability to above 0.70 for both sets of direct ratings, and to 0.58 for contrast ratings.

### Validity

Change in scenic beauty was employed as criterion measure to represent change in aesthetic quality resulting from the imposition of land-use activities. It was obtained by subtracting the average postimpact direct rating of scenic beauty from the concomitant average preimpact direct ratings. This criterion measure for each subsample was then intercorrelated with change scores for each of the direct ratings (again subtracting the average postimpact from the average preimpact ratings) and average contrast ratings of the student subsample.) Since the average score for each rating dimension was used (i.e., a multirater composite), the reliabilities of the dimensions employed in the analysis were at an acceptable level (an average reliability above 0.70 for all rating procedures). The intercorrelation of change in scenic beauty with direct rating-change scores and contrast ratings is given in Tables 10.2 and 10.3. Three direct rating dimensions (compatibility, congruity, and intactness) are significantly correlated with change in scenic beauty for two of the three samples. These variables indicate that changes in the character and coherence of the landscape seem to be associated with perceived changes in aesthetic quality. Changes in land-mass features (form) appear to be an important component of the resulting incongruity. Interestingly, none of the contrast ratings generated by the student sample correlates significantly with change in scenic beauty. However, for both the federal agency sample and the BLM/Forest Service sample, severity (of visual impact) does correlate significantly ($r = 0.76$ and $0.68$, respectively; $p < 0.01$) with scenic-

**Table 10.2 Scenic Beauty Change Scores Correlated with Direct-Rating Change Score**

| Direct Rating Dimensions (student sample) | Change in scenic beauty | | |
|---|---|---|---|
| | Student sample (n = 19) [a] | U.S. federal agency sample (n = 14) [a] | BLM/Forest Service sample (n = 14) [a] |
| Ambiguity | .38 | .27 | .08 |
| Color | .04 | .04 | −.13 |
| Compatibility | .67 [c] | .38 | .72 [c] |
| Complexity | −.06 | .19 | .15 |
| Congruity | .56 [b] | .53 | .67 [c] |
| Form | .59 [c] | .47 | .78 [c] |
| Intactness | .31 | .62 [b] | .71 [c] |
| Line | .47 [b] | −.07 | .23 |
| Novelty | .25 | .30 | .34 |
| Texture | .06 | .26 | .20 |
| Unity | .66 [c] | .09 | .52 |
| Vividness | .06 | .08 | .23 |

[a] n is the number of scenes.
[b] $p < 0.05$
[c] $p < 0.01$

*Note:* Correlations are based on average ratings of respective samples completing ratings.

beauty change. Those severity ratings do not predict from one group to the other. Thus the current data analysis indicates that contrast ratings tend not to manifest prediction of change in scenic quality that generalizes to other populations.

### Criterion Rankings

To gain more insight about *which* variables may be important for explaining change in visual quality of severity of visual impact, a separate qualitative analysis was done on data collected parallel to the Feimer and Craik (1979) study. First, after subjects had finished their quantitative ratings, they were asked to rank-order, with the most important first, criteria that they had used in rating preimpact scenes for scenic quality. Second, they were asked to list criteria in the same fashion for assessing severity of visual impact as seen in both the preimpact and postimpact scenes. The theoretical underpinnings of the approach are that after they had finished rating the nineteen sets of preimpact and postimpact scenes they would have some criteria in mind when rating the slides.

This raw data was 143 sets of two pages of rank-ordered criteria for 66 federal-agency personnel (nonvisually trained), 38 students (primarily in landscape architecture), and 39 landscape architects (U.S. Forest Service and BLM). These criteria were then sorted into categories of physical, aesthetic, and global for assessing scenic quality, and categories of visual impact (see Tables 10.4 and 10.5). Within these categories criteria were listed with their rank orders and number of times mentioned. Criteria were counted as additive only if, by content analysis, they were similar. A number of subcategories were then collapsed into the major categories in Tables 10.4 and 10.5. However, only the major criteria with their number of times mentioned and mean rank order are listed.

A number of comments can be made about each table. First are the criteria for assessing *scenic quality.* Under the *physical criteria* category landform or landform features are most often mentioned in two groups out of three, followed by lack of man-made features in two out of three groups. A surprise is the mention of climatic effects or atmospheric factors in all

**Table 10.3   Scenic Beauty Change Scores Correlated with Contrast Ratings**

| Contrast ratings Dimensions (student sample) | Change in scenic beauty | | |
|---|---|---|---|
| | Student sample (n = 19)[a] | U.S. federal agency sample (n = 14) | BLM/Forest Service sample (n = 14)[a] |
| Ambiguity | −.12 | −.16 | .17 |
| Color | .08 | −.21 | .19 |
| Compatibility | .23 | −.29 | .14 |
| Complexity | .29 | −.29 | .45 |
| Congruity | .18 | −.11 | .21 |
| Form | .13 | −.03 | .04 |
| Importance | .10 | .19 | .08 |
| Intactness | .15 | −.04 | .22 |
| Line | .25 | −.35 | −.17 |
| Novelty | .10 | −.15 | .23 |
| Scenic beauty | .19 | .07 | .34 |
| Severity | .24 | .22 | .38 |
| Texture | .07 | −.05 | .29 |
| Unity | .19 | −.29 | .19 |
| Vividness | .17 | −.01 | .26 |

[a] n is the number of scenes.

*Note:* Correlations are based on average ratings of respective samples.

three groups. Vegetative features or characteristics also play a strong role for all three groups. The mixed agency personnel respond more similarly to the landscape architects as a whole than to the students.

In the category of *aesthetic* criteria, color qualities are most often mentioned in two out of three groups, followed by variety/diversity and overall contrast. The landscape architects use more aesthetic criteria than either of the two other groups.

In Table 10.5 under the *visual aesthetic* category, the size/scale of alteration of the introduced impact, distance/scale/visibility, and spatial location are the three major variable sets mentioned beside overall contrast/clash, color, form, line, and texture pattern. Color and form are the most mentioned of the traditional variables used by BLM, which infers that the existing BLM weightings may be questioned, as was found by Feimer and Craik (1979).

In the *global aesthetic* category the criteria mentioned in all three groups are (1) obvi-

ousness/dominance, (2) fittingness/appropriateness/compatibility, and (3) naturalness. The latter two criteria are mentioned in Feimer and Craik (1979) as being highly significant in explaining people's underlying motives for their quantitative rating patterns.

The major finding that may be deduced from these two charts is that major variables are not presently included in BLM's visual contrast rating system. Some of these variables are those that can be related to the observed physical properties of landscapes, and some are not. Global nonphysically related variables do not have utility for visual impact assessment purposes because the effect cannot be identified on the physical site and therefore cannot be mitigated. Most often mentioned as aesthetic factors related to severity of visual impact were the naturalness, fittingness, compatibility, and appropriateness of the intrusion. The most prominent physical criteria cited were change in color and form qualities and magnitude of the intrusion.

**Table 10.4    Results of Open-Ended Response:   Criteria for Assessing Scenic Quality**

| | Mixed Agency Personnel (N = 66) | | | Students (N = 38) | | | Landscape Architects (N = 39) | | |
|---|---|---|---|---|---|---|---|---|---|
| | * | Criteria | ** | * | Criteria | ** | * | Criteria | ** |
| Physical | 24 | Landform features | 2.77 | 16 | Landform character-istics | 2.27 | 18 | Landform features | 2.58 |
| | 21 | Vegetative features | 3.19 | 20 | Vegetative character-istics | 2.9 | 9 | Vegetation and lifeforms | 3.67 |
| | 17 | Water | 2.47 | 7 | Water | 3.67 | 13 | Water | 2.46 |
| | 9 | Climatic effects | 3.44 | 13 | Climatic effects | 3.7 | 13 | Atmospheric factors | 3.38 |
| | 23 | Absence of man-made features/disturbance | 2.28 | | | | 17 | Man-made elements | 4.35 |
| Aesthetic | 37 | Color qualities | 2.06 | 23 | Color qualities | 2.9 | 28 | Variety/diversity of elements | 2.16 |
| | 17 | Variety/diversity | 2.06 | 23 | Variety/diversity | 2.6 | 26 | Color qualities | 3.27 |
| | 13 | Contrast | 2.2 | 24 | Contrast | 2.6 | 18 | Contrast | 2.93 |
| | 11 | Interestingness | 2.00 | | | | 8 | Interest | 3.87 |
| | | | | | | | 9 | Form qualities | 3.11 |
| | | | | | | | 5 | Line qualities | 3.2 |
| | | | | | | | 11 | Texture qualities | 3.7 |
| | | | | | | | 6 | Distinctiveness | 2.0 |
| Global | 11 | Naturalness | 1.45 | 14 | Pristineness/undisturbed naturalness | 2.86 | 12 | Naturalness/pastoral | 5.16 |
| | 13 | Composition | 2.77 | | | | 18 | Composition/harmony | 2.21 |
| | | | | 7 | Uniqueness/scarcity | 1.14 | 7 | Uniqueness/unusual | 3.43 |

*Number of times mentioned.
**Mean rank order from possible 1 to 7.

Thus, as in the correlation analysis, continuity in the general form of the landscape and the resultant compatibility of the land-use activity seem to be the most salient factors in the psychological appraisal of visual impacts. It must be stressed, however, that this analysis of rankings is only tentative. The reliability of the categories employed in this latter analysis and the consequent tallies have not yet been fully appraised.

## The Second VIA Research Increment: Stimuli, Research Participants, and Procedures

In the second round of VIA psychometric testing, twenty-five pairs of landscape scenes were employed to assess the participants' ability to use a modified VIA method. Thirty-five seniors and graduate students were trained to use the modified VIA method and were given copies of the manual developed by Sheppard and Newman (1979).

Similar to the previous years' testing, the participants were shown the preimpact 35-millimeter slide, asked to describe the existing landscape, then shown the postimpact scene adjacent to the preimpact scene and asked to describe and rate the visual impact using the modified contrast-rating forms. Again, the visual stimuli were simulated. Simulation entailed either removing or imposing the land-use activity by means of retouching and painting techniques (USDI, Bureau of Land Management,

Table 10.5   Results of Open-Ended Response:  Criteria for Assessing Severity of Visual Impact

| Mixed Agency Personnel (N = 66) | | | Students (N = 38) | | | Landscape Architects (N = 39) | | |
|---|---|---|---|---|---|---|---|---|
| * | Criteria | * * * | * | Criteria | * * | * | Criteria | * * |
| **Visual aesthetic** | | | | | | | | |
| 16 | Size of introduced impact | 2.0 | 6 | Size | 2.11 | 16 | Size/scale of alteration structure | 2.32 |
| 5 | Distance/scale | 2.0 | 5 | Distance/scale | 1.8 | 9 | Distance/visibility | 4.44 |
| 5 | Spatial location of introduced impact | 1.76 | 12 | Spatial location | 3.0 | 8 | Spatial location | 3.25 |
| 11 | Amount of Contrast/clash | 1.64 | 11 | Contrast | 3.09 | 39 | Contrast | 2.18 |
| 20 | Color qualities | 1.95 | 10 | Color qualities | 2.3 | 14 | Color qualities | 2.0 |
| 12 | Form/shape qualities | 2.23 | 3 | Form qualities | 1.67 | 13 | Form qualities | 2.07 |
| 10 | Line qualities | 2.0 | 5 | Line qualities | 2.8 | 6 | Line qualities | 2.67 |
| 4 | Textural qualities | 1.0 | 4 | Pattern | 2.75 | 6 | Textural qualities | 2.5 |
| **Global aesthetic** | | | | | | | | |
| 6 | Obviousness | 1.17 | 6 | Obviousness/blatency/obtrusiveness | 1.17 | 7 | Dominance over existing landscape | 1.43 |
| 9 | Fittingness/blending | 2.42 | 6 | Fittingness | 2.0 | 14 | Compatibility/appropriateness/fittingness | 2.92 |
| | | | 5 | Appropriateness/expectancy | 2.0 | | | |
| 18 | Naturalness | 1.61 | 9 | Unnaturalness | 1.89 | 5 | Naturalism/unnaturalness | 2.0 |
| 3 | Physical presence of disturbance | 2.67 | 8 | Overall visual change | 1.25 | 5 | Harmony w/existing landscape | 1.4 |
| | | | 9 | Aesthetic/visual quality of the setting before change | 2.33 | | | |
| **Associational** | | | | | | | | |
| 10 | Associated physical criteria | 3.11 | 7 | Associated environmental concern | 3.38 | 5 | Associated physical criteria | 2.2 |
| | | | 5 | Landform change | 2.2 | | | |
| 7 | Type of object introduced | 2.86 | 15 | Type of man-made introduced activity/structure | 3.27 | | | |

*Number of times mentioned.
**Mean rank order from possible 1 to 7.

1980b). The added landscape scenes and land-use activities were meant to create a more representative cross section of visual stimuli than before. To this end, the new visual stimuli were taken primarily of the Great Basin, canyonlands, the Great Northern Plains, and interior California landscapes with surface mining, coal-fired power plants, and geothermal energy development land-use activities.

After all rating forms and general environmental background forms were filled out, the forms were sent to Virginia Polytechnic Institute and Virginia State University, Blacksburg for keypunching and analysis. The testing was done as part of a visual analysis course taught at State University of New York, Syracuse. The following is a brief synopsis of the latest round of psychometric testing.

### Reliability

As indicated by Table 10.6, use of detailed visual contrast rating variables still falls below acceptable levels (< .70) of reliability between individual raters. The consistency of rater behavior using these detailed contrast-rating variables did improve significantly if one compares Table 10.6 results with Table 10.1 from previous testing. The additional guidance provided in the prototype manual is useful, but multiple raters are needed if significant levels of reliability are to be obtained. Table 10.7 indicates similar results for overall element components. Table 10.8 indicates reliability estimates for scale and spatial-dominance ratings.

### Validity

Ratings taken from the same SUNY, Syracuse, sample were correlated with change in scenic-beauty ratings for the same visual stimuli. In Table 10.9, those figures with asterisks indicate significant correlation with scenic-beauty change. Those variables that react in the same way as scenic-beauty change include *texture* contrast for structures, *scale* contrast for both land/water bodies and structures, and overall *spatial dominance*. Near-significant correlations with change in scenic beauty include *color* contrast for structure, *form* contrast for structures, *scale* contrast for vegetation, *scale* contrast overall, and *scale dominance*. A similar story can be seen in Table 10.10, where scale and spatial-dominance variables are highly intercorrelated with each other.

The results from the correlations and intercorrelations partially reinforce what has been found in other recent studies and in our own previous testing. First, it is much easier for people to judge the visual impact of structures than landform/water bodies or vegetation. Second, the variables that most consistently behave similarly to change in scenic beauty are scale contrast and spatial dominance for all situations, and texture, form, line, and color contrast for structures only.

## VIA Methods Applied to Wetlands and Coastal Areas

No standardized guidelines exist for conducting a visual impact assessment, but past assessments seem to have followed one of three approaches according to Palmer (1981): (1) professional appraisals, (2) predictive models, and (3) public evaluations. Professional appraisals are the most common and are discussed in the work of Baird

| Table 10.6 | Reliability Estimates for Visual Element Components of the Contrast-Rating Procedure | | |
|---|---|---|---|
| Scale | R[a] | R[b] | R[c] |
| Land/water bodies | | | |
| Color | .52 | .84 | .97 |
| Form | .35 | .73 | .95 |
| Line | .35 | .73 | .95 |
| Texture | .38 | .76 | .96 |
| Scale | .31 | .70 | .94 |
| Vegetation | | | |
| Color | .28 | .66 | .93 |
| Form | .24 | .61 | .92 |
| Line | .34 | .72 | .95 |
| Texture | .33 | .71 | .94 |
| Scale | .22 | .59 | .91 |
| Structures | | | |
| Color | .45 | .80 | .97 |
| Form | .55 | .86 | .98 |
| Line | .53 | .85 | .98 |
| Texture | .43 | .79 | .96 |
| Scale | .53 | .85 | .98 |
| Average ($\overline{X}$) | .39 | .75 | .95 |

[a] Reliability for one rater.
[b] Reliability for the average (composite) of five independent raters.
[c] Reliability for the average (composite) of the entire sample used to generate estimates (K = 35).

*Source:* Feimer, 1981.

et al. (1979) on the California coastal zone, Roy Mann (1979) on the Chesapeake Bay, and Smardon et al. (1980) on the outer banks of North Carolina. Predictive models tend to be geared more toward research than impact assessment (Palmer, 1981). The last approach, public evaluation, is based on public participation and input and is sometimes included as part of professional appraisals or the research behind the professional appraisal method.

## Professional Appraisals

### California LNG Terminal Siting

To locate potential California coastal-zone off-shore Liquid Natural Gas (LNG) sites and the types of terminals that might occupy those sites,

**Table 10.7   Reliability Estimates for Overall Element Components of the Contrast-Rating Procedure**

| Scale | R[a] | R[b] | R[c] |
|---|---|---|---|
| Color | .45 | .80 | .97 |
| Form | .47 | .82 | .97 |
| Line | .41 | .78 | .96 |
| Texture | .25 | .62 | .92 |
| Scale | .47 | .82 | .97 |
| Average ($\overline{X}$) | .41 | .77 | .96 |

[a] Reliability for one rater.
[b] Reliability for the average (composite) of five independent raters.
[c] Reliability for the average (composite) of the entire sample used to generate estimates (K = 35).

*Source:* Feimer, 1981.

**Table 10.8   Reliability Estimates for Scale and Spatial Dominance Ratings from the Contrast-Rating Procedure**

| Scale | R[a] | R[b] | R[c] |
|---|---|---|---|
| Scale dominance[d] | .54 | .86 | .98 |
| Spatial dominance | | | |
| Composition[e] | .41 | .77 | .96 |
| Position[e] | .27 | .65 | .92 |
| Backdrop[f] | .45 | .81 | .96 |
| Overall[d] | .40 | .77 | .96 |
| Average ($\overline{X}$) | .41 | .77 | .96 |

[a] Reliability for one rater.
[b] Reliability for the average (composite) of five independent raters.
[c] Reliability for the average (composite) of the entire sample used to generate estimates.
[d] Average number of raters per scene ($\overline{K}$) = 35.
[e] Average number of raters per scene ($\overline{K}$) = 32.
[f] Average number of raters per scene ($\overline{K}$) = 31.

*Source:* Feimer, 1981.

the California Coastal Commission authorized a study by Baird et al. (1979) regarding site selection and terminal feasibility for Liquid Natural Gas off-loading and storage as well as protection of the California coastal resources. The alternatives studied included island-based terminals, deep-bottom supported terminals, shallow-bottom supported terminals, floating terminals, semisubmergible, and a hybrid of land/sea-based concepts (Baird et al., 1979).

The study was conducted in three steps: design, location, and evaluation (ibid.). First, the conceptual designs for LNG storage facilities were designed by three different designer/engineer firms. These firms designed one floating and two bottom-supported facilities, as shown in Figure 10.4.

Second, zones were studied to ascertain a feasible site for an LNG terminal. This was done by the California Coastal Zone staff and consultants considering factors such as winds, waves, water depths, and safety. The result of this second stage was that seven zones off the southern California coast survived the initial screening. Of these seven, four were eventually recommended, as shown in Figure 10.5. A detailed list of reasons why zones were not recommended included terminal engineering problems; terminal system cost; operational reliability in delivering gas to California residents; public safety; adverse impacts on marine and coastal resources; conflicts with existing recreational, military, and other uses; and problems obtaining approvals (ibid.).

Third, the visual and scenic resources were evaluated. This involved three study aspects: (1) calculating the number of people exposed to views of proposed LNG facilities, (2) determining the percentage of time visible, and (3) analyzing the compatibility of the LNG activities with the coastal landscape viewsheds. The number of people exposed to a particular scene was determined from highway-use figures for coastal routes and residential-development density. The percentage of degree of visibility of the potential site zones from areas where impacts would be felt was determined from visibility data of percentage of the year that clear views of the coast were possible versus views obscured by fog.

Landscape compatibility (that is, existing industrial development versus none) was a key issue. To aid the landscape compatibility analysis, simulations (see Fig. 10.6) were created by air-brushing with watercolor dyes onto the photographs of the selected sites the various facility types at the proper scale. The simulations were useful to the Coastal Commission in three ways (ibid.): (1) policy decision-making, (2) report preparation, and (3) various workshops conducted and public presentations. The islands were undeveloped, while the coastal areas near the Ventura Flats contained oil and gas exploration development. The recommendations echoed the Coastal Commission's dual role to locate an LNG storage facility and to protect California's coastal resources. In summary, the proposed staff findings recommended a floating facility at the Ventura Flats as "the most appropriate site/facility combination" (ibid.).

### Chesapeake Bay Peer-Review Wetlands Study

To aid in the maintenance of existing Baltimore Harbor channels and the planning for future harbor development, the State of Maryland decided to locate a diked disposal area in the Upper Chesapeake Bay. A site for the facility was selected by the Maryland Department of Natural Resources (DNR) at Hart and Miller islands. The U.S. Army Corps of Engineers prepared an Environmental Impact Statement (EIS), but the DNR had outstanding questions concerning environmental impacts and contracted with Roy Mann Associates (RMA) to conduct a peer review of these questions (Mann, 1979). Environmental issues included visual impact, and the sites proposed for dredge-disposal areas also included wetland areas.

The visual impact assessment involved the evaluation of ten alternative sites. The methodology used, developed by RMA, is made up of four steps (ibid.): (1) determining significant viewable water surface, (2) defining the lateral viewing zones, (3) determining the numbers of people who had significant views of water surface, and (4) evaluating the visual quality of these views.

Given the dynamic nature of water, the surface of the dike would be visible in limitless combinations. In the first stage RMA limited its concentration to the significant viewable surface (see Figures 10.7, 10.8, and 10.9). As shown in

**Table 10.9   Correlation of Visual-Contrast-Rating Variables with Change in Scenic Beauty**

| Visual contrast rating variables | Scenic beauty change[a] |
|---|---|
| Color contrast | |
|   Land/water bodies | −.243 |
|   Vegetation | .027 |
|   Structures | .310 |
|   Overall | −.160 |
| Form contrast | |
|   Land/water bodies | −.089 |
|   Vegetation | .032 |
|   Structures | .375 |
|   Overall | .173 |
| Line contrast | |
|   Land/water bodies | −.094 |
|   Vegetation | .086 |
|   Structures | .367 |
|   Overall | .185 |
| Texture contrast | |
|   Land/water bodies | −.135 |
|   Vegetation | .074 |
|   Structures | .434[b] |
|   Overall | .251 |
| Scale contrast | |
|   Land/water bodies | −.497[b] |
|   Vegetation | −.320 |
|   Structures | .434[b] |
|   Overall | .378 |
| Scale dominance | −.359 |
| Spatial dominance | |
|   Composition | .205 |
|   Position | −.021 |
|   Backdrop | −.135 |
|   Overall | .406[b] |
| Total — Visual Impact Severity | .186 |

[a] Correlations computed across 25 scenes (i.e., $n = 25$).
[b] $p < .05$

*Note:* Change in scenic beauty is based on the difference between independent preimpact and postimpact ratings of scenes. The average (composite) ratings of the entire sample of raters were used in this analysis (see Tables 10.1–10.3 for composite reliabilities).

*Source:* Feimer, 1981.

**Table 10.10   Intercorrelations of Visual-Contrast-Rating Variables Significantly (p < .05) Correlated with Change in Scenic Beauty**

|  | Scale: Land/water bodies | Scale: Structures | Spatial dominance: Overall |
|---|---|---|---|
| Texture | | | |
| Structures | .17 | .56[a] | .18 |
| Scale | | | |
| Land/water | | | |
| bodies | — | −.64[a] | −.80[a] |
| Scale | | | |
| Structures | | — | .73[a] |
| Spatial dominance | | | |
| Overall | | | |

[a] p < .01

*Source:*   Feimer, 1981.

these figures, the significant viewable surface would be the water and wetland area that can be perceived above a minimum vertical angle or sight line (Figure 10.8), and where lateral-view exposure is more than 10° (see Figure 10.9). This delimited significant viewable surface can be further diminished by factors of distance, sea-surface characteristics, and atmospheric conditions.

The second step of the study was to determine the viewing zones, or viewsheds. RMA projected sight lines on a topographic map at 30° intervals over the full 360° around the proposed site locations and determined the impacted viewing zone from where views of the facility could be acquired (see Figure 10.10). This was corrected using aerial photos to reflect vegetation heights and building heights, which would serve to block sight lines (see Figure 10.8).

The third step was to determine the size of the affected viewing population. A considerable number of boaters use this part of the Chesapeake Bay, and figures for them were estimated using numbers of boats registered in the home port of the viewing zone. The number of residents was extrapolated from 1970 U.S. Census tract data. Automobile traffic figures

came from Maryland Department of Transportation road-use figures. These factors are shown in Table 10.11.

The last step, the visual-quality evaluation, involved constructing simulations of the facility on clear acetate and overlaying them on photographs of the potential locations. These were used to compare "before" and "after" views for each location in terms of obstruction of cross-bay views, compatibility of the dike with the foreground elements, and how much of the interior of the facility with its messy appearance is exposed to view. A rating scale of −5 to +5 was used to assess the impact.

In summary, RMA developed and applied criteria to assess the visual impact of several alternative locations of a near-shore-confined dredged-material facility. The methodology was based on professional evaluation similar to that of the previous study, but it varies in the geographic scale and range of activity.

### Cape Hatteras National Seashore Jetty Study

Maintaining the Cape Hatteras National Seashore has always been a battle against erosion. This state of constant ecological and physical change is common to barrier islands in many coastal waterways. The barrier islands of North Carolina "typically have a low vertical profile, are narrow, have a primarily sandy composition, and have exposure to high wave energy" (Smardon et al., 1980).

The channel at Oregon inlet (see Figure 10.11) has been maintained by the Army Corps of Engineers for years. Concerned with the erosion of the islands to the north and south of this channel, the Corps proposed and designed a set of twin jetties that would stabilize the area. The Corps prepared an EIS, but to settle outstanding questions on the visual impacts of this proposal, the National Park Service, Southeast Region, contracted Smardon et al. (1980) to conduct a visual impact assessment and suggest mitigative measures. Visual impacts were especially critical because the area is a heavily used recreation area as well as a wildlife sanctuary for migrating water birds.

The approach used for this study was a combination of procedures Smardon is developing for the Bureau of Land Management (Sheppard and Newman, 1979) and procedures used for

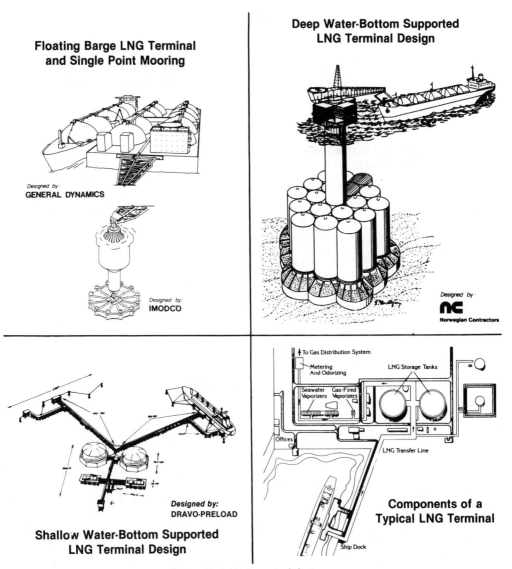

**Figure 10.4.** LNG terminal designs.

similar coastal shoreline visual impact assessments (Baird et al., 1979; Mann, 1979). It is made up of four steps: (1) describing the physical and visual environment, (2) ascertaining the type, number, and characteristics of recreational users in the area, (3) simulating the modification at key viewpoints, and (4) evaluating the visual impact and discussing mitigative measures (Smardon et al., 1980).

The first step was to describe and visually document the visual environment in its present state. The descriptive approach used a standardized vocabulary of elements of form, color, line, texture, scale, and spatial dominance (Sheppard and Newman, 1979). These same elements were later applied to the proposed modification to give a numerical rating of impact. This initial visual inventory was conducted on-site through interviews with Park Service employees and by taking color 35-millimeter slides. Care was

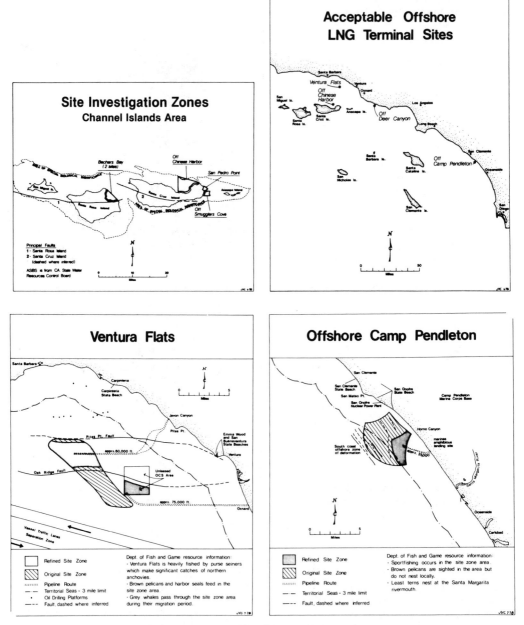

**Figure 10.5.** Acceptable offshore LNG terminal sites.

**Figure 10.6.** Preimpact scene and postimpact simulation off Santa Cruz Island.

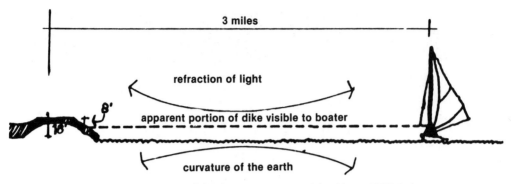

**Figure 10.7.** Visibility factors, open water (after Mann, 1979).

taken to document the camera angles and viewpoint locations and to provide scale clues within the photographs so that the simulations would be accurate (Figure 10.12).

The second step was to describe in detail the various recreational activities in the area and their general zones of occurrence. The recreational activities included swimming, sunbathing, charter-boat fishing, surf-fishing, off-road vehicle driving, beach walking, bird watching, and camping. This provided a working description for each impacted user population in terms of annual use, time of day, mode of arrival, and average amount of time per day spent in the activity. The information was derived from figures

in the EIS adjusted by information gathered in the on-site fieldwork (see Table 10.12).

The third step was to construct the simulations. The EIS provided for twin jetties constructed of either rough-cut rock transported by barge from nearby quarries in the north or cement dolos. Because of cost, Smardon et al. (1980) assumed that the rough-cut rock would be used for construction, so this material was used for the simulations.

The team selected eight possible viewpoints and narrowed them to two critical views (Figure 10.12). The two views were selected for simulation because they represented viewpoints that would have the largest number and duration of

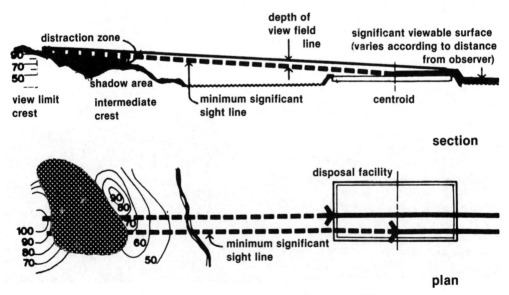

**Figure 10.8.** Distant-object visibility (after Mann, 1979).

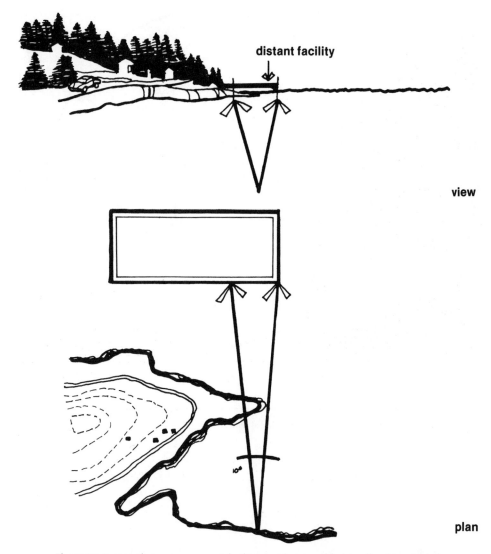

**distant facility**

**view**

**plan**

**Figure 10.9.** Lateral view exposure. A facility must be viewable laterally of terrain and objects to some significant degree if visual impact is to be assessed. A 10-degree lateral arc has been estimated as the average minimum lateral-view exposure necessary for significant visual impact to be recorded (after Mann, 1979).

recreational viewers. They also represented views where the jetties would be in the middle ground for the viewer, so they did not bias the view by putting the jetty too close to the viewer.

Because views in the Oregon Inlet area were found to be panoramic, the simulations were constructed using a series of sequential, matched color photographs of the interest area. An artist created the simulations on clear acetate overlays using colored inks and dyes, and they were mounted in a flip-up style to provide "before" and "after" views of the scene.

The fourth step, impact evaluation, was conducted by two team members trained in the Bureau of Land Management procedure (BLM, 1980a). This procedure employs professional appraisals (i.e., severe visual impact, medium, or no visual impact) with respect to the elements of form, color, line, texture, scale, and spatial dominance (Sheppard and Newman,

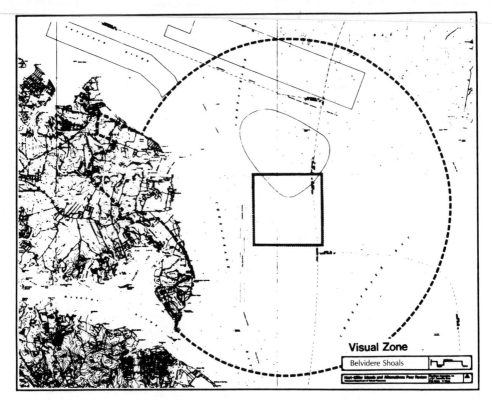

**Figure 10.10.** Sample viewing zone (after Mann, 1979).

**Table 10.11 Evaluation of Impacts on Existing Visual Quality**

| | Total residential viewing population | Selected major activity centers | Average daily traffic[2] | Recreational boaters[6] |
|---|---|---|---|---|
| Hart-Miller | 3,662 | 3,000[1] | | 19,825 |
| Black Marsh | 4,192 | — | | 19,825 |
| Hawthorn Cove | 4,779 | — | | 16,779 |
| Man O'War Shoals | 5,511 | — | | 10,183 |
| Patapsco River Mouth | 13,167 | — | 2,181,000[3] | 10,183 |
| 6-7-9 Foot Knolls | 3,899 | — | 29,890[4] | 21,607 |
| Belvidere Shoals | 4,638 | — | 29,890[4] | 21,607 |
| Sollers Point | 3,425 | — | 2,181,000[3] | 10,183 |
| Colgate Creek | 1,725 | — | 2,181,000[3] | 10,183 |
| Middle Branch | 3,841 | — | 31,620[5] | 10,183 |

[1] Maximum daily visitors; Rocky Point Park.
[2] Computed at 1.5 persons/vehicle
[3] One lane traffic; new Outer Harbor Crossing
[4] One lane traffic; Lane Memorial Bridge
[5] One lane traffic; Hanover Street Bridge
[6] Average no. of persons per boat = 2.82; includes water stored craft only

*Source:* (1) RMA telephone communication with Rocky Point County Park Manager. (3) Table 21 Outer Harbor Bridge Estimated Traffic and Revenue 1976–1985; Maryland Dept. of Transportation. (4-5) State of Maryland "Traffic Volume Map," 1974. RMA telephone communications with Bureau of Traffic Engineering, Md. Dept. of Transportation (June 1975). (6) Recreational Boating in the Continental U.S. in 1973; Coast Guard, October 1974, p. 51.

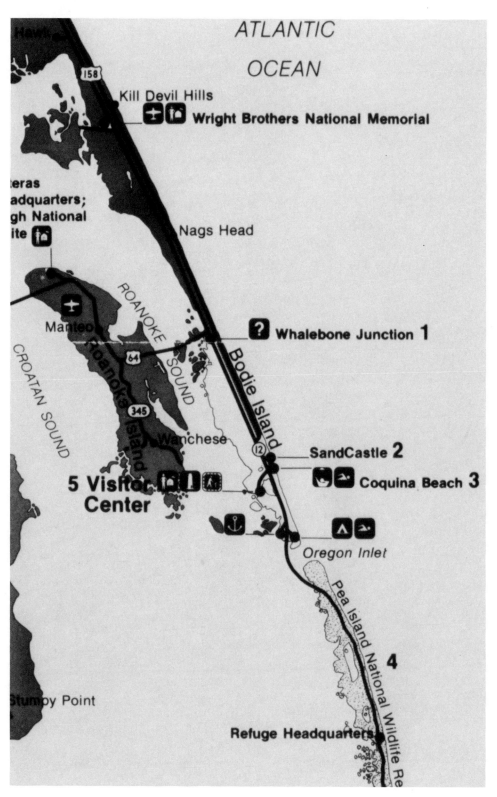

**Figure 10.11.** Oregon Inlet.

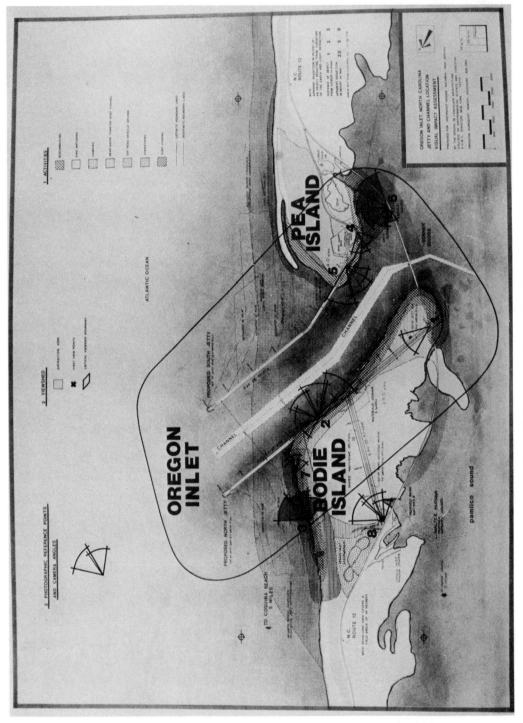

**Figure 10.12.** Oregon Inlet, visual analysis.

**Table 10.12 Comparative Recreation Activities: Effects of Jetty Alternative**

| Recreational activity | (Interdependent with all others) Camping: Oregon Inlet Campground | Bird watching (interdependent with Beach walking) | Beach walking | Off-road vehicle driving (interdependent with Surf fishing) | Surf fishing | Charter boat fishing | Sunbathing (interdependent with Swimming) | Swimming |
|---|---|---|---|---|---|---|---|---|
| Viewing duration of activity | Seldom | Substantial | Substantial | Intermittent | Substantial | Intermittent | Occasional | Intermittent |
| Annual use | 60,000 to 75,000 AVD | | | 12,000 Veh./yr. | 80,000 to 100,000 AVD | 4,164 trips | 11,000 AVD | 11,000 AVD |
| Average activity per day: ORV / NON | | 3.2 hours<br>1.4 hours | 2.1 hours<br>1.9 hours | 3 hours | 6 hours<br>3.5 hours | 8 hours<br>8 hours | 3.8 hours<br>4.4 hours | 3.8 hours<br>4.4 hours |
| Time/day | | | | | | 7 AM to 3:30 PM | | 8 AM to 4 AM |
| Time/year | March 15 to Dec. 14 | Late fall peak, all year | All year | All year | Spring/Fall | | | May 30 to Sept. 1 |
| Short-term (3-year) construction | Heavy equipment creates noise and dust. 50% reduction. Attractive nuisance. | Incompatible noise, dust. Disturbance of wildlife. | Heavy equipment creates noise and dust. | Access to some areas restricted or prohibited. | Access restricted or prohibited to surf-fishing areas. | Safety hazard to boaters from movement of construction materials by barge. Attractive nuisance. | Heavy equipment creates noise and dust. Reduced by 50%. | |
| Operation and maintenance | Noise associated with dredging for sand bypassing operation. | | 2,000 ft. of beachfront removed. Overcrowding. Sand bypassing. | 2,000 ft. of beachfront removed from ORV use. Overcrowding. Sand bypassing. | 7,000 linear feet of jetty crown for fishing off jetty. | Attract more boat fishermen near jetties. | Noise associated with dredging for sand bypassing operation. | |
| Cumulative long term | Additional pressure on NPS to expand campbround. | Increased incompatibility to bird watching activity. | Overcrowding. Decrease in quality experience. | Encourage illegal ORV use/vandalism. | Potential increase in fishing activity with attendant management problems. | Increasing incidence of small-boat accidents. | | |

1979). It involved three consecutive steps: (1) describing the existing landscape, (2) describing the landscape with the project in place using the simulations, and (3) contrasting the ratings for the existing and proposed conditions. Measures to minimize harm were suggested, such as laying the armor stone flat against the jetty side, providing guidelines for landscape treatment of the dredged spoil areas, and paving the top of the jetties to enhance recreational fishing.

In summary, Smardon et al. modified and applied criteria to assess the visual impact of twin jetties on the recreational community at Oregon Inlet. The methodology was based on professional evaluation similar to that of Baird et al. and Roy Mann Associates.

Although these VIA studies all were made for slightly different purposes, there are some common threads. The importance of visual simulation is common to all studies. It is used either to provide a vehicle for professional appraisals or to get the public to react to alternatives. Gauging the number of people affected by the visual impact of the proposed activity is another common thread. Tied with the numbers of affected viewers is a determination of affected views. In other words, what were the views of the visual impacted area that people could see? Some type of baseline determination of the landscape that is affected should be made. Do people value the affected landscape or feel strongly about it? Finally, what visual alternatives exist and how would the visual impacts be mitigated?

## Toward a VIA Methodological Framework

This discussion coalesces information presented in previous chapters as well as what we have learned from other VIA studies and research. Our objective here is to find some common procedures that serve as useful guidance in VIA of wetlands and coastal environments.

### Physical Landscape Description

The first step in VIA is to describe the wetland landscape from a physical/visual perspective. Variables specific to wetland areas such as those mentioned by Smardon and Fabos in Chapter 9 may be used, or slightly more abstract variables such as the form, line, color, texture, scale, or

spatial dominance of the existing wetland or coastal environment could be used. Rich but accurate verbal descriptors are useful, but visual documentation through photographs are essential. The VIA analyst needs to capture the visual character of the landscape before change. The perceived visual landscape changes as light conditions, seasons, and viewing angles change.

The angle of view from a key viewpoint may be established if the analyst knows which viewpoint will be most often perceived and which direction landscape perceivers will see the introduced activity. Such guidelines have been established by Litton (1973) with his landscape control points. If random shots of wetland and coastal environments are needed, Daniel and Boster (1979) developed a random technique of visually sampling an environment from all possible angles. More often than not, for wetland and coastal environments, views of wetlands or shorelines will be restricted, and Mann's process of determining significant viewable surface will need to be used. In other instances views will be unrestricted or panoramic. In such cases the photographic or media recording of the sample views should approximate what the landscape perceiver sees. So as outlined by Smardon et al. (1980) in the panoramic unrestricted visual environment of Cape Hatteras, panoramic composites of four to five 55-millimeter focal length shots were taken to be fabricated later into one continuous image. If views are more focal or enclosed, fewer photographs or smaller overall view angles can be used. All photographs should be carefully logged, including angle-of-view, time of day, film speed, lighting, and weather conditions (see Figure 10.13).

### Landscape-Viewer Sensitivity of Visual Access

The next basic step in the VIA process, which should be parallel with landscape description and documentation, is to determine who the landscape viewers or perceivers are, how many there are, and what they can or cannot see. If the VIA analyst has a situation of large numbers of landscape viewers, census data might be useful. Population census data is broken down by census tracts or blocks, which may or may not be useful when the analyst is concerned with a population spread out on a narrow shoreline or fringe of a wetland. In the latter situation

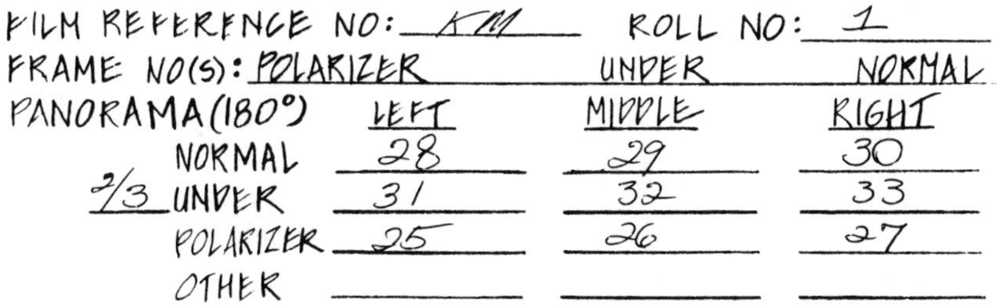

FILM REFERENCE NO: ___KM___   ROLL NO: ___1___
FRAME NO(S): POLARIZER_____   UNDER_____   NORMAL_____
PANORAMA (180°)   LEFT   MIDDLE   RIGHT
    NORMAL   28   29   30
  ²/3 UNDER   31   32   33
    POLARIZER   25   26   27
    OTHER   _____   _____   _____

**Figure 10.13.** Sample photo-log sheet.

windshield surveys from an automobile or by boat can best identify potentially affected publics. In still other cases management agencies such as the National Park Service in Smardon et al. (1980) had counts of different types of recreationalists on a yearly or daily basis. These latter sources also provided types of recreational activities that landscape perceivers engaged in. This may not be available in many cases, so the analyst may have to conduct a recreational-activity survey.

An important factor that the VIA analyst should know is what the affected public thinks about the visual impacted landscape – whether it values the landscape as it is. This is important because our VIA research indicated that people often make two decisions when asked to consider visual impact. The first one is whether or not they like the landscape. If they do value or like it, they then go on to assess the severity of visual impact from the projected activity. If they do not like or appreciate the landscape, they may not even bother with the second decision. So, existing studies that exist on the public's perception of the landscape are invaluable. If no such studies exist, the analyst must do two things: (1) ascertain preference or evaluative appraisals of the landscape as is and (2) gauge reactions to the change in that landscape.

### Visibility Assessment

Little guidance is available for visual analysts regarding visibility assessment procedures. However, Felleman has published a comprehensive monograph on the subject (Felleman, 1979) as well as a recent summary in the special visual issue of the *Coastal Zone Management Journal* (Felleman, 1982). Visibility of a given landscape is determined by the visual acuity of

the landscape observer or public and is dependent on light transmission via lines of sight from the landscape to the observer. Blocking the lines of sight is called "interposition" (see Figure 10.8). When viewing wetland or coastal landscapes, two especially relevant modifying visibility factors are (1) open water, which tends to cause partial interposition of vertical objects at distance over a water surface (see Figure 10.7), and (2) atmospheric effects, such as fog, which tend to blur or diminish what can be perceived. Another atmospheric factor is the position of the sun, which can result in front, side, or back lighting effects (Litton, 1968) (see Figure 10.14). Also seasonal lighting conditions can affect color hue, color value, sun angle, daylight time, probable light variations, and mean shadow lengths. The position of the viewer also affects what can be seen in the landscape. This is illustrated in Figure 10.15, which includes examples of observer inferior, normal, and superior positions.

Given all these variables that affect visibility of the environment itself and the viewer's ability to see the environment, the basic task at hand is to delineate (for most situations) what can be seen in the landscape via line-of-sight processes or, for VIA, where the impacting activity or land use can be seen from. Visibility or line-of-sight can be determined in the field by taking photographs, making sketches, map-notes, and videotapes, and using position markings, such as flags and stakes. For VIA visibility assessment, a recent technique is to erect a marker or even raise a balloon to the approximate height of a proposed structure to see how far away people can actually see the structure. This technique is not particularly useful for extremely low-lying horizontal modifications of the landscape. Mapped information or aerial photographs may also

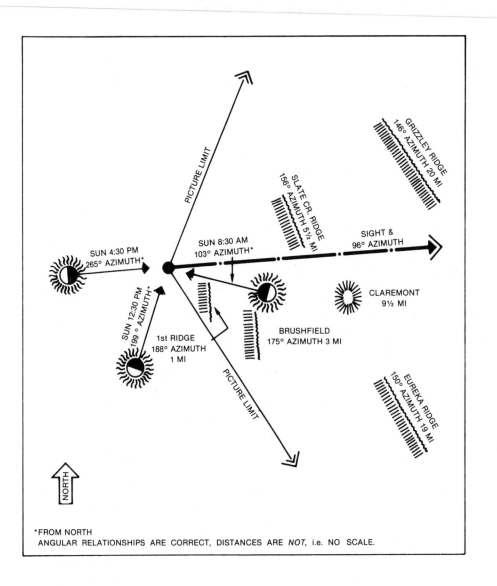

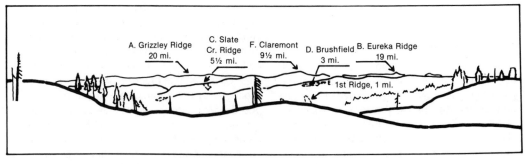

**Figure 10.14.** Light-source diagram (after Litton, 1968).

**Figure 10.15.** Superior (3), normal (2), and inferior (1) viewer position (after Litton, 1968).

be used to enhance fieldwork. This includes U.S. Geological Survey seven and a half minute quadrangles, forest-cover maps, or aerial photographs to determine where vegetation or landforms have obscured visibility via interposition. Vegetation visibility interposition will be seasonal in some cases, depending on the vegetation mix of deciduous versus conifers and length of seasons.

In some cases the analyst may be fortunate enough to have topographic elevational data or vegetation coverage converted to a computerized digital data base. For this, visibility of the landscape can be determined from any given point using computer algorithms such as VIEWIT (Travis et al., 1975). Most computer algorithms generalize the elevational data to a whole grid cell, rather than a point, so that accuracy is limited.

For wetland and coastal landscapes, gross topographic change is limited and blocking, or interposition effects of vegetation are predominant. Therefore, fieldwork complemented by vegetation mapping will prove most useful. For water-surface environments, an almost flat surface can be assumed, although slightly modified by factors reviewed from the Mann study (see Figures 10.7, 10.8, and 10.9). Lines-of-sight can be delineated from the impacting activity back toward the viewing population or affected public. If the view is not obstructed, determinations can be made about the length of shoreline or area where the public does have views of the introduced activity and the length of view: That is, in the foreground, middleground, or background (see Figure 10.16). Generally, the closer the viewer, the greater the impact. But to determine accuracy of affect and severity of impact, simulations from key viewpoints should be constructed. Line-of-sight analyses can also be used to determine view blockage. Again, if key

viewpoints are found and potential view blockage is possible, then detailed visual simulations may be needed. This is because some obstructions, such as a highway bridge on piers, may only partially block or segment views rather than completely block them. Depending on the position of the viewer looking past the highway bridge toward the landscape, some views may be blocked and others may not be.

### Determination of Key Viewpoints

The author has mentioned "key viewing points" several times. At this point in the analysis— when the analyst knows where the activity will be placed, where the viewing population is, what the activity patterns are, and the degree of visibility that the viewers have of the introduced activity—the selection of key viewpoints can be made (see Figure 10.11). If there are many possible views of the activity, there will necessarily be many key viewpoints. In other cases the viewers may be fewer in number or in restrictive situations. Visual simulations should be made of the key viewpoints to show the activity as it impacts the landscape.

### Impacting Activity/Land-Use Characterization

Once the analyst has determined what the landscape looks like and records it, who perceives it, and what is actually seen from specific locations, the question is, what is the visual nature of the impacting activity and how will it visually change the landscape? This question is partially answered by engagement in technology assessment: that is, investigating the proposed land use or activity and what it visually does in a generic way to the landscape.

In the author's research for the Bureau of Land Management, a vast array of visually impacting

| | Near Boundary | Far Boundary |
|---|---|---|
| Zones: | - - - - - - - - - - - miles - - - - - - - - - - | |
| Foreground | 0 | ¼ - ½ |
| Middleground | ¼ - ½ | 3 - 5 |
| Background | 3 - 5 | ∞ |

**Figure 10.16.** Foreground, middle ground, and back ground distances.

activities was encountered. Many of these activities were new or not well known, including forms of energy production and locatable minerals mining. Thus the analyst needs to find out as much as possible about the impacting activity in question. The Generic Visual Impact Checklist was developed by the author and Brian Dick to facilitate this (see Appendix A). Attention should be paid to ancilliary activities as well as the major impacting activity and different periods of development. Finally, all activities and subactivities should be classified in their effect on landforms, water bodies, vegetation, and structures already in the landscape. This will aid in later identification of potential visual impacts as well as accurate development of visual simulations.

There are many different forms of simulation techniques, but the basic concept is to delineate graphically what the landscape will look like with the activity in place. Note in this chapter that Baird et al.'s (1979) study used color paintings on photographic prints. Mann (1979) used perspective line drawings overlayed on black-and-white photographic prints, and Smardon et al.'s (1980) study used acetate overlays on top of multiple mounted color prints. There are many other visual-simulation techniques, and they are readily reviewed in a publication by the Bureau of Land Management (1980b).

Visual-simulation techniques include manual methods such as free-hand drawing sketches, rendering on a photograph, or using a scale model. Projection visual-simulation techniques include using overhead projectors or slide projectors to superimpose the image of the introduced activity on the image of the existing landscape. Computerized visual simulation techniques can be used to do computerized perspective rendering or to aid an artist in rendering photomontages with correct scale and perspective. Whatever visual-simulation technique is used, it should attempt to max-

imize the realistic portrayal of the impacting activity. The number of simulations depends on the number of major viewpoints of the impacting activity.

### Visual-Impact Assessment and Mitigation Summary

Given what we know about existing VIA methods as developed by researchers and agencies and as used by VRM practitioners in wetland and coastal environments, we are led to the critical question: What guidance is there for use of reliable, valid, and generalizable VIA rating methods? Will existing VIA rating methods, variables, and procedures developed by BLM and the Forest Service suffice, or are new or different procedures needed? The following are recommendations:

1. *Photographic documentation:* Little photo documentation of sites where VIA ratings have been done exists. In only one instance did we find a study where near-adequate photo documentation occurred (Environmental Associates, n.d.). Photo documentation for all sites prior to filling out VIA rating forms is absolutely essential for legal and technical reasons. This is called for in the EPA Guidelines regulations (see Chapter 2). Written descriptions are seldom adequate in themselves to capture the visual character of the area. A VIA form is a potential legal record of the site as is, and it may be needed in court proceedings if a future dispute over permit, lease, or environmental assessment occurs. Thus photo documentation, the written description, and the VIA rating of the site as is form a strong baseline for future examination. Useful guidelines for photo documentation can be found in Magill and Twiss, "A Guide for Recording Aesthetic and Biological Changes with Photographs" (1965), and Litton, "Landscape Control Points: A Procedure for Predicting and Monitoring Visual Impacts" (1973).

2. *Verbal/Written descriptive power:* The use of verbal and written descriptions of the unaltered and altered landscape needs to be improved. Landscape descriptors used for describing landscape visual-quality change are limited to only a few terms, and they are overused. Accurate descriptions may make it easier to do VIA ratings and to propose suitable measures to minimize visual impact. Interim approaches in-

clude (1) using sources of landscape-description terms that are appropriate for the environment, e.g., Litton et al. (1974) for water, wetland, and coastal environments. More long-term approaches include development of landscape adjective checklists suitable for different landscapes.

3. *Reliability of judgments:* As indicated by psychometric research, interindividual consistency in judgment is moderate for general ratings of landscape characteristics, but it is low for VIA ratings (see Feimer et al., 1979). Based upon preliminary results, three recommendations are made:

a. As many judges as possible should complete ratings for any given project, and their ratings should be averaged.
b. Ratings should be done independently of one another; joint efforts in assigning rating values cannot be considered to be more reliable than ratings by a single individual.
c. Whenever possible, high-quality simulation should be used to decrease problems raters have in conceptualizing impacts.

4. *The sophistication of VIA:* This should be comparable to the complexity, importance, or controversy of the project in question. For most projects a simple one-page rating form should suffice, especially if the project is typical and is structural in nature. If the activity or structure is special or complex, multiple independent (four or five) raters should be involved. If the activity involves extensive modification of land form/water bodies or vegetation, experienced VRM practitioner(s) should be involved.

5. *Variables:* For all typical projects/activities, the variables of *landscape compatability,*[4] *scale contrast,*[4,95] and *spatial dominance*[4] should be used as shown by the following sample rating form (see Figure 10.17). This one-page form should be supplemented by project description, location, and viewpoint delineation. Total weightings for all three variables should be equal. In a situation where a threshold of impact is exceeded or redesign is needed, visual diagnosis by a qualified experienced VRM practitioner is recommended.

6. *Diagnosis:* With a qualified VRM practitioner, this could proceed in one of two ways: (a) use of the VIA Checklist (see Appendix A) to identify specific aspects of the project that account for the unwanted severity of visual impact and can be redesigned; or (b) use of a more detailed procedure for a "reanalysis" of the project or activity in question (see Sheppard and Newman, 1979).

7. *Visual simulation:* All new or experienced VRM practitioners should use some type of visual documentation for each VIA rating. Visual-simulation methods are outlined in the BLM Manual (1980b) and in this chapter. Simulation should be used for any visually complex or controversial project or activity.

8. *Develop marker scenes:* Photographs used in visual documentation of before and after views and simulations can then be used as "marker" scenes for each geographic region and its activities (see Fig. 10.6). Marker scenes facilitate training, create a similar base of judgment, and provide examples of visually compatible and incompatible activities for wetland landscapes within that landscape region.

9. *Literature:* All VRM practitioners engaged in VIA should keep themselves abreast of the professional and academic literature (see Smardon et al. 1982) in order to make use of research findings and techniques that are particularly germane to their landscape regions or assessment projects.

## Notes

1. 16 U.S.C., Section 4321 et seq.
2. 33 U.S.C., Section 404.
3. Protection of Wetlands: Executive Order 11990, 42 Ecol. Reg. 26961 (1977).
4. General background of concepts and terminology are provided by the Prototype VIA Manual (Sheppard and Newman, 1979).
5. Note that scale contrast is a bipolar variable. Scale contrast can increase both with extremely small or large activity introductions to the given landscape. This (we think) accounts for the negative correction between scale structures and scale land/water bodies; spatial dominance and scale land/water bodies as seen in Table 10.13. This variable must be carefully handled by VRM practitioners.

## References

Ady, J.; Gray, B. A.; and Jones, G. R. 1979. A visual resource study of alternative dams, reservoirs and highway transmission corridors near Copper Creek, Washington. In G. Elsner and R. Smardon, *Proceedings of Our National Landscape,* pp. 590–97.

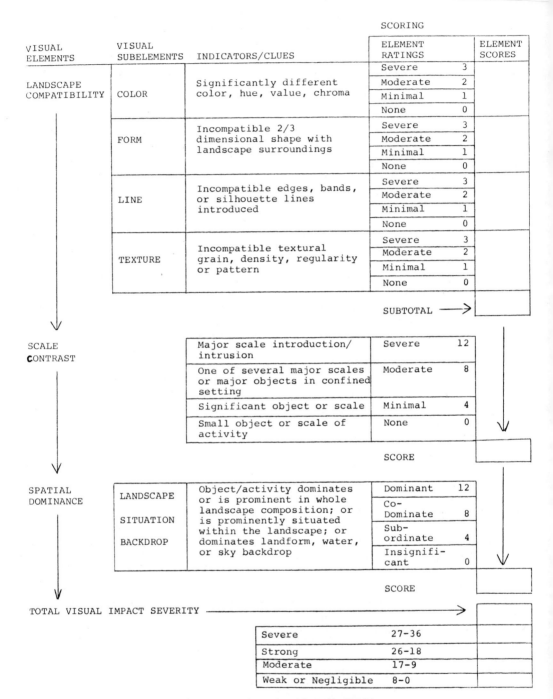

**Figure 10.17.** Second revision of basic VIA.

Baird, B. E.; Sheppard, S. R. J.; and Smardon, R. C. 1979. Visual simulation of offshore liquid natural gas terminals in a decision-making context. In G. Elsner and R. Smardon, *Proceedings of Our National Landscape,* pp. 636–44.

Craik, K. H., and Feimer, N. R. 1979. Setting technical standards for visual impact assessment procedures. In G. Elsner and R. Smardon, *Proceedings of Our National Landscape,* pp. 93–100.

Daniel, T. C., and Boster, R. S. 1979. *Measuring landscape aesthetics: The scenic beauty estimation method.* USDA Forest Service Res. Pap. RM–167. Rocky Mountain Forest and Range Experiment Station, Fort Collins, Colo.

Daniel, T. C., and Schroeder, H. 1979. Scenic beauty estimation model: Predicting perceived beauty of forest landscapes. In G. Elsner and R. Smardon, *Proceedings of Our National Landscape,* pp. 514–23.

Ebel, R. L. 1951. Estimation of the reliability of ratings. *Psychometrika* 16:407–24.

Elsner, G. H., and Smardon, R. C. (technical coordinators). 1979. *Proceedings of Our National Landscape: A Conference on Applied Techniques for Analysis and Management of the Visual Resource.* USDA Gen. Tech. Rep. PSW–35, USDA Pacific Southwest Forest and Range Experiment Station, Berkeley, 754 pp.

Feimer, N. R., and Craik, K. H., 1979. *Appraising the validity of landscape assessment procedures.* Institute for Personality Assessment and Research, University of California, Berkeley. 30 pp. plus appendices.

Feimer, N. R.; Craik, K. H.; Smardon, R. C.; and Sheppard, S. R. J. 1979. Appraising the reliability of visual impact assessment methods. In G. Elsner and R. Smardon, *Proceedings of Our National Landscape,* pp. 286–95.

Feimer, N. R.; Smardon, R. C.; and Craik, K. H. 1981. Evaluating the effectiveness of observer-based visual resource and impact assessment methods. *Landscape Research* 6(1):12–16.

Felleman, J. P. 1979. *Landscape visibility mapping: Theory and practice.* Prepared by School of Landscape Architecture, College of Environmental Science and Forestry, SUNNY, Syracuse, for New York Sea Grant Institute, Albany. 111 pp.

Felleman, J. P. 1982. Visibility mapping in New York's coastal zone – A case study of alternatives methods. *Coastal Zone Management Journal* 9 (3/4):249–70.

Guilford, J. P. 1954. *Psychometric methods.* 2nd ed. New York: McGraw-Hill.

Hendrix, W. G., and Fabos, J. Gy. 1975. Visual land-use compatibility as a significant contributor to visual resource quality. *International Journal of Environmental Studies* 8:21–28.

Jackson, R. H.; Hudman, L. E.; and England, J. L. 1978. Assessment of the environmental impact of high-voltage power transmission lines. *Journal of Environmental Management* 6:153–70.

Jacobs, P., and Way, D. 1968. *Visual analysis of landscape development.* Department of Landscape Architecture, Harvard Graduate School of Design, Cambridge.

Jones, G. R.; Jones, I,; Gray, B. A.; Parker, B.; Coe, J. C.; Burham, J. B.; and Geitner, N, M. 1975. A method for the quantification of aesthetic values for environmental decision-making. *Nuclear Technology* 25:682–713.

Litton, R. B., Jr. 1968. Forest landscape description and inventories: A basis for land planning and design. USDA Forest Service Research Paper PSW–49. Pacific Southwest Forest and Range Exp. Stn., Berkeley.

Litton, R. B., Jr. 1973. *Landscape control points: A procedure for predicitng and monitoring visual impact.* USDA Forest Service Res. Paper PSW–91, USDA Pacific Southwest Forest and Range Experiment Station, Berkeley.

Litton, R. B., Jr.; Tetlow, R. J.; Sorensen, J.; Beatty, R. A. 1974. *Water and landscape: An aesthetic overview of the role of water in the landscape.* Port Washington, N.Y.: Water Information Inc. 314 pp.

Magill, A. W., and Twiss, R. H. 1965. *A guide for recording aesthetic and biological changes with photographs.* USDA Forest Service Res. Note 77, USDA Pacific Southwest Forest and Range Experiment Station, Berkeley.

Mann, R. 1979. A technique for the assessment of the visual impact of nearshore confined dredged materials and other built islands. In G. Elsner and R. Smardon, *Proceedings of Our National Landscape,* pp. 654–59.

Palmer, J. F. 1981. Approaches for assessing visual quality and visual impacts. In K. Finsterbusch and C. P. Wolf, eds. *Methodology of social impact assessment,* 2nd ed. Stroudsburg, Pa.: Hutchinson, Ross. Pp. 294–301.

Schomaker, J. H. 1978. Measurements of preferences for proposed landscape modifications. *Landscape Research* 3(3):5–9.

Sheppard, S. R. J., and Newman, S. 1979. *Prototype visual impact assessment manual.* Department of Landscape Architecture, University of California and School of Landscape Architecture, College of Environmental Science and Forestry, SUNY, Syracuse. 84pp. plus appendices.

Smardon, R. C. 1978. *Law and aesthetics, or when is the pig in the parlor? A legal/policy overview of legal factors influence on visual landscape policy.* Department of Landscape Architecture, University of California, Berkeley. 152 pp.

———. 1979. The interface of legal and aesthetic considerations. In G. Elsner and R. Smardon, *Proceedings of Our National Landscape,* pp. 676–85.

———. 1979. *Report on BLM contrast rating and recommendations of development and implementation of visual management systems.* School of Landscape Architecture, College of Environmental Science and Forestry, SUNY, Syracuse. 6 pp. plus appendices.

Smardon, R. C.; Hunter, M.; Resue, J.; Zoelling, M.; and Standiford, R. 1982. *Our national landscape: Annotated bibliography and expertise index.* Agricultural Sciences Publications, Division of

Agricultural Sciences, University of California, Berkeley.

Smardon, R. C.; Sundquist, D.; Hunter, M. J.; and Bouchard, V., 1980. *Visual impact assessment of the Manteo (Shallowbag) Bay Project on the Oregon Inlet Area in Dare County, North Carolina.* National Park Service, Southeast Region, Atlanta, Ga.

Snedecor, G. W. 1946. *Statistical methods.* 4th ed. Ames: Iowa State College Press.

Steinitz, C., and Way, D. 1970. Section III, A model for evaluating visual consequences of urbanization on shoreline landscapes. In P. Rodgers and C. Steinitz, *A study of resource use in urbanizing watersheds.* Prepared under contract 33–68–DC–0151 by Graduate School of Design, Harvard University to Chief of Engineers, Corps of Engineers, Washington, D.C. Pp. III–1 to III–34.

The Environmental Associates. 1978. *The east-central Utah regional area visual resource inventory and analysis.* Prepared by Environmental Associates for USDI, Bureau of Land Management, Salt Lake City. 110 pp.

Travis, M. R.; Elsner, G. H.; Iverson, W. D.; Johnson, C. G. 1975. *VIEWIT: Computation of seen areas, slope, and aspect for land-use planning.* USDA Forest Service Gen. Tech. Rep. PSW–11, 70 pp. illus. USDA, Pacific Southwest Forest and Range Experiment Station, Berkeley.

USDI, Bureau of Land Management. 1980a. *Visual resource management program.* U.S. Government Printing Office, Washington, D.C. 39 pp. plus illus.

———. 1980b. *Visual simulation techniques.* U.S. Government Printing Office, Washington, D.C. 38 pp. plus illus.

Wohlwill, J. F. 1978. What belongs where: Research on the fittingness of man-made structures in natural settings. *Landscape Research* 3(3):3–5, 23.

Wohlwill, J. F., and Harris, G. 1980. Response to congruity or contrast for man-made features in natural-recreation settings. *Leisure Sciences* 3(4):349–65.

Zube, E. H. 1976. Perception of landscape and land use. In I. Altman and J. F. Wohlwill, eds. *Human behavior and the environment: Advances in theory and research,* vol. 2. New York: Plenum Publishing.

Portions of this chapter (pp. 173–78) previously appeared as "Evaluating the Effectiveness of Observer-based Visual Resource and Visual Impact Assessment Methods," *Landscape Research* 6 (1):12–16. Reprinted by permission of the Landscape Research Group.

**PART V**

# Conclusion

# 11 Conclusion

## RICHARD C. SMARDON

The preceding chapters have explored visual-cultural values and regulation of wetlands, both in the United States and in Britain, how people actually perceive wetlands, and how we can map and inventory visual characteristics of inland and coastal wetlands. Significantly, Part IV included some frameworks for evaluating wetlands for their visual, recreational, and educational values and for evaluating the visual impact of changes to wetlands themselves and from land-use changes adjacent to them. The sophistication of methodology or types of studies that can be done to assess visual-cultural values of wetlands is wide ranging.

## Complexity of Methodology

A report commissioned by the U.S. Army Corps of Engineers reviewed the wetlands assessment methodology presented by Smardon and Fabos in Chapter 9. In essence, the author of the report said the method was too complex to be implemented by the Corps. A more recent report done by the Corps, through the Waterways Research and Experiment Station in Vicksburg, Mississippi, will probably come to the opposite conclusion given the requirements of Section 404 guideline regulations from EPA (see Chapter 2). However, even with this latest

support of visual-cultural-values consideration in decision-making, there is a prevailing climate of minimizing agency involvement in private business transactions. This means that any visual-cultural assessment method must be cost effective and timely and be amenable to private corporate use as well as to agency use. Overly complex methods will not survive this decision-making climate.

## The Need for Field-Expedient Methods

Besides the general climate of minimizing complexity in decision-making is the issue of field-expedient methods. Many decision-makers do not have access to computers, elaborate visual simulation hardware, or even detailed photogrammetric maps of wetland areas. Thus field-expedient methods are needed. When resources are limited, the best available method based on sound research and practice should be used. This is why field-rating procedures and the visual impact checklist were included in this book. These techniques can be used to aid in visual impact assessment of proposed changes to wetlands and other landscapes. Likewise, Palmer demonstrated in Chapter 5 how perception-testing methods can be used with community involvement of town residents. Burgess in Chapter 7 demonstrated how visual-cultural attributes of wetlands can be mapped easily with minimum data and graphic sophistication.

## Toward the Practicum of Feasibility

The previous discussion leads us to the proposition that there are visual-cultural assessment methods of differing levels of complexity and expedience. These same methods that are used to assess, map, and evaluate visual-cultural values of wetlands have varying properties of reliability, validity, and generalizability. The practicum or general procedural rule can be postulated that more complex methods that yield higher levels of reliability, validity, and generalizability should be used in controversial situations or where there is high risk of long-term significant visual-cultural impacts. Perhaps in cases where controversy and environmental risk are less, field-expedient methods could be used. The analyst should consider the probability of contributing to cumulative visual-cultural impacts when adopting the latter strategy.

## Future Research Needs

So little substantive research concerning visual-cultural values of wetlands has been done that there is no cohesive fabric of knowledge: there are only gaps. In-depth studies have been done only for portions of the northeastern United States, the far South, and the West Coast. To the author's knowledge, no comparable studies of visual-cultural values for wetlands have been done in the Midwest prairie pothole region or in the interior Western states. Penning-Rowsell has reviewed existing studies in the United Kingdom. Most of these are professional assessments of wetlands.

Future studies need to assess the perceptual and behavior-derived dimensions of the visual, recreational, and educational values of wetlands as well as the physical attributes correlated with values. These physical attributes can then be managed to preserve or protect visual-cultural quality. Future studies also need to look at the interaction of visual, recreational, and educational values of wetlands as well as the more dynamic aspects of visual-cultural values. Some key questions need to be answered: What ecological processes can contribute to the aesthetic experience of the wetland? To what degree is the presence of wildlife correlated with the overall wetland experience when measured against more static elements, such as landform, vegetation, and water? How quickly do different wetland types change physically such that the desired visual character of the type changes?

Visual-cultural studies should be sensitive to the local or regional history contributing to wetland values. Are traditional waterfowl hunting values evolving toward nonconsumption-oriented wildlife values? Regional differences with respect to the role that wetlands play in the landscape should be carefully assessed. For instance, what is the visual role of prairie potholes in the context of the Great Northern Plains landscape? What is the role of the wetlands associated with saline lakes in the Great Basin? Unless we look at the regional landscape context, we may slowly lose major ingredients in the character of the landscape without even knowing it.

And that raises the most crucial question: How soon can we know about key attributes of national and international visual-cultural landscape heritage before it is gone and before future land-use options are forever foreclosed?

# Appendix:
# The Generic
# Visual-Impact Checklist

## BRIAN DICK and RICHARD C. SMARDON

---

### Introduction and Explanation

The Generic Visual-Impact Checklist was prepared to facilitate complete and accurate assessment of visual impact in the field by VRM practitioners. The general assumption made in preparation of the Checklist is that activities introduced in the landscape have many different subcomponents, each generating different potential impacts, regardless of site characteristics. The VRM practitioner may not be familiar with the technology or characteristics of the varied activities that are now introduced into the landscape, especially the newer energy-extraction and generation technologies. Therefore, the Checklist serves as an aid to the VRM practitioner to ensure that all general visual impacts would be considered in the evaluation of the given project. Of course the Checklist is general or generic, so unique site conditions may aggravate potential visual impacts or ameliorate them as the case may be.

All generic visual impacts listed are culled from the most complete and up-to-date sources. Documentation of visual impacts in general is extremely poor, and substantiation is even harder to find.

Activities are grouped by family: land management, resource extraction, power generation, power transmission, transportation, water-resource development, and waste treatment and industrial processing. Any specific activity impacts could be found within a project family, such as coal power plant within power generation, or could be a combination of activities and families, such as oil and natural gas activities (resource extraction) linked by an oil pipeline (transportation) to a gas and oil power plant (power generation), which in turn is linked to overhead transmission (power transmission).

As one can see from the initial listing of families and activities, there is little or no documentation of specific visual impacts. This is especially true for certain locatable mineral-mining practices, new forms of energy generation, and certain forms of material transportation.

In the left-hand column of the Checklist are abbreviations of the landscape components affected by the visual impact: vegetation (VEG), land form (LF), and structure (STR). This should help to indicate the nature of the impact as well as suggest mitigation.

On the right-hand side of the Checklist, individual sources and page numbers are noted for reference. This is an imperfect science; therefore, more rigorous or authoritative sources of documentation would be appreciated from users of this Checklist.

## General Outline

    I.    Land Management
           Agricultural
    II.   Resource Extraction
           Oil and Natural Gas Activities
    III.  Power Generation
           A. Nuclear/Thermal Power Plants
           B. Coal Power Plants
           C. Gas and Oil Power Plants
    IV.  Power Transmission
           A. Overhead Transmission
           B. Oil/Slurry Pipelines
    V.   Transportation
           A. Water Pipelines
           B. Highways/Roads
    VI.  Water-Resource Development
           Impoundments/Diversions
    VII. Waste Treatment and Industrial Processing
           A. Wastewater Treatment Systems
           B. Solid-Waste-Disposal Activities
           C. Manufacturing/Industrial Operations

## The Generic Visual-Impact Checklist: Actions and Impacts

### I. LAND MANAGEMENT
#### Agricultural Land Usage

    1. Use of herbicides
        Dead vegetation (4:330)

VEG   ⟶     Short-term adverse effect on visual quality until vegetation breaks down or is replaced

    2. Channelization projects

LF    ⟶     Results in a straight ditch instead of a meandering stream bed (4:330)

    3. Drainage and irrigation projects

VEG   ⟶     Change the landscape by changing the vegetative cover

    4. Water developments .

WATER   ⟶   Add the element of open water to the landscape (4:329)

WATER   ⟶   Change the water element from meandering stream to open expanse of water (4:329)

       5. Prescribed fire

          Returns landscape to previous condition (4:329)

       6. Brush control, mechanical disruption of soil and vegetation

VEG   ⟶   Temporary adverse effect on visual quality as a result of uprooted vegetation (4:329)

VEG   ⟶   Long-term improvement of visual quality of the landscape because of the introduction of grass (4:329)

VEG   ⟶   Breaks up monotonous landscapes and creates pleasing patterns of change (4:329)

       7. Grazing

          Presence of grazing animals (4:329)

          Enhances interest for travelers

          Reduces monotony

       8. Uncontrolled grazing

VEG, LF   ⟶   Causes accelerated erosion or destruction of vegetation (4:329)

          Sheet and gully erosion (4:329)

          Increased turbidity

          Change in odor and clarity of water

       9. Structural range improvements; fences

STR   ⟶   Introduction of structural elements in landscape (4:329)

          Visual fragmentation of view (4:329)

          Blocked or impaired view (4:329)

## II. RESOURCE EXTRACTION

### Oil and Natural Gas Activities

STR   ⟶   1. Towers, platforms, sea island piers (marine environments)

          Overboard disposal of refuse (4:390)

WATER   ⟶   Floatable material

          Accumulation on shoreline

          Debris accumulation on bottom

          Aesthetic displeasure to underwater exploration

STR   ⟶   2. Refineries, tank farms, towers, platforms, sea island piers, fencing

          Increased desirability of unspoiled scenic areas (4:390)

          Overuse of areas and deterioration of scenic appeal

          Congestion and overcrowding

STR   ⟶   Highly visible projections (4:390)

          Visual impact of truck and tank rail car traffic (4:390)

## III. POWER GENERATION

### A. Nuclear and Thermal Power Plants

       1. Plant operation

          Scale dominance to existing landscape (4:381)

STR   ⟶   Introduction of stack plume (4:381)

          Visibility degradation

       2. Building sites cuts and fills, fences, and bulk-fuel loading

                Blocked or impaired views
                    Concentrate demand on public views areas
                Cleared swaths across landscape

LF, VEG ⟶      Marred natural landform and vegetation pattern (4:381)
                Highly visible slopes of disturbed cover
LF, VEG ⟶      Marred natural landform and vegetation pattern
            3. Cooling tower
STR    ⟶      High-profile cooling tower
SKY    ⟶      Plume characteristics are dependent on meteorologic conditions

### B. Coal Power Plants

            1. Construction of facilities for extraction, clearing conversion transportation, and central station combustion
LF      ⟶      Change of surface land features and configurations (4:410)
            2. Plant site emission stacks
STR    ⟶      Strobe lights on stack (3:116)
STR    ⟶      Strong vertical line
STR    ⟶      Flashing lights attract attention (3:116)
            3. Cooling tower and evaporation ponds
SKY    ⟶      Steam plume, especially during cold weather (3:116)

### C. Gas and Oil

            1. Local power and telephone service
STR    ⟶      Introduction of support pole structures (1:82–95)
            2. Access-road construction
LF      ⟶      Maintenance road construction
LF      ⟶      Introduction of linear bands in landscape (1:82–95)
            3. Pipeline construction
STR    ⟶      Introduction of linear structures of swaths in landscape (1:82–95)
            4. Cut and fill
LF, VEG ⟶      Slopes are accentuated by the total lack of vegetation
            5. Crude-oil storage tanks
STR    ⟶      Introduction of high and massive elements (7:4)
            6. Flare
SKY    ⟶      Height and burning flame makes flare visible day and night (7:4)
            7. Exploratory drilling
STR    ⟶      Introduction of temporary drilling-rig structures to landscape (1:82–95)

## IV. POWER TRANSMISSION

### A. Overhead Transmission

            1. Transmission route selection
STR    ⟶      Visible poles and lines over streams, rivers, lakes, coastal areas (4:381)
                Increased visual access into previously inaccessible wetland areas (4:381)
STR    ⟶      Unsightly intrusions within landscape (4:381)
                Increased desirability of unspoiled scenic areas

|  |  |
|---|---|
|  | Overuse of areas and deterioration of scenic appeal |
|  | Congestion and overcrowding |
| STR $\longrightarrow$ | Highly visible vertical projections (4:381) |
| VEG $\longrightarrow$ | Cleared swaths across landscape (4:381) |
| LF, VEG $\longrightarrow$ | Marred natural landform and vegetation patterns |

2. Site-preparation field office and storage yard

General construction (5)

Clearing structural demolition and vegetation (5)

LF $\longrightarrow$   Earth work (5)

Backfill and restoration (5:145)

3. Removal of vegetation

VEG $\longrightarrow$   Recognition that vegetation (except ground covers) has or will be removed for transmission line installation (2:29)

4. Installation of overhead transmission

STR $\longrightarrow$   Dominance because of extreme closeness

A structure located less than twice its height from observer (2:29)

STR $\longrightarrow$   Excessive variety of structures

More than one type of structure (i.e., H-frame or pole) in view and/or non-synchronization of structure location (2:29)

STR, SKY $\longrightarrow$   Silhouette (2:29)

Exposure of structures with the sky as partial or full background

STR $\longrightarrow$   Focal interruption (2:29)

The interruption of lines-of-sight to a focal point by a transmission line

STR $\longrightarrow$   Concentration

A high density (real or apparent) of transmission structures in a localized area (2:29)

STR $\longrightarrow$   Spatial interruption (2:29)

The apparent division of distinct landscape spaces or patterns by a transmission line. Space division is perceived from inferior viewing positions and pattern from normal or superior viewing positions and is usually related to middle ground (2:29)

STR $\longrightarrow$   Continual feature of extended view (2:29)

Views along a right-of-way that extended from one distance zone to another, particularly through middle ground into background (2:29)

STR/LD $\longrightarrow$   Incompatible topographic alignment

Unsympathetic alignments that do not respect natural contours of existing landforms (2:29)

STR $\longrightarrow$   Scale dominance

Disparity in relative size of transmission structures and landscape elements (houses, barns) accentuated by proximity

LF $\longrightarrow$   Soil contrast as a result of grading (2:29)

Observable cut or fill necessitated by transmission-line installation

STR $\longrightarrow$   Special-feature compatibility (2:29)

The violation of landscape and/or cultural elements that are both singular and significant in a context of the project area as a whole (i.e., waterfalls, lakes, cultural centers)

LF $\longrightarrow$ Edge violation

The visible crossing of a regional linear feature or line of transition from one landscape to another (i.e., valleys, ridge lines, or between different landscape types, such as forest-field or mountain-plain).

5. Transmission towers

Rigid, unnatural appearance, medium contrast to the form and lines expressed in natural landscape

B. *Oil pipelines*

1. Pipeline (9:3–312)

LD, VEG $\longrightarrow$ Alter small-scale landforms and remove vegetation cover

Change in established scenic and open-space values

LF $\longrightarrow$ Permanent primitive road is likely to remain

STR $\longrightarrow$ Above-ground valves and pipeline bridge across rivers are visible

STR/VEG,
WATER $\longrightarrow$ Pipeline at river crossing; oil spill would create an oil-covered area along the river until vegetation could reestablish itself (9:3–317)

2. Pump stations (9:3–313)

STR $\longrightarrow$ Introduction of pump-station structure to landscape

Above-ground power-line transmission towers

## V. *TRANSPORTATION*

A. *Highways/roads*

1. Road alignments, cuts, fills, retaining walls, cribs, re-vetted embankments (4:267)

LF, STR $\longrightarrow$ Drainage-way terraces

Contrast between natural landforms and engineering features of highway significant if visible from public recreation area, residential areas, or scenic highways

STR $\longrightarrow$ Urban or existing development patterns and engineering features of highway

Significant if visible from residential areas or from commercial operations that benefit from view

LF $\longrightarrow$ Increased prominence of land or landscape features visible from highway

Control or prevent development that would visually degrade lands or landscape features prominently seen from highways

LF/STR $\longrightarrow$ 2. Embankments (highway above grade) berms, elevated highway (on structures, fences, and barriers landscaping) (4:267)

Blocked viewlines along visual corridors (valleys, stream courses, streets)

Sever visual continuity of open-space network

Fragmentation of open-space expanse

Isolate open-space areas from connection with larger open-space systems

Fragment image of community or neighborhood as a discrete cohesive unit

Disorientation or confusion of visitor or resident

Block or reduce view from residential areas or commercial operations that benefit from view

Decreased residential and commercial property values and rents

Decreased patronage to commercial operations

Reduce affiliations to community by residents blocked off by highway

Blocked viewlines to landmarks in community from residential and recreational areas and commercial operations that benefit from view

Decrease patronage to commercial operations

STR ⟶ Elevated or above-grade highway out of scale with adjacent urban development

Highway is dominant element in view of community or neighborhood

Scale of highway overpowers scale of community or neighborhood

Decreased property values

Contrast between scales

3. Fill slopes, grading cut slopes and faces vegetation clearing (4:266)

LF ⟶ Highly visible erosion and/or bare earth or rock scars

Significant if visible from public recreation area, residential areas, or scenic highway

4. Landscaping of cut slopes, fill slopes, graded areas, landscaping of median strips and highway shoulders, revegetation of cut slopes, fill slopes, graded areas revegetation of highway shoulders

VEG ⟶ Contrast between existing vegetation and revegetated or landscape area

Significant if visible from public recreation area, residential areas, or scenic highways

STR ⟶ 5. Night lighting, vehicle reflections, vehicle lights, vehicle movement (4:266)

Glare visible in recreational or residential areas

Visual distraction from pursuit of recreational, residential, or commercial activities

## VI. WATER RESOURCE DEVELOPMENT
### A. Impoundment

WATER,
STR ⟶ 1. Impoundment (4:346)

Block viewlines along visual corridors (valleys, stream courses)

Sever visual continuity of open-space network

Fragmentation of open-space expanse

Isolate open-space areas from connection with larger open-space systems

2. Grading, flooding, draining, filling, clearing (4:346)

LF $\longrightarrow$ Creation of permanent, highly visible landscape (drawndown rim, shoreline clearing, cut and fill faces) that vividly contrast with surrounding landscape

VEG $\longrightarrow$ Creation of areas of highly visible dead, dying, decaying, or unhealthy vegetation
Degrade visual attraction of area to residents and visitors
Degradation of recreational potential

LF $\longrightarrow$ Creation of mudflats (drawndown rim), erosion scars
Loss of visual appeal to residents, recreational users, or visitors
Degradation of recreational potential

VEG $\longrightarrow$ Exposure of stumps and vegetation debris
Degrade visual attraction of area to residents and visitors

STR $\longrightarrow$ Engineering feature of the project out of scale with landscape
Significant if visible from public recreation areas, residential areas, or scenic highways

WATER $\longrightarrow$ Water body out of scale and character with surrounding landscape
Significant if visible from public recreation areas, residential areas, or scenic highways

## VII.  WASTE TREATMENT AND INDUSTRIAL PROCESSING

### A.  Wastewater Treatment Systems

STR $\longrightarrow$ 1. Night lighting, vehicle reflections, vehicle lights
Glare visible in recreational or residential areas (4:425)

2. Pipelines

STR $\longrightarrow$ Storage of unattractive materials, equipment, and unsightly excavation piles
Temporary decrease in visual access to surrounding areas (e.g., residential and commercial views) (4:425)

STR $\longrightarrow$ 3. Landscaping, project structural facilities (tanks, ponds, operations building, incineration facilities) (4:425)
Alter and/or block viewlines to scenic attractions from public viewing areas (scenic highways, public recreation areas)
Alter and/or block viewlines to scenic attractions from commercial operations that benefit from affected view
Decrease profits to operation
Decrease commercial property values
Alter and/or block viewlines to scenic attractions from existing or potential residential development
Decrease in property values
Alter and/or block viewlines along visual corridors (valleys, stream courses, streets)
Sever visual continuity of open-space network
Fragmentation of open-space expanse
Isolate open-space areas from connection with larger open-space systems
Siting of project in open-space area that forms vivid edge of community and distinguishes community from adjacent communities

Blurring of community definition as a distinguishable unit

4. Fences, project structural facilities (4:424)

STR, LF  ⟶  Contrast between natural landforms and engineering features of project

Significant if visible from public recreation area, residential areas, scenic highways, or commercial operations that benefit from affected view

STR  ⟶  Contrast between urban or commercial development pattern and engineering features of project

Significant if visible from residential areas or from commercial operations that benefit from affected view

5. Berms, fills, grading, cut slopes and faces, vegetation-clearing-treatment lagoons (4:424)

LD  ⟶  Highly visible erosion and/or bare earth or rock scars

Significant if visible from public recreation area, residential areas, scenic highways, or commercial operations that benefit from affected view

6. Landscaping of cut slopes, fill slopes, graded areas revegetation of cut slopes, fill slopes, graded areas (4:425)

VEG  ⟶  Contrast between existing vegetation and revegetated or landscaped areas

Significant if visible from public recreation area, residential areas, scenic highways, or commercial operations that benefit from affected view

## B. Solid-waste-disposal activities

LF  ⟶  1. Landfills of trash and garbage

Blown to adjacent property or into water

Litter left on beach

Attraction of insects, gulls, and rodents

Physical annoyance, disease vectors

Broken glass, sharp objects, rusty debris

Bodily injury

Increased public disregard for area

Increased litter, vandalism, misuse

Olfactory discomfort

2. Automobile junkyards (4:434)

LF, STR  ⟶  Low compatibility with surrounding landscape (can be ameliorated to some extent by fencing)

Intrusion within visual scene

Increased desirability of unspoiled scenic areas

Overuse and deterioration of scenic appeal

Congestion and overcrowding

3. Offshore disposal of solid wastes (4:434)

Accumulated organic sludge on bottom

Introduction of sewage and industry liquors

WATER  ⟶  Unappealing water color and noxious odor

Intrusion within coastal scene

Increased desirability of unspoiled scenic areas

Overuse and deterioration of scenic appeal

Congestion and overcrowding

4. Landfill operation and completion (4:434)

LF    $\longrightarrow$    Visual impact of new landform in creation and completion
      Possible blocking of views

LF    $\longrightarrow$    Shape, height, and form incompatible with immediate surroundings
      New land use stimulated by completion of the landfill may be compatible with immediate surroundings

LF, VEG $\longrightarrow$  Final landscaping may add or detract from final landform

## C. Manufacturing/Industrial Operation

STR   $\longrightarrow$    1. New plant construction/operation (4:457)
      Low compatibility of manufacturing activity located within sight of a recreational facility, historical area, or unique ecological setting

STR   $\longrightarrow$    Vertical structures of the plant visible from great distances
      Building colors and design conflict with natural coloration and surroundings

SKY   $\longrightarrow$    Plant gaseous emissions visible great distances

      2. Power pylons and wires; bulk refining and processing utilities (4:458)

STR   $\longrightarrow$    High visible projections
      Intrusions within the view

STR   $\longrightarrow$    3. Power pylons and wires; utilities, fences, railroads, tanks, elevators and warehouses, building-site cuts and fills, structures solid-waste disposal, bulk refining and processing
      Visual intrusions
      Increased desirability of unspoiled scenic areas
      Overuse and deterioration of scenic appeal
      Congestion and overcrowding
      Blocked or impaired views
      Concentrated demand on public-view areas
      Increased demand on public-view areas
      Congestion and overcrowding of area
      Overuse and deterioration of area and facilities
      Insufficient space to accommodate parking

LF, VEG $\longrightarrow$  4. Building-site cuts and fills (4:458)
      Cleared swaths across landscape
      Marred natural landform and vegetation pattern
      Highly visible slopes of disturbed cover
      Marred natural landform and vegetation pattern

## Sources

1. Oil and Gas Environmental Assessment of BLM Leasing Program, Miles City District, U.S.D.I., Bureau of Land Management. February 1980.

2. An Assessment Methodology for Transmission Line Visual Impact, prepared by Kane and Carruth, P. C. Landscape Architects, 1977; David B. Carruth, Randall Arthur, Douglas R. Snider.

3. Draft, West-Central North Dakota, Regional Environmental Impact Study on Energy Development, USDI, Bureau of Land Management, State of North Dakota. 1978.

4. Environmental Assessment Resource Handbook (1st ed.), Environmental Impact Assessment Project, Oregon State University Extension Service, Corvallis. 1976.

5. Study of Environmental Impact of Underground Electric Transmission Systems by EDAW, Inc., Environmental Planning, San Francisco. May 1975.

6. Final Environmental Statement by the U.S. Nuclear Regulatory Commission, Office of Nuclear Reactor Regulation, for Montague Nuclear Power Station, Units 1 and 2, February 1977. Proposed by Northeast Nuclear Energy Company, Docket Nos. 50–496, 50–497.

7. Trans-Alaska Pipeline System, Visual Impact Engineering Program/APSC Prepared by R & M Consultants, Inc., the Collins Dutot Partnership Hok Associates. September 1975.

8. Choosing Transmission Tower, Office of Environmental Planning, State of New York Department of Public Service. 1975.

9. Final Environmental Impact Statement, Crude-Oil Transportation System: Valdez, Alaska, to Midland, Texas (as proposed by Sohio Transportation Company).

10. National Forest Landscape Management, Vol. 2, Chap. 5, Timber, U.S., Forest Service, Agriculture Handbook No. 559. 1978.

11. Landscape Architecture Technical Information Series, published by American Society of Landscape Architects in cooperation with Surface Environment and Mining Program of U.S. Forest Service, Vol. 1, No. 3, "Creating Land for Tomorrow." 1978.

# Index

# About the Authors

Richard C. Smardon, M.L.A., is Senior Research Associate and Coordinator for Research and Community Service at the School of Landscape Architecture, College of Environmental Science and Forestry, S.U.N.Y., Syracuse. He is the editor of a special issue on visual resources management for the *Coastal Zone Management Journal* and of the proceedings of the *Our National Landscape* conference, and he is on the editorial board for the *Northeastern Environmental Science Journal*. His interests and activities include community cultural landscape image assessment, visual impact assessment, and urban ecosystems.

William E. Hammitt, Ph.D., is Associate Professor of Forest Recreation in the Department of Forestry, Wildlife and Fisheries at the University of Tennessee, Knoxville. His major research interests are in the areas of recreation behavior, on-site visual preferences, environmental cognition, and recreation resource management. The author of more than fifty published articles and past associate editor of the *Journal of Leisure Research*, Dr. Hammitt's current research involves the management of trail landscapes and parkway vistas for the visual preferences of park visitors.

Michael S. Lee, M.L.A., is a landscape architect with the city of Arvada, Colorado, and an active member of the Colorado Chapter of the American Society of Landscape Architects. His papers cover work on landscape assessment methodology.

Molly Burgess Mooney, M.L.A., is a landscape architect with her own design practice in Sheridan, Wyoming. She is active in Wyoming's historic preservation movement, and serves as a consultant for the state office.

James F. Palmer, Ph.D., Research Associate and Curriculum Director for the Program in Environmental Studies at the College of Environmental Science and Forestry, S.U.N.Y., Syracuse, holds graduate degrees in landscape planning and forestry. His past work focused on rural and wildlands environments, while his current work is concerned with the role of nature in the lives of urbanites.

Edmund C. Penning-Rowsell, Ph.D., is Reader in Geography and Head of the School of Geography and Planning at Middlesex Polytechnic and Director of the Polytechnic's Flood Hazard Research Center. He is a consultant for national and regional agencies, and his published research covers geomorphology, landscape evaluation and planning, flood plain management, and the economics of flood alleviation and land drainage schemes.

Rowan A. Rowntree, Ph.D., a specialist in forest ecology and biogeography, conducted research on watersheds and estuaries in California under fellowships from the Conservation Foundation and Resources for the Future. His publications include articles and chapters on the ecological foundations of estuary planning.